SECURITY AND GOVERNANCE IN SOUTH ASIA

SOME OTHER RCSS PUBLICATIONS

- *The Simla Agreement 1972: Its Wasted Promise* (Manohar, 2001);
- *Security Studies in South Asia: Change and Challenges* (Manohar, 2000);
- *People-to-People Contact in South Asia* (Manohar, 2000);
- *South Asia at Gun Point: Small Arms and Light Weapons Proliferation* (RCSS, 2000);
- *CBMs in South Asia: Potential and Possibilities* (RCSS, 2000);
- *Confidence Building Measures in South Asia* (RCSS, 1999);
- *Ethnicity and Constitutional Reform in South Asia* (Manohar, 1998);
- *Regional Economic Trends and South Asian Security* (Manohar, 1997);
- *Diplomacy and Domestic Politics in South Asia* (Konark, 1996);
- *Nuclear Non-proliferation in India and Pakistan: South Asian Perspectives* (Manohar, 1996);
- *Refugees and Regional Security in South Asia* (Konark, 1996)

RCSS Newsletter

A quarterly bulletin is published containing reports on RCSS activities as well as work of other centres and institutions involved in South Asian Strategic studies, and articles of contemporary interest to the countries of the region.

RCSS Policy Studies

19. Governance in Plural Societies and Security: An Overview (May 2000)
18. Third-Generation Indian Perception of the Kashmir Issue (May 2001)
17. Coping with Disorder: Strategies to End Internal Wars in South Asia (October 2000)
16. Law and Order Situation and Gender-based Violence: Bangladeshi Perspective (October 2000)
15. Potential for Military Among Bhutanese Youth (September 2001)
14. Order, Welfare and Legitimacy in the Regional Context of South Asia: *An Ultima Thule* (August 2000)
13. Energy Crisis and Sub Regional Cooperation in South Asia (August 2000)
12. Defence Expenditure in South Asia: India and Pakistan (June 2000)
11. Defence Expenditure in South Asia: Bangladesh and Sri Lanka (April 2000)

Others

- *Directory of Individuals and Institutions Engaged in South Asian Strategic Studies* (1998).

Security and Governance in South Asia

Edited by

P.R. CHARI

REGIONAL CENTRE FOR STRATEGIC STUDIES
COLOMBO

MANOHAR
2001

First published 2001

ISBN 81-7304-438-4

Published by
Ajay Kumar Jain for
Manohar Publishers & Distributors
4753/23 Ansari Road, Daryaganj
New Delhi 110 002

Typeset by
Kohli Print
107 Radhey Shyam Park
Delhi 110 051

Printed at
Lordson Publishers Pvt. Ltd.
C5/19 Rana Pratap Bagh
Delhi 110 007

Contents

Preface

Among the many transformations we are witnssing at the dawn of the twenty-first century, a crucial issue is related to the concept of security. The fundamental question that arises and which needs to be asked is what is it that we want to secure? In the earlier era of strong state nationalism, the answer was obvious. It was the territory of the nation state and, as a corollary, all that furthered a nation's interests in this task. This could be achieved essentially at the expense of another country or a group of states. This idea held sway till the end of the Second World War and continued for much of the Cold War. It was common then, in the name of this nationalism, to expect citizens of a state to unquestionably lay down their lives in defence of this cause. This no longer holds. Countries today find it difficult to justify the loss of a single citizen's life in conflicts, whether near or far from home. Because increasingly in people's perceptions they have slipped in priority compared to other issues. What then is security?

In truth security is far too interdependent an issue to be defined in purely military terms. In a rapidly integrating and globalising world other factors and concerns have come to acquire greater salience. It can no longer be my security against yours, but my security and your security in a single planet where all are equal stakeholders. Full realization of this and a clearer definition will perhaps take some more time yet, but the concept and relevance of *human security* vis-à-vis *state security* is growing and entering the international debate.

There is now a growing salience in people's minds on three fundamental human aspirations; *freedom from fear*, *freedom from want* and the hope of leading a *life of dignity*. These are challenged today, not so much by war or conflict, but other perhaps even more serious and immediate conditions. Three of the more important issues, particularly in Asia, are perhaps the impact of *globalization* particularly on developing nations, the challenges to *governance* in plural societies and the adverse impact of a degrading *environment*.

It was with this aim and with support from the *Ford Foundation* that the *Regional Centre for Strategic Studies* in:tiated a project on *Non*

Traditional Security Issues in South Asia, as part of an Asia wide programme, to examine these emerging conditions of security. The topics addressed in this first phase were *Globalization and Security, Governance in Plural Societies and Security* and *Environment and Security.*

To conceptualize and develop the programme a planning and coordination conference was held at Rajendrapur in Dhaka in October 1999. Twenty leading intellectuals from South Asia came together to consider the various facets related to this emerging concept of security and shape the project.

The current book, *Security and Governance in South Asia* is a result of a two year long study and workshops. My sincere thanks to P.R. Chari, the Project Director for his input and personal expertise as a senior practitioner in this very area for managing the project with such distinction. Contributions have come from five eminent intellectuals and experts from different countries of South Asia in what is truly a pathbreaking effort at generating greater understanding on this important issue of our times.

Executive Director DIPANKAR BANERJEE
RCSS
June 2001

CHAPTER 1

Security and Governance in South Asia: Their Linkages

P.R. Chari

INTRODUCTION

The end of the Cold War a decade ago signalled the end to several widely accepted certitudes in the international system. But the mitigation of superpower rivalries, erosion of bloc politics, cessation of ideological predilections, and the triumph of liberal democratic values did not lead to any diminution of international tensions and conflict. Instead, the epicentre of these tensions and conflicts moved more certainly into the Third World, and the focus of these discords shifted from the external to the internal sphere. A seminal change has occurred now in the theatre and nature of conflicts. The Stockholm International Peace Research Institute (SIPRI) has recognized this change in the post-Cold War era; its annual statistics confirm that intra-State conflicts now greatly outnumber inter-State conflicts. For instance, the SIPRI Yearbook (2000) informs that: 'There were 27 major armed conflicts in 25 countries throughout the world [in 1999]. Only two of the conflicts were interstate. . . . [M]ore than 1000 people died in each of the 14 conflicts in 1999.'[1] Incidentally, the two inter-state conflicts identified by SIPRI relate to those between Ethiopia and Eritrea, and India and Pakistan over Kashmir.

A marked reduction in inter-state conflicts, that had earlier been promoted and nourished by superpower and bloc rivalries, has also occurred. SIPRI notes that: 'Foreign military intervention remains the exception and is not becoming the rule.'[2] The marked increase in intra-State conflicts within the Third World is attributable to the exacerbation of latent tensions and instabilities; their historical roots lie embedded in persisting ethnic, religious, communal and linguistic asymmetries. Many of these asymmetries lay dormant during the colonial and Cold War era: a 'decompression effect' resulted after the Cold War ended, leading to the eruption of internal conflicts arising out of a plethora of ethno-nationalist, socio-economic and communal-religious reasons.

THE SOUTH ASIAN SECURITY *PROBLÉMATIQUE*

This is specially true of South Asia. Despite being the *karma-bhumi* (action theatre) of Mahatma Gandhi and the birthplace of three of the world's oldest religions, South Asia is a very violent place. Over the last half century, it has witnessed major inter-State conflicts and mass migrations; several insurgencies afflict its subregions; its societal contradictions have precipitated class and caste wars; besides, ethnic, communal and sectarian violence remain endemic to the region. South Asia also exhibits an unusual phenomenon. Despite their common vulnerability to subregional dissension, South Asia has a long history of its constituent countries providing moral and material assistance to support dissidence in their neighbours; indeed, aggravating the security problems of their neighbours has become a not uncommon instrument of their foreign policies. It would be tedious to cite the several illustrative examples available, but major instances are India's training and equipping the Mukti Bahini to liberate Bangladesh in the 1970s, and Tamil militant groups against the Sinhala government in Sri Lanka during the 1980s, and the proxy war launched by Pakistan in Kashmir in the 1990s.

A significant accretion to internal conflicts, therefore, distinguishes the security *problématique* in South Asia exacerbated by the malevolence of inimical neighbours. Two other characteristics of the regional situation require mention; they were noticed several years ago, but have not changed over the intervening period.[3]

- First, India's size, natural resources, population, gross domestic product, and other traditional attributes of power cause uneasiness among its South Asian neighbours. Their ingrained belief that unless India displays large-heartedness and magnanimity towards its neighbours it will not gain their confidence, fails to appreciate India's concerns with activities prejudicial to its national interests that occur in its geostrategic environment.

- Second, the generally estranged nature of Indo-Pak relations has indubitably vitiated the regional security milieu; it also prejudices the diligent efforts by SAARC to utilize the regional cooperation instrumentality to soften the edges of suspicion and forge peace and stability in South Asia. The sequential nuclear tests conducted by India and Pakistan in May 1998 and the subsequent Kargil conflict between them provided the exception to the general rule that democracies and nuclear weapon states do not war against each other. These two major events have greatly vitiated the prevailing atmosphere of deep mutual suspicions and animosities between India and Pakistan.

The crisis in South Asia was also recognized several years back to have three interrelated dimensions;[4] these have not changed over the years. They comprise the following.

- The growing polarization of society along ethnic, linguistic and religious lines, and an undermining of social values through which diverse communities had lived together in a pluralistic society.
- The failure of centralized structures to share political power and give effective representation to all strata of society, leading to growing militarization and use of coercive State power to quell resurgent nationalism.
- The collapse of an approach to development that has generated endemic poverty, growing interpersonal and interregional disparities, erosion of the ecology and growing dependence on foreign aid.

More recently, human security, which emphasizes the security of the individual over the security of the State, has gained larger recognition. The concept of human security is still evolving, specially the manner in which it interfaces with more conservative notions of security, but its evolution derives from prevailing inadequacies with current definitions of security. The raison d'être for the State, in terms of Hobbesian dialectics, is related to the preservation of internal and external security. This understanding proves inadequate if awkward questions are asked to interrogate the security *problématique* like 'Security for whom?', 'Security of what values?' and 'Security by what means?' Further, if these questions were to be asked in the context of the security of the State and the individual, very different answers would accrue.[5] Still, an increasing attention to human security seems inevitable since the wave of democratization and globalization in the international system has released new forces of egalitarianism in national polities. It would be feckless to believe that the individual's desires for greater human security would not be also heightened, specially with the rapid diffusion of information technology spurring the revolution of rising expectations in the people of South Asia.

In the light of the foregoing, an understanding of South Asian national security requires the military and non-military threats in the region to be considered. The compulsions of external and internal security of the State, however, have led to its centrality being emphasized, military security being exaggerated, and its propensity to centralize power being encouraged. This has increased after the nuclearization of the subcontinent in May 1998 added a new dimension to military security in the national security policies of India and Pakistan—the two major States in South Asia. This perception has also influenced their smaller neighbours. Apropos, the composition of the national security decision-making elite in South Asia, comprising their armed forces, police, paramilitary forces and intelligence services, ensures an inability to adopt a holistic view and appreciate the non-military aspects of national security. Their sensitization to the need for including human security within this holistic paradigm to discern the totality of security threats to the State and its citizens has yet to occur.

Significantly, these elite are often part of the problem, and not the solution, to insecurities in the region, especially when civilian regimes are weak and divided. The police, for instance, are largely perceived as oppressors of the people in South Asia, rather than their saviours by ensuring the maintenance of law and order and public safety; their open utilization in political infighting explains their immunity to being disciplined. At another level, it has been noticed that

> The Cold War effectively militarized the study of security; thus mainstream security studies 'has traditionally devoted less attention to the goal of security than to the means by which it is pursued. More accurately . . . the field has tended to focus on *one* set of means . . . that is, military statecraft'. This left little opportunity to advance either broader conceptions of security more in line with the development needs of countries, or alternative means of achieving security.[6]

A theoretical foundation was laid, thereby, for emphasizing the military as distinct from the non-military and human aspects of security.

The reality is just the reverse. Under the rubric of nuclear deterrence, the likelihood of a nuclear or major conventional conflict occurring between India and Pakistan has receded. Some discussion is proceeding fitfully on the viability of limited war despite the obtaining Indo-Pak nuclear stand-off with the Kargil conflict serving as the exemplar. However, there is no answer to the objection that a limited war in a nuclearized environment could escalate into a conventional war and further to a nuclear exchange, hence planning for a limited war in this milieu amounts to fecklessness. The probability of the internal and non-military sources of insecurity and problems of human insecurity excoriating the South Asian countries are far more real, which derives from the manner in which their domestic polity is functioning. The wasteful use of state resources, a non-consensual and plebiscitary approach to politics, an unresponsive administration and so on are adding to the prevailing misgovernance of the State, resulting in an exacerbation of its internal and non-military security problems, and inhumane governance.

THE ISSUE OF GOVERNANCE

This brings us to the role of governance in providing military and human security. Governance is distinct from 'ruling' and its connotations with 'command' and 'dominance'. The dictionary informs us that governance comprises the 'act, manner, fact or function, of governing'; the 'manner of governing' most closely approximates the role of governance for this discussion, but it has been described more elaborately.[7] The United Nations Development Programme (UNDP) defines governance 'as the exercise of economic, political, and administrative authority to manage a country's affairs at all levels. It comprises mechanisms, processes, and institutions through which citizens and groups articulate their interests, exercise their legal rights, meet their obligations, and mediate their differences.' The Organisation for Economic Cooperation and Development (OECD) describes it more crisply by stating that: 'The concept of governance denotes the use of political authority and exercise of control in a society in relation to the management of its resources for social and economic development. This broad definition encompasses the role of public authorities in establishing the environment in which economic operators function and in determining the distribution of benefits as well as the nature of the relationship between the ruler and the ruled.' These and other descriptions of governance confuse process with prescriptions to achieve normative objectives.

Views regarding good governance and the means to procure it also vary and tend to be impressionistic. But the concept of humane governance has acquired a new salience, which includes 'a combination of good economic governance, good political governance, and good civic governance'.[8] Proceeding on the assumption that the processes of governance in South Asia have been captured by identified special interest groups, it is evident that good political governance requires decentralization of powers to the people; accountability and transparency in public affairs; access to prompt and affordable justice; elimination of discrimination against women and minorities; and, finally, maintenance of peace and social cohesion within states. Good economic governance requires a middle course being charted between market-driven laissez faire and command/control economies. They must be supplemented by adequate budgetary allocations to the social priority sectors; a progressive taxation system; efficiently targetted subsidies for the poor; and equitable access to credit and land. Similarly, good civic governance envisages civil society being strengthened by voluntary and private sector activism, and that the deprived and underprivileged sections of society would organize themselves to reduce their dependence on the State and defend their rights and freedoms. Good citizenship, good corporate and employer behaviour, good-neighbourly activity and self-policing of rights violations are further aspects of good civic governance that require pursuit.[9]

These criteria may appear hopelessly idealistic and unattainable in the foreseeable future. At the very minimum, however, good governance policies include:

- promotion of efficiency and transparency in public administration;
- respect for human rights and the rule of law; and
- a greater role for civilian bodies in monitoring and managing the security sector.'[10]

So much is clear. South Asia is noteworthy for examples of poor governance. Scarce resources are inefficiently deployed or frittered away, the administration is getting increasingly divided on ethnic and sectarian lines, law enforcement is arbitrary and political leadership is obviously inadequate. This situation derives largely from lack of a participatory government accompanied by a rapid erosion of political government. Greater transparency, access to information and oversight mechanisms to regulate the functioning of the State's machinery is cardinal to reversing this parlous situation. In their absence a 'We-They' syndrome has developed between the governing elite and the governed masses with the bureaucracy becoming the masters rather than the servants of the people. Moreover, the international financial institutions have become increasingly sensitive to the need for linking structural adjustment programmes with good governance: this, it is realized, would be more productive than imposing conditionalities on donee countries that have often worsened their economic and social predicament.[11]

A word is necessary here on the irresistible phenomenon of globalization, which makes national frontiers pervious to the entry of ideas, goods, technology and population flows. Their potential to both enhance and diminish military, non-military and human security is apparent. Globalization can permit synergy to be developed with external forces, enabling the eradication of poverty, deprivation, illiteracy and disease. On the other hand, globalization can also lead to the exploitation of vulnerable population groups by promoting consumerism, smuggling of drugs and arms, and trafficking in women, children, and people desperately searching for a better quality of life. Adaptation to the demands of globalization would unavoidably be required of national governments.

LINKING SECURITY AND GOVERNANCE

There is little policy coherence in South Asia on recognizing an overall conception of national security in its several facets and balancing the needs of State and human security. There is also the problem of reaching consensus on these issues and the long-term objectives to be sought. This dilemma is accentuated by the difficulty that arises in reconciling the competing ends of ensuring State security from external assault and internal disruption, whilst also providing greater outlays for social and economic development. Ultimately, hard political decisions need being taken from the budgetary perspective, appreciating the scarcity of resources, the political issues embedded in their allocation and the difficulties of additional revenue mobilization.

Disconcertingly, there is little debate, leave alone recognition, of the place of good governance in managing the State in South Asia, although the pursuit of dharma provides an especially indigenous flavour to this issue. Ethical and moral principles in statecraft and in life lay the foundations of dharma. 'The aim is social welfare, not the welfare of a particular group only but of the whole world, for 'the entire world of mortals is a self-dependent organism'. Yet dharma itself is relative and depends on the times and the conditions prevailing, apart from some basic principles, such as adherence to truth, non-violence etc.'[12] It would overstate the case to urge that a unique theory of governance applies to South Asia as opposed to Western concepts. The essential question is 'whether a body of universally applicable principles could be found to assess the governance function, and whether such a body of principles could be assembled with enough "conceptual integrity" and "clarity" to be accurately called a model or paradigm . . .'.[13]

In truth, a regional perspective could only derive from national policies regarding these questions; this is not visible in any of the South Asian countries since the linkage between security and good governance has rarely been recognized. Neither has it been appreciated that the actors concerned with national security management must include, apart from the military, paramilitary forces, police and intelligence agencies, the judiciary, media, civil society and business interests. They have vital roles to play in the security sector. An important duty has also to be performed by oversight mechanisms, whether established by parliamentary or constitutional authority, to ensure that the rule of law is not infringed: this is essential for the credibility and integrity of the governance processes and the management of national security.

The nexus between security and governance in South Asia is the underlying theme of this volume; explaining this nexus offers the challenge in this exercise. Scholars in the region have contributed individual country studies, which reflect different perspectives on this issue. The caveat needs early mention here that overstretching the concept of security could eviscerate it of all meaning. As perceptively noted: 'Once anything that generates anxiety or threatens the quality of life in some respect becomes labeled a "security problem", the field risks losing all focus. Such an agenda is conceivably rich, and is certainly inclusive, but can also be off-puttingly vague.'[14] This problem becomes acute if a central place is accorded to ensuring human security, apart from State security, and assessing the adequacy of the governance processes to ensure its provision. One way out of this difficulty is to review the direct and indirect threats to human security and classify them according to their visibility and immediacy.[15] An element of discretion and uncertainty would always persist, but this methodology is useful to differentiate between the threats to human security that are remediable by the State and by societal action. Thus a reconceptualization of the very concept of national security in South Asia is possible by restricting the ambit of security to what threatens the State and human lives: this would include, apart from the military, non-military and non-traditional threats identifiable, human security, and others like States failing or becoming totalitarian.

A similar conceptual overstretch would occur by extending the meaning of governance to embrace all aspects of societal activity. Clearly, there are some aspects of humane governance (like women's empowerment) that require social engineering: this lies partly in the sphere of State action, and partly in the area of social reform. Expectations in regard to governance must, therefore, be tempered with a pragmatic understanding of what is remediable by the State, and what lies in the domain of civil society. The State cannot be wished away in matters relating to humane governance. Although the nation State concept is believed to be the source of many of its problems like the integration of minorities, there is no solution possible to the quandary as to how it might be disinvented. Moreover, many issues relating to humane governance like promoting literacy and providing basic health cannot be entirely left to private effort and requires the intercession of the State.

AN OVERVIEW OF THE STUDY

A word is necessary now to explain the manner in which this study was effected. A concept paper was circulated in advance to the authors. It proceeded on the assumption that a military security perspective was inadequate to understand the magnitude or nature of the threats to national security in South Asia. It was, therefore, necessary to take into account the non-military and newer threats to security and pass under review concepts like human security and humane governance to appreciate their implications for national security. Thereafter, it was necessary to discern the systemic challenge to their governance processes and clearly establish the linkage between misgovernance and insecurity in these countries. Some other issues requiring attention were identified to be the culture of militarization in several regional countries with their armed forces playing a decisive role in decision-making; the security aspects of the crisis of governance in South Asia; and the remedial measures possible to reverse this situation.

The real challenge in this study, however, lay in establishing the nexus between State and human security, the respective roles of the citizen and the State in providing humane governance, and the precise linkages between security and governance. The authors were requested to keep these perspectives firmly in mind whilst writing their essays. A gist of their findings is given below.

Holding Bangladesh to be a grossly misgoverned State, Amena Mohsin indicts the several State institutions concerned with governance in the country, like Parliament, the electoral process, political system, military and the Constitution itself as being responsible for this state of affairs. These institutions acquired an undemocratic character following the failure of the political leadership to arrest their polarization, hence, the polity has yet to evolve and ensure a minimum level of security for the citizens. Military and quasi-military regimes have ruled the country between the military take-over in 1975 and 1990, which distorted the political process. The State has created politicized ethnic and religious minorities, whilst nationalist differences divide the dominant Bengali community: this further undermines the people's security. The paper recommends democratization of State institutions and the SAARC process to grapple with the national security issues in Bangladesh.

In 'Trenches, Boundaries and Spaces', Meenakshi Gopinath argues that the Human Security paradigm affords a viable perspective to locate the concerns, dilemmas and tensions of governance in a pluralistic society like India; it would also be hospitable to the gender perspective. The period after the 1980s is discussed in this paper when the secular ideal and the Nehruvian development paradigm began to be severely tested. The first section of the paper foregrounds contemporary challenges to governance from demands to *institutionalize* diversity. The next section focuses on the new people's movements that emerged around issues of human security. The final section addresses the concerns surrounding the management of security in a nuclearized environment, and the growing culture of militarism. The demarcation of *internal* versus *external* security is interrogated, underscoring the need for imaginative dealing with border-States that represent the *internal-external* interface.

Lok Raj Baral identifies the issue of plurality as possessing a sociological and political perspective, whilst relating it to security in the special case of a multicultural country like Nepal. He notes that the political elite have little commitment to the democratic political development of the country or to good governance for achieving this objective. Social and economic disparities have widened as a result of the non-traditional sources of insecurity being left unattended. Even the letter and spirit of the Constitution has been neglected by these elite, to the detriment of the poor and deprived sections of the population.

Dwelling on the situation in Pakistan, Shahrukh Rafi Khan has sought to demonstrate two points. First, elections to the local bodies that are being contemplated by the military government in power are not a straightforward exercise in devolving power to the grass-roots level for the better delivery of services via people's participation and self-management. To be effective, this exercise would entail at the very minimum the redistribution of assets, and civil service, electoral and judicial reforms so that human security is ensured. Second, it would be preferable to devolve accountability (besides financial and administrative authority) to the lowest tier at which a particular service is delivered. An indicative model for such devolution of authority has then been presented, which could also provide an exit strategy for the military government.

The chief contention in Paikiasothy Saravanamuttu's chapter is that the problem of governance in Sri Lanka stems primarily from the failure to acknowledge the pluralism available to society through constitutional guarantees, political institutions and culture. The cumulative effect is a crisis in the legitimacy of the State, manifested in the protracted ethnic conflict. This crisis of legitimacy can only be resolved by a new social contract between the State and the citizen, enshrining the values of democratic pluralism and diversity. The chapter traces the political developments in Sri Lanka, whilst further arguing that this crisis of legitimacy has bred and sustained a zero-sum political culture in which the partisan politicization in the pursuit of power and its consolidation has become paramount. Consequently, the space for the full exercise of democratic rights and a robust civil society has become restricted. It is only through the appreciation and institutionalization of pluralism and diversity as sources of strength rather than as threats to the State and polity that governance could be anchored in society.

The inadequacy of a military approach to national security in South Asia is argued in the concluding chapter. It identifies the crumbling of democratic institutions, alienation of minority communities and the growing criminalization of politics in South Asia as lying at the heart of the problems of governance and security in the region, before speculating on the remedial action possible.

NOTES

1. *SIPRI Yearbook 2000: Armaments, Disarmament and International Security*, (Oxford: Oxford University Press, 2000), p. 14. SIPRI defines a major armed conflict to involve the use of armed strength between the military forces of two or more governments, or of one government and at least one organized armed group, resulting in the battle-related deaths of at least 1,000 people in any single year and in which the incompatibility concerns control of government and/or territory.
2. Ibid., p. 8.
3. These are discussed in P.R. Chari, ' Security Aspects of Indian Foreign Policy', in Stephen Philip Cohen, ed., *The Security of South Asia: American and Asian Perspectives* (Urbana and Chicago: University of Chicago Press, 1987), pp. 50–2.
4. 'Editorial Overview: The Crisis and Promise of South Asia', in Ponna Wignaraja and Akmal Hussain, eds., *The Challenge in South Asia: Development, Democracy and Regional Cooperation* (New Delhi: Sage, 1989), p. 18.
5. These questions are debated in Kanti Bajpai, 'Human Security: Concept and Measurement', Occasional Paper No. 19: OP: (2000), Joan B. Kroc Institute for International Peace Studies, University of Notre Dame, Indiana. The paper also compares the approaches towards ensuring human security urged by the UNDP and Canada; the Canadian approach prescribes a greater role for the State and global cooperation to achieve its objectives.
6. Dylan Hendrikson, *A Review of Security-Sector Reform*, Working Paper 1 (London: The Conflict, Security & Development Group at the Centre for Defence Studies), 1999, p. 16.
7. Cf. 'Views on Governance', in *Human Development in South Asia 1999: The Crisis of Governance* (Karachi: Oxford University Press, 1999), Box 2.1, p. 29. These views include, apart from the UNDP and OECD, those of the World Bank and the Commission on Global Governance. Together, they present a universal recognition of what 'governance' implies and should comprise.
8. Ibid., p. 28.
9. Ibid., pp. 31–7.
10. The Conflict, Security & Development Group, *Bulletin*, October 1999, p. 3.
11. Ibid.
12. Jawaharlal Nehru, *The Discovery of India* (New Delhi: Oxford University Press, 1986), Fifth Impression, p. 107.
13. M.J. Vinod, ' Conceptualising Good Governance: Questions of Democracy and Development', *Mainstream*, vol. XXXVIII, no. 45, 28 October 2000, p. 16.
14. Lawrence Freedman, 'International Security: Changing Targets', *Foreign Policy*, Spring 1998, p. 53.
15. Kanti Bajpai suggests this methodology: op. cit., n. 5 above, pp. 22–7.

CHAPTER 2

Governance and Security: The Experience of Bangladesh

Amena Mohsin

Despite much hype by the ruling Awami League regime on American President Bill Clinton's short visit to Dhaka on 20 March 2000, two things became obvious to political observers. First, the US President recognized the role played by non-governmental agencies in Bangladesh in bringing about human development and ensuring human security. Second, this recognition is a sad reflection on the misgovernance or failure of governance by the State. Rehman Sobhan has argued that 'the character of the Bangladesh state is a society which is not so much over or misgoverned but is barely governed at all'.[1] The latter part of the statement has some merit, but the syndrome of 'barely being governed' is an aspect of misgovernance by the state, which attempts to overgovern by its attempts to centralize and overpoliticize its institutions. It is indeed ironical that a people who had revolted against misgovernance are caught today in the same vortex of misgovernance.

This paper defines governance as the manner in which people are looked after or cared for by the State. In doing this, it takes cognisance of the modes, institutions and manner of governance, which are responsible for the nature and quality of the polity that a State develops. The manner and modes of governance are linked to the notion of security. The term 'security' is used here in a broad and comprehensive sense. Security includes not only the territorial security of the State but also, more importantly, the human security of the people. Human security implies the physical and psychological security of a people and the creation of institutions that enable them to participate and be responsible for the maintenance of their own security in a democratic manner. This paper argues that the dichotomy of security between military and human is faulty, and, to some extent, deliberate, since it only serves vested interests. Scarce national resources are diverted to military security, endangering the security of the people. The militarization of the State also has repercussions on inter-State security, which also endangers the security of the people.

The failure of the State to deliver basic services to the people, widespread corruption and appropriation of State resources by the regimes in power and the opposition, weak political institutions, lack of democratic spirit in the party in power and in the Opposition has turned Bangladesh into one of the most violent and polarized societies in the region. This process is not unidirectional, nor is it a post-Independence phenomenon. The creation of the State itself was marked by violence. Polarization existed within the rank and file of the politicians and freedom fighters during the liberation war. Violence was rampant thereafter, and it polarized independent Bangladesh on the course adopted by the new state. This was exacerbated by the institutions established and the manner of their governance. The post-Independence regime failed to integrate these diverse forces into a coherent body, which had its consequences for human security within and outside the State. *This paper argues that State institutions and structures of governance are responsible for human insecurity in Bangladesh.*

The paper is divided into three sections. The first examines the limitations of the State due to the Constitution, the electoral process and Parliament, and how they impact on human security. The second section reviews the militarization of Bangladesh politics and its consequences for human security due to the intervention of another State institution, viz., the military. Finally, the paper argues the need to creatively change the institutions to make them participatory, democratic and people-centric.

MISGOVERNANCE, POLARIZATION AND SECURITY

The State of Bangladesh inherited a polarized polity at birth. This had its roots in the nationalist struggle against British colonialism.[2] The Partition of India divided the country on communal lines into Hindus and Muslims, whilst the independence of Bangladesh divided the people along nationalist lines into 'Bengalis' and 'Bangladeshis'; communalism and chauvinism were latent in both these processes. These divisions reflected in the nature of the political elite and the institutions devised by them for governance, viz., the Constitution, Parliament and the electoral process, which exacerbated this polarization.

The Bangladesh Constitution is a highly nationalist and undemocratic document, ensuring the hegemony of the dominant Bengali nation in all spheres of life. The Constitution of 1972 adopted nationalism as one of the fundamental principles of State policy, along with democracy, secularism and socialism. This State-sponsored nationalism was chauvinistic and clearly identified itself with the dominant Bengali population in the State. Article 9 of the Constitution defined Bengali nationalism as:

> The unity and solidarity of the Bengali nation, which, deriving its identity from its language and culture, attained sovereign and independent Bangladesh through a united and determined struggle in the war of independence, shall be the basis of Bengali nationalism.[3]

The State thereby acquired a distinct Bengali character. It might be pointed out here that Bengali nationalism, emphasizing the Bengali language and culture was the basis of the independence movement of the East Bengalis within the State of Pakistan. This secular brand of nationalism was considered to be a logical tool to counter the Islamic brand of Pakistani nationalism. Its adoption as the basis of State nationalism and the State's endeavour to impose Bengali nationality on the entire population, however, was beset with problems as Bangladesh is home to about 45 different ethnic communities. The Constitution also declared Bangladesh to be a homogeneous unicultural country. By denying space to the ethnic communities, the political elite of Bangladesh only replicated the hegemony that it had fought against within the State of Pakistan.

These provisions of the Constitution were unacceptable to the ethnic communities in Bangladesh, more specifically the hill people of the Chittagong Hill Tracts (CHT). They perceived their cultural identity and survival as a distinct community to be threatened by the imposition of Bengali nationalism. Manobendra Narayan Larma, the lone representative of the hill people in Parliament at that time, refused to endorse this Constitution and lamented that there was no space and recognition within it for his people. Thereafter, Larma formed the Parbattya Chattagram Jonoshonghoti Samiti (PCJSS), a political platform for the hill people: subsequently, a military wing, the Shanti Bahini, was added to it. The formation of the PCJSS signalled the break of the hill people from the State-sponsored model of nationalism and gave rise to an insurgency movement that was to continue for the next two decades. This insurgency took its toll on human security. The CHT underwent full-scale militarization and the region was placed under military control (discussed later). The CHT's problem was essentially political but the State's attempt to impose a military solution only revealed the hegemonic character of the State. It was seen by the hill people as a demonstration of Bengali power to further consolidate Bengali hegemony. This widened the divisions between the hill people and the Bengalis.[4]

The military takeover after 1975 was followed by the introduction of Islamization into the Constitution and the polity. This move was ostensibly undertaken for political reasons. The military regimes wanted to distance themselves from the Awami League and also from 'Hindu' India. It was identified as being too pro-Indian, and was accused of selling out to India. Religion was, therefore, used as a political tool to consolidate the position of the military regimes. The Constitution was given an Islamic orientation through the insertion of '*Bismillahir-Rahmanir-Rahim*' ('in the name of Allah, the Beneficent, the Merciful') at the beginning of the Constitution and before its preamble. The principle of secularism was dropped and substituted by the principles of absolute trust and faith in Almighty Allah. Article 12, by which communal political parties were banned in Bangladesh, was dropped from the Constitution. Article 9, which stressed the linguistic and cultural unity of Bengali nationalism, was omitted. Instead of being called Bengalis, Article 6 clause 2 envisaged that the citizens of Bangladesh would be known as 'Bangladeshis'.[5] The state thereby shifted from Bengali nationalism to 'Bangladeshi nationalism', which emphasized Bengali culture and language and incorporated the elements of territory and religion in its fold.

Islam, being the religion of the dominant Bengali community, came to be identified as an element in this State-sponsored model of nationalism. In 1978, Islam was declared to be the State religion with the provision that other religions could be practised in peace and harmony. The State's identification with and promotion of one particular religious community placed the other religious communities at a disadvantageous position. This turned the Bengali Hindu community and the other ethnic groups into minorities, who were ethnically and religiously marginalized. The seeds of religious polarization were, thus, sown by the adoption of a Bangladeshi model of nationhood.

The Bengali Muslim community has also polarized along these two models of nationhood, with each side accusing the other of anti-State activities. Supporters of Bengali nationalism accuse their opponents of being anti-liberation elements, while the latter accuse the nationalists of a sell-out to India. The civil and political society in Bangladesh is violently polarized today along these two models of nationhood.

The national electoral process too is beset with problems. The 'one person, one vote' principle ensures the rule of the majority while the minority communities remain unrepresented and unheard. The electoral process is also masculinized and corrupt. There is no binding residency rule for the candidate in the constituency from where he/she contests or gets elected; consequently they are increasingly dependent on intermediaries who work on their behalf during elections. These are mostly thugs and hooligans who have no political affiliations but work for money. Thus, money and muscle power are the mainstay of the electoral process.

The Election Commission's office, though autonomous, is not free from government influence. The Election Commission's Secretariat works under the Prime Minister's office. It is no surprise, therefore, that there are constant allegations by the Opposition of vote-rigging during the bye-elections. In fact, the Opposition parties have boycotted all the bye-elections held by the present Awami League regime. Similarly, the Awami League, then in Opposition, had launched an anti-government programme against the then BNP regime in 1994 on allegations of vote-rigging in the Magura bye-elections. This movement ultimately led to the passage of the 13th Amendment to the Constitution, which provides for national elections being held under a non-partisan caretaker government. One could argue that this would free the elections from the grip of a partisan government and ensure *free and fair* elections. The picture, however, is not so clear. The caretaker government is dependent on the district and thana-level administration, i.e. the Deputy Commissioners (DC) and Thana Nirbahi Officers (TNO) for holding the elections as they serve as returning officers. The police are also called upon to maintain law and order. The partisan nature of these two institutions is well known, since the government is constantly accused of politicizing the administration.

However, this politicization started immediately after Independence with the introduction of the district quota system, spoils system recruitment, two years antedated seniority for freedom fighters, and induction of large numbers of outsiders into the civil service, especially army officers, to perpetuate the power base of the regimes.[6] The political parties and the bureaucracy have used the polarized situation within the political system and the bureaucracy to their advantage. The polarized and partisan nature of the administration was revealed most starkly in 1996 when the bureaucracy came out in open support of the Opposition to force the government to resign.

Significantly, the examination results of the Public Service Commission (PSC) examination held in 2000 and the appointments made thereafter have caused much controversy. It was said that the ruling party influenced the examination results and the appointments. Some 17 student leaders and activists of the ruling Awami League party have been appointed to the police cadre. It has been alleged that they were appointed, not on merit basis, but by obtaining unbelievably high marks (like 180 out of 200) in the viva voce. These marks are not compatible with their written examination marks. All the 11 members of the PSC appointed by this regime are affiliated to the ruling party.[7] The ruling party has refuted these allegations, but the Opposition continues to make this an issue. Significantly, perceptions of politicization of the administration are strong in the general population. Hence, there appears to be an urgent need to give more authority to the Election Commission with powers to recruit its own officials.[8]

The muscle and money engulfing the electoral process makes it difficult for women and the poorer segments of the population to participate in national politics. The absence of meaningful women's participation in the electoral process is indeed deplorable, since women constitute 48.59 per cent of the total population (according to the estimates of 1989). This implies that almost half the population is excluded from effective participation in national politics. It also needs emphasis that the presence of a few women at the helm of political leadership does not necessarily guarantee gender-sensitive politics or the introduction of feminist perspectives into politics. This is evident from the violent nature of politics in Bangladesh. The absence of structures for the meaningful representation and participation of women leads to a masculinization of the women involved in politics as politics or 'public life' is considered the domain of men and conducted within a masculinized paradigm.

The absence of a residency requirement for the candidate is also a serious problem. It has created a wide gap between the voters and the person who supposedly represents them. The power of hooligans resulting from this situation and the capital-centric politics has further undermined the democratic process.

The national Parliament is a single-house, 330-member body. The 300 members are directly elected, while 30 seats are reserved for women who are nominated by the elected members. Nominations are normally given in return for services or connections. These nominees have no contacts with the people, and are looked upon as mere 'showpieces'. They remain inaudible, and invisible serving merely as vote casters for the nominating party. In view of the cosmetic nature of women's representation, civil-society members have increasingly called for a change in the existing situation. The reservation provision expires in April 2001. There have been demands for direct elections and an increase in the number of reserved seats for women representatives. It is argued that the reservation of seats is required for a further period of time so that women can make themselves visible and become effective participants in politics, apart from women in politics gaining general acceptance in this period.

It is interesting that the mainstream parties have not agreed to change the existing system, but have further agreed that Pajeros would be made available to all the MPs. This only highlights the elitist nature of Bangladesh politics where women and the poor remain under represented. There are also a very insignificant number of women in the ministries. Tables 2.1 and 2.2.[9] underline the dismal state of women's representation in the national Parliament and the cabinet positions held by them.

There is literally no reservation for the minorities: those who get elected do so from the platform of the mainstream political parties. These parties have their own agendas and cater to the majority rather than minority aspirations. In the present Parliament, only 8 members are from the Hindu community, and 3 from the Chakma community. Of the 11 elected members, 10 are from the Awami League (1 independent candidate having joined the Treasury Bench after his election), and 1 from the BNP. The minority community members who get elected from these parties are bound to toe their party lines, as voting against the party position would result in loss of the seat. Three seats are reserved for the CHT, but they are for the geographical area and not for the hill people.

It needs pointing out that in 1979–80, the state had undertaken a policy of Bengali settlement in the CHT as part of its anti-insurgency strategy. Consequently, the Bengalis today constitute 50 per cent of the total population of the HT. Due to this demographic change in the region, Bengalis can also get elected from the region. One of the major demands of the PCJSS has been to reserve three seats for the hill people in Parliament, but this was rejected by successive regimes in Bangladesh. However, one could point out that even if three seats were reserved for the hill people, there is very little these three representatives could achieve in a House of 330.

TABLE 2.1: REPRESENTATION OF WOMEN IN ELECTIONS

Year of Election	No. of Women Succeeding in General Seats	Percentage of Successful Women Candidates	Reserved Seat for Women	Percentage of Women Candidates to total seat
1973	0	0	15	4.8
1979[a]	0	0	30	9.0
1979[b]	0+2	0.7	30	9.0
1986[c]	5	1.7	30	10.6
1986[d]	3+2	1.7	30	10.6
1988	4	1.3	—	—
1991[e]	8	2.7	30	11.5
1991[f]	4+1	1.7	30	10.6
1996	7	2.0	30	11.21

In 1973 and 1979, (a) women candidates contested the elections but no one got elected. In the 1979 (b) bye-elections, two women candidates got elected. In 1986 (a) Sheikh Hasina got elected from three constituencies: consequently, there were bye-elections for two seats and two women got elected from there (b) In 1988, the reserved seats for women remained inoperative. In the 1991 (a) elections women won eight seats, out of which Khaleda Zia won five. In the bye-election for the four seats, i.e. 1991 (b), male candidates were put up by the BNP. The Awami League had put up one woman candidate, but she was not elected, so the four seats were occupied by four male BNP candidates.

TABLE 2.2: REPRESENTATION OF WOMEN IN CABINET

Government	Total No. of Ministers	Total No. of Men Ministers	Total No. of Women Ministers	Percentage
Sheikh Mujibur Rahman (1972–5)	50	48	2	4
Ziaur Rahman (1979–82)	101	95	6	6
Hossain M. Ershad (1982–90)	133	127	4	3
Begum Khaleda Zia (1991–6)	39	36	3	5
Sheikh Hasina (1996–)	46	42	4	8.69

The manner in which Parliament is conducted is highly autocratic, with little scope and space for the participation of the Opposition. There have been allegations of the microphones of the Opposition members being switched off during debates. The Opposition has constantly alleged that the television (government-controlled) coverage of Parliament sessions has been quite partisan. The Opposition had, in fact, undertaken gheraos (encircling and locking in) of the television station in protest against their alleged partisan role. The Opposition has now made the streets its protest ground on the plea that it is not allowed to talk in Parliament. It is probable that the Opposition makes out an exaggerated case, but it is equally true that the neutrality of the Speakers of Parliament has always been suspect. The Speaker and the Deputy Speaker have normally been elected from the majority party, and they retain their party affiliations and seat after their elections to these positions.

The above processes and institutions have created an extremly polarized situation, having serious security implications. The State has created politicized minorities that have the potential to destabilize the political system. The ethnic polarization, as pointed out earlier, gave rise to an insurgency situation in the CHT for almost two decades. Apart from the hill people, the plains Adivahis also resent their economic and political marginalization within the Bengali-dominated state. The BAGACHASH, a Garo student's forum, has threatened to carry out a movement like that of the hill people if the State does not take cognisance of their political and economic rights, which would include constitutional recognition of their cultural distinctiveness and customary land rights.[10] While one might dismiss these manoeuvres, this does not obviate the fact that deep grievances against the State of deprivation exist within the minority community. They do not feel that the State has secured their cultural, economic and political rights. More importantly, they perceive their existence threatened by the State institutions and policies.[11]

Apart from the ethnic communities, the religious minorities also feel insecure due to the Islamization clauses of the Constitution. The declaration of Islam as the state religion, they allege, has put members of the other religious groups in a subservient position. The continued existence of discriminatory laws like the Vested Property Act, which had its origins in the Enemy Property Act of Pakistan, is a cause of much dismay and resentment among the Hindu community. This Act was passed in 1965 and consisted of the following major provisions:

India is declared as an enemy country;

All interests of the enemy, i.e., nationals and citizens of India, those residing in the territory occupied/captured/controlled by Indian firms, companies as well as in the lands and buildings situated in Pakistan, to be taken over by the custodian of Enemy Property for control or management;

The benefits arising out of trade or business or lands and buildings should not go to the enemy, so that it may not affect the security of the state of Pakistan or impair its defence in any manner.[12]

The Act was kept in operation through various proclamations even after the end of the war. Paradoxically enough, the Bangladesh State retained the same Act. On 26 March 1972, the Bangladesh Government enforced the Bangladesh Vesting of Property and Assets Order (Order 29 of 1972). By this Order, the properties left behind by the Pakistanis (non-Bengalis, Biharis who left for Pakistan) and the erstwhile enemy properties were combined into a single category. This was a clear violation of the spirit of the liberation war, which was based on a secular plank. The Hindu community regards it as being discriminatory on political and economic grounds. It is one of their major causes of insecurity. The Hindu community has lost much of its property and has been subjected to much harassment due to this law.[13] According to one estimate, the total number of Hindu households affected by the VPA is 10,48,390. The total land dispossessed is 1.05 million acres.[14]

The Hindu-Bouddha-Christian Oikkyo Parishad has consistently called for a repeal of this discriminatory law. In view of these constant protests, the government set up a Parliamentary subcommittee under the Ministry of Land to recommend the repeal of the Vested Property Act. The committee has formulated a Draft Bill. But this Bill has several loopholes. It recommends that properties that are not legally vested in the ownership of the government and those which have been declared as enemy or vested property after 16 February 1969 would not be considered as vested property under the proposed law. The fact of the matter is that most Hindu property has been declared vested property after this period. The proposed Bill further visualizes that nothing contained in the proposed law shall affect the proprietorship status of the vested property if it has been taken over by the government, a government institution, any other institution or individual, has been sold or has been handed over permanently by the government on the directives of a court. These cases cannot be questioned in any court.[15] These provisions negate and defeat the spirit and objectives of the proposed law. It also states that the original owners must produce their land documents before the tribunal set up for the settlement of the land issue within 180 days of the promulgation of the law, else it would be taken over as government property. The 180-day time period is considered to be insufficient by the affected community. Besides, the law also provides that in the absence of the original owner, the property would be passed on to the successor according to Hindu inheritance laws. The present Hindu law deprives women of any right to inheritance, and in such cases this provision would be discriminatory against women.[16]

Thus the State, through its own actions, has jeopardized the basic security of its minorities, both ethnic and religious. This has its ramifications for state politics and adds to the polarized state of national politics. A further consequence of this insecurity is an emigration to India, which affects inter-State security and also incites the communal forces in India. While it is true that many Muslims have crossed borders in search of economic opportunities, the fact remains that many Hindus have done so for economic as well as personal security reasons.

Women have also been marginalized by these policies. The growth of fundamentalist forces has endangered their security, and there has been an increase in the number of fatwas (religious edicts) in the rural areas. It has also strengthened the masculinized values of the State that promote patriarchal values and marginalize women. These values of Bangladeshi politics can be appreciated from the fact that the present Opposition, led by a woman, has supported a fundamentalist group protesting against the decision of the High Court to ban fatwas. This is being done in the most violent manner, not only by calling for hartals (total shutdown of all work), but by declaring the two judges who gave the ruling, as '*murtad*' (banished from religion).

The present spate of hartals (February 2001) has already claimed the lives of more than a dozen people. It has turned into a battle of muscle and guns between the ruling and Opposition parties. In the process, the resolution of the question of issue of fatwas, so important for empowering women, seems to have got lost in the vortex of power politics. With elections coming up by the middle of the year, violence has become the main tool in the hands of the ruling and Opposition parties for capturing power. This is a sad reflection on the unhealthy state of politics in Bangladesh where resort to violence is fast replacing institutional politics as the mode of governance. It is important to note that the masculinization of society is inextricably linked with the militarization of the polity,[17] which serves the interests of a vested group, while the women, children and the people suffer.

Apart from disrupting the growth of a healthy democratic process, these developments have also affected the economy. Instead of in Parliament, street protests and frequent hartals has become the Opposition's norm. Hartals take a heavy toll of the economy since all normal economic activities come to a halt. Its toll in terms of human suffering is staggering and immeasurable.[18] Hartals have made politics more violent, as both the ruling and Opposition parties openly use small arms.

According to one estimate, there are 80 terrorist syndicates in the State, out of which 28 are in the capital, Dhaka. The country has about 2,00,000 illegal weapons, and Dhaka has 50,000. Everyday, about 9 people are killed within the country: out of this, 4 are victims of these illegal arms. The country has turned into one of the important transit routes for drugs and small arms. Alarmingly (but not surprisingly), these arms are proliferating within the country under the patronage of the political parties.[19] Many innocent people have been caught in the cross-fire and bomb explosions. They have either died or been crippled for life. According to one report, 170 persons were injured and 30 persons died due to bomb explosions between 1998 and 1999. Among the dead, 10 were children and another 10 children were seriously injured.[20] The politicians seem oblivious to this human suffering. In fact, each dead body provides more fodder for their violence, as they claim the dead to be their partymen.

The academic sphere has also been severely affected by the regular shutdowns of academic institutions by the opposing political forces, at times for months together. A dangerous consequence of such negative politics is the lack of interest towards studies among students at all levels. A normal four-year course at the university now takes seven to eight years to complete. The consequence is a heavy brain drain, whilst important human resources are being wasted. A national daily recently reported that the Chittagong University campus has turned into a den of drug addicts. Among the important reasons cited for this state of affairs are sessions being extended, uncertainty of getting a job, and domination of the student's dormitories by student leaders belonging to the major political parties. These leaders are engaged in drug trading in the campus.[21]

This violent situation keeps the parties, both ruling and Opposition, from concentrating on important issues, like the environment, city planning, health, nutrition, education, and transportation that affect human security on a daily basis. A glaring example of this is the dengue epidemic that has gripped the country at present. The WHO warned the government of this outbreak about two years back, but neither the ruling nor the Opposition parties made an issue of it. Consequently there are at least 4–5 reported cases of death occurring daily due to dengue.

MISGOVERNANCE, MILITARIZATION AND SECURITY

The post-Independence government of Bangladesh was beset with the herculean task of massive post-war rehabilitation. Expectations, often unrealistic, were raised by the euphoria surrounding independence. Arms were available openly, the economy was in tatters, and the military was ideologically divided. The State was in dire need of visionary leadership. The Awami League regime failed to provide any direction to the people. Sheikh Mujibur Rahman, the 'Father of the Nation', acted more like a party leader than a state leader. Lawlessness and nepotism became the order of the day. The State acquired an authoritarian character. In 1974 the Special Powers Act (SPA) was passed which gave sweeping powers to the law enforcing agencies. This law became a tool for oppressing the Opposition. In 1975, the country shifted from a multiparty system to a one-party regime, press freedom was banned, and political opposition, too, was banned.

The military remained divided, but was frustrated with this state of affairs. The defence budget was gradually reduced. In the 1973–4 budget, it was little more than 16 per cent, in 1974–5 it came down to 15 per cent, and in the 1975–6 budget estimates it was less than 13 per cent. The regime did not take any steps to reconstruct the training institutes and cantonments that were destroyed during the liberation war. The military resented the formation of the Jatiyo Rakkhi Bahini (JRB, or 'National Security Forces') whilst it was being neglected. The JRB was given special powers and took orders from the President. The military considered the JRB to be a parallel institution and a threat to its corporate interests.[22]

On 15 August 1975, Sheikh Mujib was assassinated by a group of disgruntled majors. The military coup brought the military to the helm of affairs. During 1975–90 the country remained under military and quasi-military rule under Generals Ziaur Rahman and H.M. Ershad respectively. During this period, Bangladeshi politics became distorted and militarized in two very important ways: (*a*) the military as an institution has become a *factor* in Bangladesh politics; (*b*) civilian politics were militarized and polarized.

Zia emerged as the strongman following a series of coups and counter-coups in November 1975. The army was torn by internal conflicts. The freedom fighters were divided along ideological lines. One group wanted a conventional army, whilst the other advocated the case for a revolutionary army on the Chinese model. There were divisions between the repatriated officers (those who were interned in Pakistan) and the freedom fighters. Mujib had given two years seniority to the freedom fighters: the repatriated officers resented this, as they had to serve under their juniors. Zia tried to redress this problem by promoting H.M. Ershad and Kazi Golam Dastagir, two of the seniormost repatriated officers. Zia also appointed Ershad as the Deputy Chief of Staff, which was resented greatly by the freedom fighters. He crushed a revolt on 7 November 1977 and hanged its leader, Col. Taher, getting himself entrenched in power. The movement for a revolutionary army was thus stopped. The JRB—an element of much resentment within the army—was dismantled and incorporated into the army. Zia rapidly expanded the size of the military, raised its salaries, allowances and other benefits. The military budget increased substantially, as indicated in Table 2.3.[23]

The militarization of the administration started during his regime; for instance, while at the beginning of 1980, the number of military officers appointed to top civilian positions was 41, by the end of the year the number went up to 79.[24] Though Zia's cabinet consisted of civil-military bureaucrats and technocrats, it was dominated by the military, as it was placed under the supervision of Zia's Principal Staff Officer (PSO), the most intimate of his confidantes from the army.[25]

The intelligence services were also brought under the military. In 1977, Zia appointed a senior general as the director general of the National Security Intelligence—a civilian body, but the principal organ for intelligence gathering. This tradition was to continue long after his death. But the Director General Forces Intelligence, the military organ

TABLE 2.3: MILITARY BUDGET

Year	Million Dollars
1975	42
1976	86
1977	136
1978	140
1979	135
1980	138

of intelligence gathering, gained the upper hand in terms of credibility and reliability. These developments had far-reaching political implications for a society like Bangladesh, which lacked stable political institutions.

Ershad, the second military ruler of Bangladesh, continued and expanded the policies initiated by Zia. Unlike Zia, Ershad did not face any dissension or opposition from within the military. By 1982, when Ershad seized power in a bloodless coup from the Sattar civilian regime, the military had been cleansed of its internal factionalism and had started claiming a constitutional role for itself in the administration of the country.[26]

Ershad formalized the entry of military officers into the foreign and civil services on the basis of a quota system: 25 per cent of the posts in the Foreign Service were allocated to the armed forces. The police forces were also brought under the control of the military. Ershad literally colonized the administration with military personnel. Important bodies of national importance like the National Economic Council, Committee on Food, Agriculture and Rural Development, Energy and Mineral Resources Committee, Export-Import Committee, Government Purchase Committee, Promotion and Service Restructure Committee, Pay Fixation and Administrative Reorganisation Committee were either led or dominated by military men. They also established dominant positions in business circles, including the disinvested and private banks, insurance companies, industrial units, and so on. Ershad also offered expensive plots of lands and house building loans on easy terms to military officers.[27]

The allocations to defence in the annual revenue budget were increased on an average by 18 per cent while the total yearly budget increased by 14 per cent. In contrast to the policy followed by earlier regimes, new pay scales were introduced in August 1985, which brought about parity of salaries between military and civilian employees. It is important to note that military personnel enjoy benefits and allowances not enjoyed by their civilian counterparts.[28] On 20 September 1986, the government issued the Warrant of Preference. It gave preference to the Chiefs of the Army, Navy and Air Force over Members of Parliament. About 40 per cent of Ershad's successive Councils of Ministers were drawn from the military.

The military rulers of Bangladesh, both Zia and Ershad, realized quite early in their rule that, in a highly politicized society like Bangladesh, it was not possible to rule either by reliance on the support of the military or by use of its coercive power. Their quest for legitimacy at home and abroad turned them on the path of civilianization of their administration. In the process, however, Bangladesh politics got militarized. This took place in two ways. First, the military got involved in the process of party building, and retired military personnel got inducted into politics; second, the military became a factor in regime sustenance and regime change.

For Zia, legitimacy was not a problem. He was a popular and valiant freedom fighter. His personal honesty was never in doubt. More importantly, he had not come to power by design: rather, he was catapulted onto the political scene by accident, although he was the main beneficiary of the August 1975 coup. At the national level, the government passed the Political Party Regulations (PPR) in July 1976 that allowed domestic politics with government permission. About 60 political parties applied and 21 of them, including the Awami League, were allowed to operate. Zia legitimized his own presidency by holding a presidential referendum on 30 May 1977. He resigned from the Army, and, in September 1978, launched his own political party, the Bangladesh Nationalist Party (BNP). During this process of civilianization, however, the military intelligence and the NSI were extensively used for setting up new political organizations, disrupting the Opposition, undermining their unity, getting support and buying off opponents. Soon, the military became the most significant political party.[29] Martial law ended after the inauguration of the elected Parliament in 1979.

Zia's civilianization process, however, brought him into conflict with senior military officers, especially the freedom fighters. They were displeased by Zia's leaning towards the rightist forces that, they believed, had undermined the spirit of the liberation war, and were also alarmed as civilianization meant a lesser role and power for the military in state affairs. This was unacceptable to his associates, who had nurtured him in power. Zia was assassinated on 31 May 1981 in a military coup.

The military elite 'allowed' the civilian government of the BNP to survive for a while, largely due to the popularity that Zia enjoyed among the soldiers and the general public. But soon after, Army Chief Gen. Ershad pressed for the military having a constitutional role in State affairs. Then he forced the Sattar regime to form a National Security Council. It included the three Service Chiefs of the armed forces, the Prime Minister, and the Vice-President, with the President as its head. The military thus became part of the decision-making body of the government. The regime, however, took time to institutionalize this. The military realized that the government was buying time: it could not wait any longer. Finally, on 24 March 1982, Ershad seized power in a bloodless coup and martial law was imposed.

Ershad ruled for nine long years, but could never make himself acceptable to the civil and political society of Bangladesh. He was considered a usurper who had seized power from an elected civilian regime. This made Ershad dependent on the military. Yet, the need for legitimacy drove him towards civilianization of the government. On 21 March 1985, a referendum was held to ensure his continuation in the presidency till the holding of presidential elections. Ershad resigned from the Army, and, in January 1986, floated his own political party, the Jatiyo Party.

Once again, the military intelligence played a crucial role in the formation of this party, buying allegiance and creating splits within and among the political parties that had united in an anti-Ershad movement. Thus, the Awami League was persuaded to participate in the parliamentary elections of May 1986. Money and arms were given to trade unions and student leaders. Intelligence officers also played a significant role in devising administrative reforms that would offset Zia's achievements in the rural sector.[30]

Ershad was sworn in as the elected President on 23 October 1986 and martial law was withdrawn on 10 November 1986. All the elections held by his regime were regarded as farcical and 'managed' by the military. Despite the civilianization of the government, Ershad, unlike Zia, could not distance himself from the military, as he failed to gain general acceptance by the people. He had to resign in 1990 in the face of a massive upsurge against him. Ershad turned to his constituency, the military, for support. But they too withdrew their support, as they could gauge the pulse of the people. Thus, regime changes in Bangladesh, till 1990, took place through the Army, either by its action or inaction. The military has thus become a factor in Bangladesh politics. More importantly, the introduction of Bangladeshi nationalist politics has polarized the political parties; consequently, the political leaders remain divided on core national issues, which hampers political stability and the growth of viable political institutions. The military, however, has established itself as a coherent body.

This fact is well understood by the civilian regimes. The two successive civilian Prime Ministers maintained their control over the military through the Armed Forces Division. They also retained the portfolio of

Defence. Despite civilian attempts to control the military, they made conscious efforts to keep the military satisfied. Both the BNP and the Awami League have committed to build a modern military in their party manifestos. This is especially significant for the Awami League, which had been accused of neglecting the military. More importantly, fundamental changes were brought about by the military regimes in the Constitution that changed the ideology of the Awami League. But the party is in no position to amend the Constitution. It is indeed an irony that Hasina has to woo the same institution that wiped out her family and changed the ideals of her father.

The military budget has remained high during the two civilian regimes. During the BNP regime, it took up, on an average, 16 per cent of the revenue budget of the State. At present (that is under the Awami League), the military consumes about 18.7 per cent of the revenue budget. This is an extremely high economic and social cost to be paid by a country which, according to the Human Development Indicators (HDI) published by the UNDP in 1999, ranks 150 out of 175 countries. Its HDI is the lowest in South Asia. Despite having one of the lowest life expectancy and highest infant mortality noted in the world, the country allocates only 2 per cent of its GDP for health and social welfare.[31] Bangladesh also has about 700,000 child workers. This suggests that Bangladesh accounts for 5 per cent of the world's total number of working children. It also implies that roughly 4 per cent of Bangladesh's total population are working children.[32]

It is interesting that much of the defence expenditure has been allocated for national security, although the country has yet to evolve a national security policy. This became evident during the controversy following the purchase of MiG-29 aircraft by the Bangladesh Air Force from Russia, and Ashok Leyland trucks for the military from India. The Opposition questioned the rationale of buying military equipment from India, when the defence strategy of Bangladesh is based on the notion that India is the enemy. The Bangladesh military also has strong defence ties with China, and the latter is one of Bangladesh's major arms suppliers. Given India's unfriendly strategic relations with China, the Bangladeshi move appears to be based on ad hocism rather than a well thought out defence policy. Questions were also raised about the appropriateness of buying the MiGs for the Air Force. Civil-society members also questioned the high costs involved in the purchase of these aircraft, whilst important human security issues like environment, health, education, children's rights, and human rights remain neglected.

The political parties also have a high percentage of ex-military officers: five of the ministers of the BNP were ex-military officers. The present defence adviser to the BNP chairperson is a former military chief. Twelve senior military officials, three of whom had served as Service Chiefs, were nominated by the Awami League in the 1996 general elections. Five of them got elected. An Awami League MP, Gen. Safiullah (retd.), who was a former military chief, heads the present parliamentary committee on defence.

The military takeover in 1975 gave an impetus to the full-scale militarization of the CHT. During this period, gross violations of human rights took place. As mentioned earlier, Bengalis were settled in the hills from the plains to change the demographic composition of the region. By 1991, Bengalis became 50 per cent of the total population of the Hills. Military activities and Bengali settlements made thousands of people homeless. Around 50,000 crossed over to India as refugees, and around the same number became internally displaced persons. Anti-insurgency activities and market-oriented developments like plantation of commercial crops and creation of Reserve Forests (RF) affected the fragile ecosystem of the region; this marginalized the hill people who depend on forest resources, regarding it as their communal property. The CHT issue created inter-State security problems between Bangladesh and India, with each accusing the other of encouraging and providing sanctuary to each other's insurgent groups.

Apart from direct militarization, politics has been militarized in other ways. The long years of political protests against the Ershad regime—a fallout of the military takeover—has increasingly made the political parties undemocratic and fascist. There is no internal democracy within them. Though the party manifestos provide for elections to leadership posts in the parties, there are usually no contenders. Politics has become personality- or cult-oriented, rather than institution-based. The Awami League continues the Mujib cult, with his daughter Sheikh Hasina being the main leader in the party. Similarly, the BNP continues to harvest Zia's charisma, with his widow carrying the mantle of the party. It needs to be pointed out here that, although Mujib and Zia remain the main icons of their respective parties, both Sheikh Hasina and Khaleda Zia have consolidated their positions in their parties through their own leadership qualities. Street agitations have made the parties dependent, however, on thugs. Violence is adopted as a normal course of political settlement.

The anti-Ershad movement saw the militarization of student politics.

The student wings of the political parties have emerged as their main bastions of power. Arms were supplied to the student wing of Ershad's Jatiyo Party by the military intelligence to counter the Opposition's student wings.[33] The latter also acquired arms through various means with the connivance of their parties. These armed cadres have now been institutionalized within the political parties. Many of the cadres owe no allegiance to any political party: money being their main objective, they can be easily bought. Money and muscle have thus acquired a central position in Bangladesh politics. The armed cadres are nurtured by the political parties in the academic institutions. Education has become hostage to their politics, adding to the insecurity and sufferings of thousands of students. University and college hostels remain under their control. Rival factions have fought many 'battles' for hall 'capturing'. Students seeking seats in these hostels have to get the blessings of the *boro bhais* (big brothers). They oblige them by joining party processions and meetings. Consequently, many students have been drawn into this cycle of violent politics.

The academic institutions have also been politicized. At the university level, teachers are divided into different colours like blue, pink, white—each symbolising a political party. Promotions and entry into university teaching positions is largely influenced by these university party politics. The chief executive makes even the appointment of the Vice-Chancellor on partisan rather than academic considerations. It is, therefore, not surprising that persons having a third class in their academic results are appointed to the post of Vice-Chancellor of a state university. This situation makes the university administration dependent upon the armed student wings of the parties. Such a situation in the highest academic institutions of the country leads to stagnation of the younger generation. Consequently, brilliant students are leaving the country, causing irreparable damage to its future.

Militarization has also endangered the security of the common people, as thugs in the armed party cadres often act in connivance with the police forces. These armed cadres possess small arms of different types. This has increased the crime rate and also made politics extremely violent and criminalized. Political parties harbour or hire these thugs, who are often professional killers, to come to power, stay in power, or even to eliminate political opponents. The weapons are often smuggled across the borders. According to one report, there are 30 arms trafficking routes to Bangladesh, which includes land, air and sea routes.[34]

Public institutions responsible for the security of the people are not trusted by them. They regard the police as one of the most corrupt and least trustworthy institutions. There have been numerous cases of rape and death in police custody. For instance, there were 16 reported cases of rape by military and police personnel in 1998. There were 12 reported cases of rape by security personnel in 1999, and 6 such cases in 2000. Attempted cases of rape by security personnel were 11 in 1999, and 6 in 2000 (one was by the Indian BSF).[35] The police hierarchy, on its part, has also expressed its concern on the rising crime rates in the country in one of its quarterly review meetings held in September 2000. It has blamed the politicians for interfering in police functioning, and underlined the existing political chaos and the indifference of police officers to the causes behind the proliferation of crime. They also felt that due to politicization, many good officers have been sidelined, while inefficient ones, who are not even fit to run a police station, are on the ascent.[36]

In the name of curbing increasing lawlessness, the government has taken resort to special laws like the Public Safety Act (PSA) 2000, which authorizes the security personnel to arrest any person on suspicion without bail. This is a gross violation of basic human rights. Predictably enough, it is being used against political opponents, rather than actual terrorists. Consequently, the Public Safety Act has become the 'Public Insecurity Act', and is being challenged and opposed by civil society. It is important to note that a parliamentary subcommittee recently revealed that in the last 24 years, a total of 69,010 persons were detained under the SPA (promulgated in 1974), of which 68,195 were later released by the High Court because of vague, indefinite and weak grounds of detention. In other words, in more than 98 per cent of the cases, the High Court found the government to have misused this law to detain people who were not guilty as charged.[37] Yet, the law continues, along with the PSA.

There is thus a correlation between misgovernance and militarization of state politics, each abetting the other, and adding to the insecurity of the people. The State, by acquiring special powers through different Acts, is increasingly becoming an autocratic body while the people remain insecure in their homes, streets and work places.

CONCLUSION

Misgovernance, militarization and insecurity appear to be the hallmark of the Bangladesh State. The roots of this predicament lie within the structures of the State that increasingly lead it towards acquiring a hegemonic and non-democratic character. The State has retained these characteristics with and without military rule. Consequently, Bangladesh is one of the most misgoverned States. It is futile to expect the politicians to change their attitude towards politics within the prevailing structure. They look upon it as a game of power where the general people only count to capture State power, and can be bought or manipulated by money or muscle power.

The military, though largely responsible for the polarized and violent state of Bangladesh politics, is well aware of the divisions and weaknesses in the political system. The failure of the political leadership to reach a consensus on minimum core issues only strengthens the position of the military vis-à-vis the civilians and makes them a factor in politics. The civilian regimes try to keep the military satisfied by increased expenditure on defence. This takes its toll on human security and sharpens the divisions between the civilian population and the military, adding to the polarized nature of the polity.

This is not the *Sonar Bangla* ('Golden Bengal') that the people had dreamt of during their struggles and sacrifice. The pillars of governance must rest on genuinely democratic and participatory structures to ensure security for the people. For this purpose, this paper suggests the following:

REMEDIAL MEASURES

DEMOCRATIZATION OF THE CONSTITUTION

The Constitution must recognize that Bangladesh is a multinational society. The constitutional emphasis on one language, one culture and a uniform academic curriculum should be abolished. Instead, the State must develop the languages and cultures of the non-Bengali communities. The Constitution must recognize the customary rights and privileges of the ethnic people, specially in the context of land issues. The constitutional provision for equality of women in all spheres of life remains unfulfilled due to the patriarchal nature of the society. The Constitution should have specific provisions for the realization of equal rights for women. The Constitution is not sacrosanct, and has been amended 13 times. These changes can be brought about by amendments, provided the political will exists, which is difficult to come by at present, but could be created if the other structures and processes undergo a process of democratization as suggested below.

DEMOCRATISATION OF THE PARLIAMENT

The Bangladesh Parliament is a highly gendered and hegemonic institution. Women, minorities and the poor remain under-represented. There is a demand from the non-governmental agencies and civil society organizations to increase the representation of women. Reservation of seats for women and their election through direct elections has been suggested to make them accountable to the people. At present, they remain accountable to the party, as they are party nominees. Demands have also been made to make it mandatory for the political parties to nominate a certain percentage of women during elections. This needs to be ensured either through a constitutional amendment, or by consensus among the political parties. In case of failure to do so, the Election Commission must cancel the contesting of elections by the defaulting party. This paper does not propose the reservation of seats for minorities in Parliament, as this would heighten the majority-minority dichotomy. Instead, it suggests that each party must have specific provisions for the minorities in their party manifesto and must nominate indigenous people during elections. In this context, one can also suggest the strengthening of local government institutions and their coordination with the national parliament in some fashion so that grass-roots voices may be heard in Parliament. The neutrality of the Speaker must also be ensured. There should be a constitutional provision for electing two Speakers, one from the ruling party and the other from the Opposition, to serve in rotation. This would save Parliament from a single Speaker (from the ruling party) autocracy.

REFORMING THE ELECTORAL PROCESS

The autonomy of the Election Commission has largely been circumscribed by its dependence on government institutions, which are partisan and corrupt. It is, therefore, important that the Election Commission should have its own institutions for conducting the elections. Apart from conducting elections, it should be responsible for updating and checking the voter's lists during the inter-election period. It should also undertake programmes for educating people at the grass-roots level on their voting rights and the importance of fair elections. At present, the floating population and expatriates are not included in the voter's list. Attempts should be made to incorporate them. The candidate's residence in their respective constituencies should be made mandatory. This would make politics people-centric and not capital-centric. The Election Commission must have the power to demand accounts of their expenses and also declaration of residence by the candidates. If a candidate violates these requirements, the candidature should be cancelled.

DEMOCRATISING THE POLITICAL PROCESS

The Election Commission should make it mandatory for political parties to conduct internal elections. The term of the party leadership should be limited to a maximum of two years. Persons having criminal records and convictions for financial corruption should be debarred from contesting elections and holding public office. The parties must ensure adequate gender and minority representation, and have a code of conduct. They cannot harass the people by enforcing forced shutdowns of the academic institutions, calling hartals, and holding public meetings during peak hours at public places, disrupting normal public activities. A ban should be placed on the student wings of political parties. They have lost their historical role: instead, student politics is increasingly being seen as a form of terrorism. This would be difficult to ensure if the administration and the teaching community remain partisan. This paper suggests a total ban on politics by teachers and government officials.

REDEFINING NATIONAL SECURITY

The policy planners in Bangladesh are yet to evolve a consensus on what constitutes 'national' security. The realists make a case for military security, but are hard pressed to identify the exact nature of the military threat. The political settlement of the CHT conflict has reinforced the reality that conflicts, whether internal or external, have their roots in socio-economic and political, rather than military causes, and their solution demands the strengthening of the relevant forces rather than the military. It is time 'national' security was redefined as 'human' security. It must be emphasized that a community cannot base its security on the insecurity of others: the costs are immense in economic, societal and environmental terms. True power can only come from collective empowerment. Bangladesh's national security should be formulated on these lines, clearly defining the real sources of threats.

EMPOWERING CIVIL SOCIETY

It is imperative that the civil society empowers itself and holds the political process accountable. This requires a greater awareness and informed objectivity by the members of civil society. The media can play a constructive role here. The seminars, workshops and public dialogues organized by different citizen's forums and institutions, like the Fair Election Monitoring Agency (FEMA) and others, in association with mainstream newspapers, highlighting issues of governance ranging from public toilets to seats for women in Parliament are examples of building a critical and informed civil society. The academic curriculum also needs to be democratized and reorganized. At present, it is biased towards the Bengali community and ignores the non-Bengalis who do not find themselves represented in history books within this curriculum. This, too, strengthens a culture of intolerance and ethno-centrism. The academic curriculum must reflect the cultures, history and lives of the different communities in Bangladesh.

STRENGTHENING REGIONAL COOPERATION

The SAARC process should be reinvigorated. Many issues like disaster management, environment, transborder migration, trafficking of women, and small arms proliferation have regional security implications. Minority discontent in one state derives overt and covert support from neighbouring states, thus complicating the security environment. Small arms proliferation, trafficking of women and drugs are regional issues, so SAARC can provide a platform for considering these issues at the highest political level. There should be a greater exchange of ideas and information at the people-to-people level. SAARC scholarships could be provided for this purpose, and SAARC student's visits and exchanges could be encouraged. Visits by the elected members of the local government institutions could also be arranged so that they may learn from each other's experience and strengthen the sense of a South Asian community at the grass-roots and local levels. So far, SAARC has remained state-centric; attempts at people-to-people level cooperation have been confined to the elite, with the general people remaining outside its ambit. For creating a genuine South Asian ethos and security community in South Asia, it is necessary to democratize and decentralize the SAARC process.

The realization of these propositions requires concerted efforts by civil-society members. Non-governmental agencies have a vital role to play in sensitizing civil and political societies in this regard. Governance has become a captive of the ruling class: it is time the ruled try to coordinate themselves, and, with the ruling group, to make governance a people's agenda. Only by sharing power in a realistic, rather than an abstract and theoretical sense, can the people be genuinely free from the present elitist form of governance. Bangladesh, at present, may have the trappings of a democracy, but in reality it is 'partycracy'. The culture and spirit of democracy are absent. Only a truly democratic society, with participation by all the segments of the people, can ensure good governance and security.

NOTES

1. Cited in Subhash C. Kashyap, 'Institutions of Governance: the Parliament, the Government and the Judiciary', in V.A. Pai Panandiker, ed. *Problems of Governance in South Asia*, New Delhi: Konark Publishers, 2000, p. 95.
2. For an exposition of this view, see, Imtiaz Ahmed, 'Governance and the International Development Community: Making Sense of the Bangladesh Experience, *Contemporary South Asia*, vol. 8, no. 3, 1999, pp. 295–309.
3. *The Constitution of the Peoples Republic of Bangladesh*, Government of the People's Republic of Bangladesh, 1972, p. 5.
4. For details, see Amena Mohsin, *The Politics of Nationalism: The Case of the CHT*, Dhaka: UPL, 1997.
5. Constitution op. cit., n. 3 above.
6. Kamal Siddiqui, *Towards Good Governance in Bangladesh: Fifty Unpleasant Essays*, Dhaka: UPL, 1996, pp. 18–19.
7. *Daily Star*, 20 November 2000.
8. For a detailed discussion on election reforms see Imtiaz Ahmed, 'Electoral Process in Bangladesh: Rationales for Reform, in Devendra Raj Panday et al., eds., *Comparative Electoral Processes in South Asia*, Kathmandu: NESAC, 1999, pp. 12–31.
9. Nazmunnessa Mahtab, 'Women in Politics: Bangladesh Perspective', paper presented at an international seminar on Women in Politics organized by the British Council, Dhaka, 9–10 October 2000.
10. The author was present at this meeting that took place in Dhaka in March 1999 to welcome the new Garo students within this forum.
11. Personal interviews with the author.
12. Abul Barkat et. al., *Political Economy of the Vested Property Act in Rural Bangladesh*, Dhaka: ALRD, 1997, pp. 31–5.
13. For details, see Amena Mohsin, 'National Security and the Minorities: The Bangladesh Case', in D.L. Sheth and Gurpreet Mahajan, eds., *Minority Identities and the Nation-State*, Delhi: Oxford University Press, 1999, pp. 312–32.
14. *Daily Star*, Dhaka, 30 January 2000.

15. *Janokontho*, 25 November 1999.
16. *Bhorer Kagoj*, 16 October 1999.
17. For an exposition of this view, see, Ann Tickner and Hans J. Morgenthau's, 'Principles of Political Realism: A Feminist Reformulation', in Rebecca Grant et al., eds., *Gender and International Relations*, Milton Keynes, U.K. Open University Press, 1991, pp. 27–41.
18. For a detailed exposition of the politics of hartal, see Imtiaz Ahmed, 'Political System and Political Process in Bangladesh: Consensus on Intolerance and Conflict' *The Journal of Social Studies*, no. 78, Dhaka: CSS, 1997, pp. 71–89.
19. *Prothom Alo*, 13 February 2001.
20. *Star*, 6 October 2000.
21. *Independent*, 18 November 2000.
22. Maj. Gen. M. Ibrahim (retd), *Shena Bahinir Obbhontore Atash Bochor* (*Twenty-Eight Years Within the Military*), Dhaka: Mowla Bros., 1999, p. 29.
23. *IISS*, London, 1985, p. 172.
24. Ali Riaz, *State, Class and Military Rule: Political Economy of Martial Law in Bangladesh*, Dhaka: Nadi New Press, 1994, p. 228.
25. Mahmud S. Ali, 'Civil-Military Relations in the Soft State: The Case of Bangladesh', *ENBS/EC* Research Paper, No. 1/6-94, 1994, p. 30.
26. *Holiday*, Dhaka, 6 December 1981.
27. Rupak Bhattacharya, 'Unrest in the Bangladesh Army on May 18–20, 1996: Implications for the Bangladesh Polity', *The Journal of Social Studies*, no. 81, Dhaka: CSS, 1998, p. 6.
28. Talukdar Maniruzzaman, *Politics and Security of Bangladesh*, Dhaka: UPL, 1993, p. 83.
29. Ali, op. cit., n. 25 above, pp. 30–1.
30. Ibid, p. 42.
31. *Daily Star*, 26 May 2000.
32. *Weekend Independent*, 13 October 2000.
33. Former student leaders of Dhaka University have stated this to the author.
34. Neila Husain, 'Problems of Proliferation of Small Arms in Bangladesh', in Dipankar Banerjee, ed., *South Asia at Gun Point: Small Arms and Light Weapons Proliferation*, Colombo: RCSS, 2000, pp. 8–12.
35. *ASK*, Documentation Unit, Ask, Dhaka, 2000.
36. *Daily Star*, 9 September 2000.
37. *The Daily Star*, 9 October 2000.

CHAPTER 3

Trenches, Boundaries, Spaces: The Dialectics of Governance and Security in India

Meenakshi Gopinath

The Fabian and Liberal aspirations that informed the initial euphoria of India's 'tryst with destiny' derived from convictions that independence from colonial rule would usher in freedom and democracy. The vicissitudes of the nation building trajectory were to dramatically highlight the contradictions between economic growth and social equity, citizen's rights and State policy, people's security and the processes of governance.

Fifty years later, this discourse is being challenged even as the development paradigm and the secular agenda are being recast. This paper examines the discursive terrain of the politics of democratic governance and security in contemporary India. The challenges to a pluralist ethos are traced through the leitmotifs of cultural rights and minority identities, the tensions between people's security and 'national' security, and the rise of a new nationalist assertion that generates militarism.

This paper also explores the ideational and societal processes that impact the evolving discourse since the 1980s. In viewing these unequivocally through a gender lens, it makes a case for *engendering* both security and governance.

The scripts regarding *secularism* and *development* are being rewritten since the 1980s. In the evolving equations between the State and the market, the shifts in economic policy and programmes of structural adjustment effected by globalization, the welfare orientation is on the wane. The legislated consensus on the pillars of nation building and social transformation is also under strain.

*The author wishes to thank Manjri Sewak of WISCOMP whose inputs and insights have helped shape this essay.

The challenge to secularism more especially from the forces of right-wing majoritarianism coincides with the retreat of the State. This lays the State open to the charge of collusion with reactionary forces in society. Pressures from different sections of civil society have affected governance processes, impairing the rights of minority groups in particular. Further, there is growing recognition that the Nehruvian model of development by concentrating on aggregate growth, failed to deliver on equity and social justice. This has spawned social movements that interrogate the premises of nation building and reconstruction from the perspective of human security.

Significantly, these movements have led to people's mobilization outside political parties, by building alliances across geographical and occupational spaces. There is a conscious strategy to move beyond 'insensitive' party politics to explore the area of people's power and activism. These non-violent movements seek to push the boundaries of representative democracy to assert the rights of direct participation in decisions governing the lives of citizens. They also reflect a sense of fatigue and betrayal about the failure of political parties to move beyond entrenched vested interests and vote banks. However, these protests find the State unwilling or unable to negotiate the changing terrain, but clinging to an obsolete vocabulary of governance.

There is another dimension to this script. Indian federalism now includes new actors in the legislative and executive decision-making processes. Regional parties and hitherto marginalized caste and class groups have significantly altered the contours of governance and the legitimacy of the Westminster model of parliamentary practice. The logic of this process saw the Gujral Government grappling with the unpredictable dynamics of coalition making in 1997. Its two successor BJP-led Governments have had to balance the diverse pulls of a now 23-party Nationalist Democratic Alliance (NDA). While apostles of 'strong governments' see this as 'destabilizing', the reality is that coalition governments are here to stay. They reflect the complexity and diversity of Indian society that must rightfully find their way into decision-making in a democratic federal polity. But the unease with coalitions has led to a reluctance to evolve new rules of the game, and new strategies to provide coherence and stability. The result is a pre-occupation with retaining power at all costs, and compromises with stated ideological positions. Strategic planning is the casualty in this day-to-day crisis management process.

The general elections of 1999 indicated the changing preferences of the electorate towards regional and State issues. Described as the 'municipalization' of the national election, the process revealed that voters want effective governance rather than grand national agendas. The most important component of this agenda at Independence was constructing a unified, national society, out of heterogeneous ethnic, religious and linguistic groups. Communal challenges have multiplied over the last decade, and the grammar of nationalism is being re-fashioned. Even the official invocations to non-violence and Gandhi have waned. Instead, a strident discourse on 'national power' and 'honour' is shrinking the space for dialogue and negotiation.

The rationale that motivated the ruling elite to reverse earlier positions, and see nuclear weapons as the kingpin of India's security strategy, may have roots in this denouement. Some sociologists link this phenomenon to the ascendancy of the 'new' middle class and its dream of India as a major superpower, sustaining a homogenized nationalist agenda in a diverse and pluralistic society. The crucial challenge for governance in India is to find the balance now between investing in people and meeting threats to 'territorial integrity'. These threats are by no means only 'external'. Human lives remain imperilled due to internal conflicts—guerrilla wars, separatist movements, political and ethnic violence. Vulnerable sections of the people continue to be denied access to basic human security in terms of water, food, nutrition, health services, education and housing owing to the failure of governance.[1]

The scale of violence targetted against ethnic, religious and sectarian minorities is on the increase. Between 1954 and 1994, there were around 15,000 communal riots in India, resulting in 13,301 casualties.[2] Inter-caste violence in India claims hundreds of lives each year. In 1996 alone, 36,000 crimes were reported against Scheduled Castes and Scheduled Tribes.[3] Violence against women shows an alarming increase, specially in northern India. According to conservative estimates, there were 23,000 cases of dowry deaths in India between 1994 and 1998.[4] In 1996 alone, there were more than 4,000 *reported* cases of child rape.[5] Religion still continues to be the most combustible manifestation of conflict. Nearly 2,000 people died in communal rioting that followed the demolition of the Babri Masjid in 1992, which touched major urban centres.[6] More recently, Christians have been targetted in Gujarat, Orissa, Madhya Pradesh and Bihar.

Yet, the endemic causes of conflict are seldom addressed. The most contentious issues revolve around ethnic status, religion, language, distribution of assets and lack of employment. Inequitable distribution of wealth and imbalances in regional growth have also fuelled discontent and growing insecurity. The State, too, in the use of coercive powers for the maintenance of 'law and order', has proved to be a serious threat to the security of citizens. Although the Terrorist and Disruptive Activities Act (TADA) lapsed in May 1995, 1,502 detainees continued to be held as of January 1997.[7] Another draconian Act, the Armed Forces Special Powers Act (1972), confers sweeping powers to the military and grants immunity to the armed forces from prosecution. The indemnity provided by Article 34 of the Constitution to public servants and any other person for any action taken by them for the maintenance and restoration of order in disturbed areas has created its own distortions. Approximately 8,300 people have been killed in Jammu & Kashmir and the north-east since 1995, and at least 2,000 have been held in long-term unacknowledged detention by security forces in these areas. There have been an estimated 200–400 extra-judicial killings in Jammu & Kashmir in 1997 alone.[8]

RECASTING GOVERNANCE AND SECURITY

The conventional security discourse, stemming from the Cold War, is inadequate to evaluate the emerging threats to security in South Asia, which are a complex amalgam of domestic and external factors, linked with the crisis of governance.[9] In India, intra- State conflicts being more frequent than inter-State conflicts, the losses from terrorism and insurgency are far greater than during all its conventional conflicts taken together. The loss of life during the decade-long insurgency in Punjab exceeded that incurred in the past four Indo-Pak conflicts taken together. Insurgency in Kashmir since 1989 has resulted in even higher casualties.[10] These factors coupled with rampant corruption and criminalization of politics debilitates State capacity to grapple effectively with threats to security.

National security, apart from its external dimension, gets internally oriented when the processes of democratization gather momentum and force a broadening and expansion of the meaning of national security, making it less elitist. In this situation, the State's military capabilities become less relevant for achieving the security needs of the citizenry. As Achin Vanaik has pointed out, externally determined security threats justify strong military capabilities. When security risks are internally determined, purely military solutions become counterproductive.

Changes in the international system suggest moving beyond realist perspectives on national security. The growing strength of transnational corporations, GATT, WTO, the IMF, the World Bank and international money markets, with their astronomical financial flows have put unprecedented pressures on the autonomy of States like India.[11]

The paradigm of 'human security' suggests an alternative approach. Challenges from both external military threats and internal conflict to 'national security' can be addressed in a non-reified manner from the vantagepoint of those most directly affected, namely the citizens. Human security, as formulated by Lloyd Axworthy, includes security against economic deprivation, and includes an acceptable quality of life and a guarantee of fundamental human rights. Recognizing the importance of non-State actors, it sees good governance, sustainable development and social equity as important to global peace as arms control and disarmament. It recognizes the links between environmental degradation, population growth, ethnic conflicts and migration.[12]

In the human security paradigm, the primary *referent* of security is the human person. The importance of the State is not discounted, but it is treated as co-equal to individual security. In terms of *values*, human security encompasses a State of well-being in which individuals or groups are assured protection from physical and mental harm, and freed from fear and anxiety. It incorporates freedom from want and a vision of life with dignity and respect for personal and cultural identities. It is a concept firmly based in the Universal Declaration of Human Rights and in the idea of equal enjoyment by women and men in the rights it guarantees. *Threats* are reckoned as both direct and indirect, from other States as well as non-State actors and also from structural sources arising from relations of power at various levels—from the family upwards to the global economy. In this approach, force is not seen as an effective *means* of dealing with multifarious threats to personal safety and freedom; human development and humane governance are preferred instruments of security. If coercion is necessary, then sanctions are a first recourse.[13]

The essence of good governance in India would involve enabling processes that interrogate—and, if necessary, subvert—existing structures of dominance and authority. Democracy and citizen empowerment become crucial components, and in a plural, stratified and fractious society, the test of good governance must be premised on how the State and civil societies democratically negotiate *difference*.

The litmus test would be how the security architecture responds to these processes. The term 'governance' is replacing 'executive' in post-modernist social science discourse. Yet, in India, even though the State has weakened, it retains significant capacities to impact the security of its citizens. The State is simultaneously a source of insecurity for a large section of its citizens, when it acts complicitously with unjust, undemocratic structures in society.

What is significant for governance in India is that the State is neither consistently 'protector' or 'predator'. It oscillates between these roles depending on which group or interest is negotiating its agenda or seeking entitlements or benefits by democratic appeal. It has been argued that the Indian State's project of social transformation is not above bargaining and compromise. It is not open, however, to negotiation by vulnerable categories of citizens. In its attentiveness to some powerful interests, the public agenda is open and inclusionary, while towards others it is severely exclusionary. The core projects of the State are, it is argued, rendered differentially open to negotiation, and so it is not a problem of too little or too much democracy, but of its selective availability.[14]

In India, the challenge to governance is made more complex since the State is not an independent actor in its ability to implement declared objectives. The constraints regarding citizens' security are underpinned by economic and social inequalities. Recognizably, the poor are voiceless and politically marginalized. Social inequalities are not merely the result of class differences, they also derive from caste, gender and community and these often overlap class inequalities. The complexity of Indian society, as it is fractured along several axes—class, caste, gender, religious community—and sometimes along more than one axis simultaneously, has created the group characterized as 'doubly disadvantaged'.[15] These groups—women of minority religions or dalit communities, tribals, oustees due to development projects—constitute a sizeable segment whose security needs have been met with a singular lack of responsiveness. Their continued marginalization poses the greatest challenge to humane governance in India today.

DEMOCRACY AND DIFFERENCE

The manner in which democracies deal with divisions and deliver on equality of citizenship, whilst accommodating and welcoming difference, is the most formidable challenge to governance. The question is how to arrive at a conception of citizenship based on democratic choice that guarantees equal rights without jeopardizing minority rights or undermining justice.

The decade of the 1990s has seen a multiplication of political conflicts around religious, caste and regional identities in India. Yet, no single event, in recent Indian political history after the anti-Sikh riots of 1984, has highlighted the fragility of the political and constitutional commitment to secularism as the demolition of the Babri Masjid in December 1992 and the violence in its aftermath. It represents a defining moment in the assertion of processes that undermine governance and the security of minority groups in particular.

Moreover, the growth of community conflicts has coincided with a deinstitutionalization of the Indian State. The normative and organizational pillars of the post-Independence Indian State—secularism, socialism and nationalism of the Nehruvian oeuvre—and the civil bureaucracy, have weakened. Simultaneously, the size of the electorate has multiplied, competition for State-controlled resources has increased, traditional social hierarchies have eroded, and the struggles for democratic inclusion have spread. The combination of an organizational vacuum with the intensification of democratic aspirations has encouraged mobilization along multiple lines.[16]

Lower-caste struggles have also broadened the parameters of democracy and this consciousness is one of the major antidotes to unbridled majority assertions. Yet, the ascendancy of Hindu nationalism has become a decisive factor in shaping the discourse of Indian politics, with the State alternating between the roles of helpless spectator and complicitous ally. Hindu nationalist mobilization, by undermining minority rights, challenges democratic process. It draws sustenance from the urban, upwardly mobile groups and trading classes, and draws rigid boundaries between communities. The rise of compulsive consumerism, intense internal competition, new opportunities and expanding horizons for upward mobility following the Green Revolution in north India had a destabilizing influence on the emerging middle class, which began to search for an emotional anchorage. Organized Hindutva, while never challenging the material interests of these classes, was able to effectively insert a system which raised solidarity to a new, intense, emotional level through its inherent militancy.[17]

Whilst being essentially patriarchal, the movements of the Hindu right induct and politicize women. Their inclusion (as Tanika Sarkar argues) does not deny consumerist individualism to women. It allows them a new activist role, earlier withheld, and constructs a revitalized moral vision of domestic and sexual norms that promise to restore the comforts of old sociability and familial solidarities.[18] Integral to this mobilization strategy is the perception of the Hindu 'endangered woman' who could become a 'potent weapon for violent mobilization'. This has made her a metaphor for the cause of a Hindu motherland. In bouts of communal violence, the community dissolves into the figure of the threatened woman, and violence becomes a necessary condition of male honour.[19] This was in evidence during the Mumbai riots of 1992–3 when women became the symbols of honour or dishonour for two hostile communities.

The growing need to assert and protect 'Indian culture and values' cannot be isolated from a larger global pattern. Cultural imperialism, accelerated by the communication revolution, has not merely triggered 'Talibanization' processes in the Islamic world the announced agenda of the central government to reform the education system, contain the 'deleterious' impact of Western culture and infuse pride in India's 'rich cultural heritage' reflects similar concerns. The reductionist view of culture reflected in it is deeply problematic for a culturally diverse country like India. The need for such reform was mooted in October 1998 at a conference of state education ministers. It endorsed teaching Sanskrit and the Vedas and Upanishads, but was silent on other Indian languages and scriptures. Though rejected by the majority of state ministers, the then BJP President Kushabhau Thakre went on record saying that withdrawal of the proposal was only a 'temporary retreat'.[20]

Similar exercises in rewriting history textbooks were witnessed in Madhya Pradesh and Uttar Pradesh in the early 1990s. The recent controversy over the withdrawal of the '*Towards Freedom*' series by the Indian Council of Historical Research (ICHR) has led intellectuals and politicians to organize protests against the increasing influence of the Hindu right in academic and research institutions like the ICSSR, ICHR and prestigious think-tanks. Similarly, key appointments to policy-making organizations dealing with culture, history and education are clear attempts to expedite saffronization.

The sudden growth of madrassas with generous funds received from the Middle East and the reported funding of Christian missionary institutions by Western sources spur and legitimize these moves. The perception among sections of the majority elite that successive governments have built vote-banks by appeasing minorities at the cost of national security contributes to their misgivings, making it difficult to deal with fundamentalist fringes in religious communities. The recent repeal of the UP Hindu Public Religious Institutions (Prevention of Misuse of Funds) Act, 1962 reveals the capitulation of the State government to the Vishwa Hindu Parishad, a right-wing Hindu organization involved in social mobilization efforts.

The recent acquittal of Shiv Sena chief Bal Thackeray repeats this story. Accused of inciting communal violence leading to the Bombay riots of 1993, Thackeray was acquitted by a magistrate in Mumbai on 25 July 2000 on the grounds that the case was 'time-barred'. This overlooked the serious indictment by the Justice Sri Krishna Commission of Inquiry of Thackeray's role in inciting the worst ever communal violence in Mumbai.[21] On 9 August 2000, the Mumbai High Court adjudicated that the dismissal of the riots cases against Thackeray were 'improper' and admitted the state government's appeal. Thackerey's subsequent release demonstrated the capitulation of the Indian State to blackmail by Shiv Sena hooligans, who held the city to ransom and paralysed essential services.

These events brought into focus the selective invoking by the State of 'hate speech' offences in violation of sections of the Indian Penal Code. Some of them include promoting enmity between groups (Sec. 153A), undermining national integration (Sec. 153B), injuring or defiling a place of worship (Sec. 295), outraging religious feelings (Sec. 295A) and criminal intimidation and public mischief (Secs. 503–6). It is interesting that, following the demolition of the Babri Masjid and vandalization of numerous churches and mosques thereafter, the State failed to invoke Sec. 295 (injuring or defiling a place of worship). Yet, it was quick to invoke the law against painter M.F. Hussain on the grounds that his paintings hurt the religious sentiments of the Hindu community. The violation of constitutionally established norms of conduct and their contravention whilst seeking recourse to justice exposes the limitations of the juridico-legal apparatus, calling into question the impartiality of the law-and-order machinery. Besides, the communalization of the security forces in Mumbai, Kashmir and Punjab, and the Provincial Armed Constabulary (PAC) in UP during inter-community riots represents yet another threat to the fabric of the polity.

Since the late 1990s, a new target has been found in the Christian minority community.[22] Christian missionaries are seen as a threat by the establishment in that they have provided quality education throughout the country. The inability of government schools to match their standards has proven to be a thorn in the flesh. In addition, these schools have provided economic and educational opportunities for hitherto disenfranchised dalits and other groups, many of whom embraced Christianity in the process. The charge of 'forcible' conversions against the missionaries has added a new contention to the debate. The killing and public torture of priests, the rape of nuns and the burning of Bibles have become standard practices of intimidation in Gujarat, UP and Orissa. The report of the National Minorities Commission on these incidents states that these were motivated acts of robbery. But the link between the areas where these incidents occurred and the prominence of the VHP or the Bajrang Dal (considered storm troopers of the Hindu Right) in these regions has been highlighted in parliamentary debate.

What is seriously in jeopardy here is India's claim to be a practising secular democracy. These crimes are violative of the Articles in the Indian Constitution that guarantee equality before the law, non-discrimination on grounds of religion, race, gender, caste (Art. 15), protection of the freedom of speech, expression and movement (Art. 19), protection of life and personal liberty (Art. 21), protection against arrest and detention (Art. 22), freedom of conscience and freedom of religion (Art. 25). However, these constitutional guarantees provide little comfort to those affected by communal violence.

The issue of 'conversions' strikes at the core of Hindutva since its ideology presents all past religious differences as dissent from *within*—tribals as incomplete Hindus, Buddhists and Sikhs as breakaway Hindus, who can be reclaimed—and invokes Hinduism as a supreme assimilative power and a practice ingesting diverse traditions and sects.[23] Kumkum Sangari has shown that conversions signify acts of rejection, dissent, choice and freedom of movement within a multi-religious society. In India, these movements have created links or overlapping religious networks by altering relationships *between* belief systems and generating reconfigurations *within* belief systems. . . '.[24] These 'partial conversions' blur the distinctions between 'minority' and 'majority', but become a more vulnerable target for competing political claims than those groups that can be slotted under 'separate cultures'. Conversion in the Indian context has historically created interfaces, parallelisms and meeting grounds between religions, and yielded interweaving practices that question congealed identities.

DEMOCRACY AND CULTURAL RIGHTS

A key question in the context of governance and citizenship is how to imbue societal practices and structures with 'human' dignity. This requires the acknowledgement that whereas formal political arrangements recognize the importance of protective discrimination of the socially and economically marginalized, *cultural deprivation* has not been squarely addressed. It has been argued that 'the protection of cultures, particularly minority cultures becomes a group right'.[25] The right of a culture to exist flows from the citizen's right to culture. But this right means little when the culture itself is threatened. The concern about preserving minority culture is embedded in various provisions of international law concerning the rights of persons belonging to minorities.[26] The cultural rights of minorities can be grounded in a larger framework of human rights: two categories of rights constitute the absolute minimum for national minorities: *cultural self-determination*, and their participation in decision-making at the national level.[27] The Indian Constitution grants minorities the right to preserve and develop their culture and make institutional arrangements by establishing educational institutions. This right is in the nature of a restriction on the powers of the State.

One of the symbols used by the community to mobilize political support is included within the phrase 'cultural rights'. Often there is not a tactical alliance, but a *contest* between State and community over the issue of cultural rights, especially their regulation by law.[28] The crucial issue for governance in the context of cultural rights is that they do not easily fit into the neat classifications of: (*a*) individual rights and (*b*) collective rights. Also, the responsibility of the State for ensuring the rights of individuals to preserve their culture entails commitment to its protection, which is a complex issue. There is also the conundrum as to how relations between different collectivities, on the one hand, and the collectivity and the individual on the other, should be governed.

In the context of 'secular' governance, the question that must be asked is: for the democratization and secularization of civil society, would the best route be secular policies imposed by the State, or should this be accomplished by leaving space for the transformation of communities? The complexity of the issue increases if one sees it additionally through the *gender lens*. The contradictions and conflicts between individual rights to citizenship and the community, between different *kinds* of community, and between the *state* and *community* appear starkly when viewed through this lens. It raises basic questions about the nature of Indian secularism and its impact on women. How secularism proceeds with articulating the complex and contested interrelationships between 'women' and the notions of nation, community and citizen is significant.[29]

The complicities of the patriarchies of religion, community and the State were highlighted in the public debates following the Shah Bano judgment where an indigent divorced Muslim woman filed for maintenance under Sec. 125 of the Criminal Procedure Code.[30] The ulema's position that the Supreme Court judgment granting her relief was interference in Muslim Law stirred up a controversy which became a major political issue, with thousands of Muslims demonstrating against the court decision. Capitulating to pressure, the Rajiv Gandhi Government enacted The Muslim Women (Protection of Rights on Divorce) Act 1986, which exempted Muslim women from the purview of Sec. 125 of the Criminal Procedure Code. Many feminist groups and progressive sections of the Muslim community saw it as a setback for Muslim women.[31]

Feminist opposition then was based on the understanding that there are basic similarities between religious patriarchies. Women become the symbols of community identity: any attempt to change the position of women is perceived as an assault on the community. Personal laws are defended as part of ancient religious tradition, but the reality is that they were codified in the colonial period. This led to a vociferous demand for a Uniform Civil Code (UCC). Since the mid-1980s, however, there has been a discernible shift in feminist positions, marked by a cautious and nuanced approach towards the UCC.[32] This was based on a growing realization that a potentially progressive initiative was being hijacked by the Hindu right's agenda of integration and assimilation, causing further insecurities within religious minorities.[33] At present, only the BJP, among all the political parties, is committed to the adoption of a UCC.

The mobilization around the Shah Bano case must also be seen against the backdrop of the 1980s when Muslims, like Christians today, were facing a major threat to their security. Many riots took place in that period, providing momentum to the movement. With progressive elements seeking reform from within the community, the clerics are unlikely to be able to carry the day.[34] The public debate on the UCC has invariably been cast in terms of the integrity of the nation, which is seen under threat from the existence of plural systems of legality. Conversely, resistance to the UCC comes from community leaders on the grounds that it destroys the cultural identity of minorities. It has been argued that the UCC debate has polarized around the twin axes of State and community, rendering invisible the issue of gender justice and that the debate on the UCC has rarely surfaced in public consciousness as a feminist issue.[35]

From the feminist perspective, the *unqualified* right of communities to cultural identity is difficult to accept since patriarchies can be as oppressive as State structures in denying 'their' women individual rights. Yet, the growth of majority communalism makes the translation of this concern in legal terms problematic. The issue of women and community is a metaphor for the problems involved in governance and the security provided to citizens in the context of cultural rights. It also highlights the reluctance of the State to intervene proactively for the benefit of the *doubly disadvantaged* within communities.

The couching of the UCC debate as a majority versus minority issue highlights the ambiguities and paradoxes central to secularism as the cornerstone of the constitutional intention. The leitmotif of 'secularism' in the Constitution straddles these contradictions. It simultaneously posits the separation of religion from the public arena, while also asserting the need for the State to regulate religious practices, both by non-intervention (declaring certain areas of jurisprudence to be the prerogative of religious leaders), and by intervention (ensuring financial accountability of religious trusts, etc.)

The critique of the State, consequently, on this question from the 'secular' position has, therefore, been that it does not intervene enough (as in its reluctance to enact a UCC), or that it intervenes too much (as when government passed the Muslim Women's Act in 1986). The State traverses a slippery slope in being the neutral arbiter between religious communities and the agent of social justice *within* communities.[36] The sharp reaction and resistance of representatives of the Christian community to the centre's proposal to introduce the Indian Divorce (Amendment) Bill, 2000, intended to remove gender discrimination for divorce, must also be seen in this context.

The current debates on the UCC reflect the breakdown of the earlier consensus on one of the frames of reference that informed the democratic project of the Indian State. From the perspective of a discourse of governance, this calls for a concerted democratic interrogation of the politics of homogenization that is being scripted as an enterprise to bring people into the 'national mainstream'. Still, it is widely believed that the pluralist fabric of society will provide the necessary corrective to this trend.

Rajni Kothari's claim that the unique blend of 'creative nationalism' and 'persisting pluralism' that produced India's democratic culture is still with us and is woven into whatever remains of the institutional fabric of the polity, is cause for comfort. It suggests an in-built resilience to surmount these new challenges. Kothari identifies six major parameters of the shift within Indian society to a new set of actors seeking a different political order based on 'genuine' democracy: (1) the growing assertion of the 'dalit' movement in politics; (2) large-scale politicization of caste groups and minority communities at the lower reaches of the social hierarchy; (3) the empowerment (through progressive social enactments) and coming into decision-making processes of hitherto disempowered groups like the Scheduled Castes (SC), Scheduled Tribes (ST) and Other Backward Castes (OBC); (4) the rise of small regional parties addressing local issues, following the general disenchantment of the electorate with the political elite (both leaders and political parties) and consequential lack of good governance; (5) the shift towards a more federal system of governance even more than envisaged by proponents of State rights; and (6) the growth in the consciousness and confluence of secular forces as a result of the ascendancy and stridency of communal and fundamentalist forces.[37]

Hindu nationalism can be seen at one level as a conservative backlash, a xenophobic desire among the relatively privileged, to resist the broader democratic transformation that has intensified political mobilization among the lower castes and minorities. So the process of questioning and subverting social hierarchies and the agendas that legitimate them will not always be a peaceful one.

ALTERNATIVE POLITICS, ALTERNATIVE DEVELOPMENT

The closing decades of the twentieth century have witnessed a series of people's resistance movements that interrogate prevalent State positions on 'security' and development. These movements exemplify the political assertion of erstwhile-marginalized sections of civil society which are demanding humane and responsive governance. Focusing attention on the complicity of the State with indigenous elite, and the new inequities of power and privilege unleashed by globalization, they appeal beyond the nation state to international civil society, invoking issues of human security. The networks opened up by globalization afford them linkages outside national boundaries in common cause. This erodes the nation states' claim to the exclusive allegiance of its citizens.

The Nehruvian paradigm of development stands challenged today as never before, with 600 million people barely managing to survive and subsist, and the benefits of 'planned development' accruing to less than a third of the population. The playing out of the dialectic of '*India versus Bharat*' has dramatically highlighted the contradictions between the 'modernizing' aspirations of the Indian nation state and its commitment to meaningful democracy. In the words of Partha Chatterjee: 'The two domains—one of sovereignty and the other of governmentality, corresponding respectively to a discourse of rights and a discourse of policy—were brought together into the political arena of the nation State in the Nehru era.'[38] The lack of fit between the political language of rights and the economic language of utility and efficiency got reflected in the processes of governance.

Some of these movements, which stand out as particularly important from the perspective of this paper, are those mounted against the erosion of human security like dismantling of workers' rights, the right to health, the right to land and the right to biodiversity. These movements interrogate the developmental priorities of the Indian State, but also the co-mingling of the sanction of the State and the new market power of global capital. They highlight the fact that the deregulation of national economies and privatization of State assets invoked by the idiom of globalization indicates that governments are no longer willing, or able, to protect the sources of livelihood of their citizens.

The fact that many of these movements have substantially large numbers of women and are in some instances led by women, point to the real possibility of the so-called 'soft issues' entering decisively into the discourse for redefining security. An important aspect of this trajectory is that while business and commercial interests are actively championing the 'freeing of civil society' from State control, these movements are bringing added pressure on the State to govern in a manner that is sensitive to the people's agenda for security, in directions that rebuild 'living democracies' and 'living economies'. They have succeeded in highlighting the contradiction between the State discourse on the priorities of development on the one hand and people's security on the other.

The Indian State at the turn of the new century stands pulled in two different directions as reflected in the changing contours of contemporary debates among policy makers, intellectuals and professionals on governance and rights. At one end, there is pressure to integrate more efficiently into the world economy, and, on the other, the demand to respond to vulnerable sections of society and deliver on the promises of social equity reflected in its early 'welfarist' commitments.

The priorities of the development agenda in the decades following Independence have created a new category of subaltern, the internal refugee. New groupings of these displaced and dispossessed people have emerged, cutting across the ideological, geographical and class spectrum to pose a new kind of challenge to the Indian State. Though their success is uneven, they explore the possibilities of 'peoples' power', outside the ambit of parliamentary politics. They reflect a conscious strategy that recognizes the decline of political parties and their inability to effectively and democratically mediate State-society relations. They reject a notion of politics that is exclusively State centred even as they epitomize a critique of the corruption of State functionaries who routinely collude with local and powerful elite to corner the benefits of development activity and routinely extract commissions from projects meant to provide basic amenities.

The Indian experience has been that large-scale State projects in the name of enhancing security or providing 'development' have essentially been directed by modernizing elite, far removed from and insensitive to the needs and concerns of local communities. Largely of technocratic inspiration, they treat people as objects of the development process, become conduits of largesse for middlemen, contractors, politicians and bureaucrats and benefit the already advantaged.[39]

The interrogation of governance practices in India today comes, not *directly* from arguments for democracy, but from mounting protests on questions of survival, against displacement by mega-projects of people from their habitats, ways of life, cultures and on issues of food and water security and what has come to be termed 'belief security'.[40] From the 1980s onwards, several movements have mobilized around issues of human security. They have drawn sizeable numbers of women, and in some cases are led and organized by women. To cite a few examples:

1. The Bhopal Gas Peedit Mahila Udyog Sangathan ('Organization of Women Gas Victims of Bhopal') addressing issues of compensation, relief and rehabilitation to the victims of the huge industrial disaster

in 1984 caused by the gas leak from a Union Carbide factory in Bhopal.

2. The North Balasore Missile Base Resistance representing the indigenous struggle of the people of Baliapal (Orissa) against the setting up of a National Test Range for missiles, which brought to the fore the conflict between the State perception on national security and the people's right to a secure and safe life.
3. The more recent Navdanya movement, which, like movements of farmers in Karnataka, Maharashtra and Punjab, protests against the adverse impact of India's accession to Agreements on Agriculture under GATT and its concessions to multinationals on the sources of livelihood of substantial sections of those living in rural India and the potential threat to food security. It has also mounted pressure on international civil society to contest attempts by countries like the United States to patent indigenous products like *neem*, basmati rice and turmeric.
4. The Campaign for the Right to Information spearheaded by the Mazdoor Kisan Shakti Sangathan (and led by Magsaysay awardee Aruna Roy) in the villages of Rajasthan, which has emerged as the fulcrum of the citizens' movement for access to information on government allocation and spending. The recent tabling of the Right to Information Bill in Parliament is a culmination of the campaigns launched by people's movements like the MKSS across the country, representing public ire at the opacity and lack of accountability of government structures and asserting the peoples' right of access to official documents. The campaign has worked successfully in Madhya Pradesh, Goa and Tamil Nadu, where the state governments have passed legislation to guarantee the right to information. The impact of this legislation will result in altering patterns of accountability.

The 74th and 75th Constitutional Amendments, initiated by the Rajiv Gandhi Government, introducing 33 per cent reservation for women at the panchayat level, despite initial scepticism, have dramatically altered the contours of governance and priorities of resource allocation at the levels of local government. Efforts to extend such access to Parliament and State assemblies though the 81st Amendment Bill have encountered stiff resistance within and without party structures, further highlighting the obstacles to gender equity in governance.

It is, however, in the controversial debates surrounding the Narmada

Bachao Andolan (NBA) and its resistance to the Sardar Sarovar Project[41] that the challenge which these movements represent to the State, is most dramatically highlighted. They reflect a contest and conflict over the management and control of natural resources in a democracy, and the social process and choices that control the use and application of technologies. The NBA has become a symbol of the struggle over democratic meaning and the growing consciousness against iniquitous unsustainable development. With the exception of Jayaprakash Narayan's (JP) call for 'total revolution' in the early 1970s, the NBA is undoubtedly the single most sustained and significant non-violent movement in post-Independence India. Begun in 1985, and viewed by most political parties as 'anti-development', it draws workers and supporters from diverse socio-economic, professional, geographic and ideological backgrounds. It is the first movement in India to effectively use its linkages with international civil society to mount pressure in international fora on institutions like the World Bank.[42] The JP movement gained momentum by its assertion of democratic liberties against the excesses of the authoritarian regime of Indira Gandhi, and in the process, hastened the induction of the Backward Classes and groups into the electoral process. The NBA has focused on the disarticulation and marginalization of vulnerable sections resulting from the misgovernance associated with the development activities of the Indian State, and its upholding a paradigm that privileges technocracy over livelihood. The NBA brought to the fore issues raised by earlier lesser-known movements on behalf of the to-be-dispossessed: issues of social justice, economic efficiency, environmental sustainability and cultural survival.

In the 1980s and 1990s, through a series of strikes, fasts, processions and *padayatras*, the NBA widened its support base. This was necessary because a powerful pro-dam movement and a lobby that received the overt and covert support of the State apparatus confronted it. Its offices in Gujarat were systematically targetted and its adherents attacked by both the police and a pro-liberalization press. While the public debate has tended to polarize into a big dams vs small dams controversy, the NBA itself has raised legitimate concerns about issues concerning the 'resettlement' and 'rehabilitation' of oustees, and the potentially devastating impact of the project on the environment.

It is in this context that the judgment of the Supreme Court in October 2000 on a Public Interest Litigation (PIL) petition filed by the NBA in 1994 assumes significance, and is of grave importance for issues of citizens' rights and democratic governance. By a 2 : 1 majority, the apex court ordered the Gujarat government to proceed with the construction of the dam. Although the controversy about whether big dams are necessary or not is far from settled—and there is a vast body of technical and scientific literature arguing for both positions—the pronouncements of the court have evoked strong reactions. While there is euphoria and relief from the expected quarters, these pronouncements are being seen as a severe blow to movements for people's empowerment and the dispossessed who sought relief from the court against insensitive governance.[43] Significantly, the findings of the World Commission on Dams' Country Report for India has laid out in detail the massive failure that large dams represent.[44] Expert case studies of individual dams showed that the actual human and material costs incurred in their construction generally exceeded their putative benefits.

The judgment of the apex court also reflects an approach to governance, to litigation, to court behaviour, which has been described as conservative in the extreme. Aspects of the judgment are seen as eroding the principles underlying PIL and more recent trends in favour of freedom of information and of transparency and accountability of governments and private institutions. Proponents of judicial activism see this as a baffling departure from the judiciary's laudable efforts to 'rescue the people from the egregious failures of the executive and the legislature'. The incredulity is, however, not shared by those who cite the 'selective' nature of judicial activism and its implicit class preferences.[45]

What constitutes 'public purpose' has always been contested within the constitutional discourse. No policy or statute exists to give legal protection to oustees from land acquired for 'public purpose'. The doctrine of Eminent Domain provides the State protection from effective appeal, and the State, in concert with large companies, could read into 'public purpose' and 'eminent domain' enabling clauses to divest the poor and vulnerable of their land in 'benefit zones'. The fact that large projects have displaced approximately 21.3 million people since Independence and that nearly 75 per cent of those dispossessed were not rehabilitated throws up important questions for governance. The importance of a coherent policy on rehabilitation and resettlement cannot be overstated. The future prospects for humane governance will depend on the imagination with which this concern of security is addressed.

THE MANAGEMENT OF SECURITY: PEOPLE AND NATION

The Indian State faces the challenging task of balancing the competing demands of *national security* and requirements of human security of increasing numbers of newly articulate groups.[46] Since the 1980s, this conflict has occurred in the State's management of internal security. The link between militarization as social process and militarism as world-view is firmly established in contemporary social science discourse. The 1980s marked the decade when the militarization trend manifested itself. Civilian regimes, unable to tackle the rising tide of communalism, casteism and militant regionalism politically, came to rely on the police and armed forces to maintain internal stability, and perform such diverse tasks as quelling communal riots, providing relief during natural disasters, maintaining essential services during strikes, and counter-insurgency and anti-terrorist operations.[47]

The use of draconian anti-people Acts that were used to contain dissent during the 1975–7 Emergency under Mrs. Gandhi[48] continued into the 1980s with more such legislation added to the list. The Armed Forces Special Powers Act gave almost carte blanche powers to the security forces in the North-East: it was extended to Punjab in 1983 and Kashmir in 1990. The Terrorist and Disruptive Activities Act (TADA) gave vast powers to the States in 1985. It was made more rigorous (the burden of proof being shifted to the accused), and its powers extended to the centre in 1987. The TADA, which was widely misused and had acquired a distinct anti-Muslim orientation in the 1990s, was revoked in 1995.[49] But other special regulations remain in force.

Significantly, it was during this period that the military establishment got involved in politically volatile situations whilst grappling with insurgencies that were qualitatively different from the early communist armed struggles in Telangana, and pockets in Mumbai, Uttar Pradesh, West Bengal, Travancore, Tripura and Manipur during 1948–51, or the Naxalite or Maoist movements for economic and social reform in the late 1960s. The insurgencies in the closing decades of the twentieth century—Assam, Punjab and Kashmir—interfaced the internal and external dimensions of security, since they were located in border States, with arms, money and moral support for terrorist and insurgency activities coming from unfriendly or hostile neighbouring States.

In India, the tensions between the assertions of ethnicity and nation building have spawned violent, separatist movements with demands ranging from autonomy to independence. The conflicts in the north-eastern States (Assam, Nagaland and Tripura), Punjab and Kashmir, are generically described as 'terrorism', but are variegated. They do share a certain social basis and historical context, having arisen in opposition to insensitive and myopic ruling-class politics. But they have a specific causation and express particular grievances against and alienation from the formal structures of governance.

The erosion of democratic institutions began with the Emergency. The steady decline of the Congress party prompted it to enter opportunistic alliances with undemocratic forces in the States for short-term political gains. The consequent undermining of democratic, moderate voices in these regions from the 1980s have been contributing factors. The failure of state governments to undertake meaningful development activities and the centre turning a blind eye to corruption and nepotism in the state administration enabled secessionists and fundamentalists to gain legitimacy. The insurgency in the north-east, Punjab and Kashmir highlights the vulnerability of the federal State when governance is unresponsive to pluralist aspirations.

The movements for autonomy and secession in the border states of Punjab, the north-east and Kashmir share common characteristics. They mobilize and build their ideology on ethnic and religious identity, systematically construct an 'outsider' as the 'other', appeal to sectarian sentiments and can be communal. They target innocent civilians to dramatize their cause, advocate terrorist tactics and are militarist. They are hierarchical, centralized and essentially patriarchal in orientation and methodology.[50] They are mostly atavistic and prone to disintegrating into various factions.

The State response to these movements has demonstrated tactics and strategy that favour militarism over dialogue and reconciliation. The flushing out of terrorists by extensive military operations has required combing operations where lawful citizens are mistaken for terrorists. Police torture, wrongful confinement, custodial death and rape are widespread. The excesses of the militants are met with the might of the State, resulting in abrogation of the rule of law, and breakdown of institutions and processes of democracy. The suffering of civilians caught in the crossfire (with women and children being the worst victims)[51] has highlighted the fragility of a federal structure that treats the failed promise of development as a law-and-order problem. An estimated 60–65 per cent of India's military and paramilitary forces are deployed in anti-insurgency operations. The hazards of over-reliance on containment as a tool of governance have far-reaching implications for a plural society. The strengthening of such mechanisms outside democratic accountability narrows democratic space, but also contributes to a brutalization and criminalization of official agencies and institutions.

The militarization of the Indian State also has important external manifestations. The Indian Armed Forces have (on instructions of the civilian authority) been drawn into the task of external diplomacy to consolidate Indian hegemony in South Asia.[52] The creation of Bangladesh in 1971 was a major milestone in carving out this hegemonic role. It found expression in the 1980s through Indian military operations in Sri Lanka and the Maldives. Operation Pawan involved engaging the Indian Peace Keeping Force (IPKF) in Sri Lanka (1987–90) to disarm Tamil militants fighting for an independent homeland, and Operation Cactus entailed the Indian Armed Forces intervening to save the democratic government in the Maldives in 1988 from a coup attempt. Underpinning these operations is a new brand of coercive diplomacy projecting India's military capabilities and unwillingness to countenance 'outside interference' in South Asian affairs. India's consistent position has been to prefer bilateral arrangements to multilateral processes within SAARC: this has led to consternation in the smaller countries of the region, not just Pakistan, which was evident in Sri Lanka against the IPKF, in anti-India protests in Bangladesh during the Khaleda Zia regime, and more recent violent protests in Nepal.

The political ascendancy of the BJP after 1998 has seen the emergence of a discourse which links national security with cultural nationalism and militarism which has resonance within the strategic establishment and a section of civil society. This was evident in the jingoism during the Kargil war, and labelling any critique of India's strategic choices or nuclear programme as 'anti-national'.

The concern within the security establishment that 'India lacks a tradition of strategic thinking' is gaining greater currency and finding more persistent articulation,[53] reflecting a more assertive realism in defence and foreign policy. Its growing acceptance coincides with the waning of the Nehruvian security paradigm with its mix of idealism and political realism, but emphasis on compromise and peaceful settlement of disputes. While the process began after the debacle with China in 1962, the more definitive break came with the Indo-Pak war of 1971. With the first Indian nuclear test in May 1974, intervention in Sri Lanka in 1987, and sustained references to threats from anti-national forces colluding with a 'foreign hand', the stage was set for a new security paradigm that privileged defence security. Both internal and external dimensions of security came to be seen from this perspective. With the break-up of the Soviet Union, and the belief that the primary threat to India comes from China, Pakistan, and, less credibly, from the remaining superpower, the preferences of the strategic elite became significant in determining India's nuclear posture.[54]

The May 1998 tests moved India decisively from its position of nuclear ambiguity—around which since 1974 a political consensus had obtained—to one of minimum nuclear deterrence.[55]

There are good reasons to doubt that the Pokhran tests and the Pakistani retaliatory blasts at Chagai have better served the goals of Indian security. The Kargil conflict following these nuclear blasts represents the first major military confrontation between India and Pakistan in nearly 30 years, and demonstrated the fallacy of the argument that the likelihood of conventional war is reduced by nuclearization of the two countries.[56] That nuclearization would allow expenditure on conventional forces to be reduced was based on a thesis that nuclear deterrence subsumes conventional deterrence. This has given way to an acknowledgment in the Draft Nuclear Doctrine that 'highly effective conventional military capabilities shall be maintained to raise the threshold of outbreak both of conventional military conflict as well as that of threat or use of nuclear weapons'.[57]

The scathing indictment in the Kargil Review Committee Report on the conduct of operations is cause for concern. The report highlights the crisis of national security management, revealing the skewed nature of decision-making in defence matters. It blames the Research and Analysis Wing (RAW), the external intelligence agency, for failure to forewarn the military in time. Its categorical statement that 'an objective assessment of the last 52 years will show that the country is lucky to have scraped through various national security threats without too much damage'[58] raises significant questions about the efficacy and sustainability of the command and control systems required in a nuclearized environment. Satellite-based early warning, intelligence and damage assessment facilities are non-existent today, and are not likely to be available for several years.[59]

Within the realm of techno-strategic discourse, what is significant is not that facts are 'manipulated', but that significant questions are not allowed to enter the debate. The idea that nuclear weapons denote a substantial *qualitative* change in the nature of weaponry since they kill non-combatants (women and children), and that they are indiscriminate, uncontrolled and genocidal in character, has never seriously entered the discourse.[60] The idea that science is one of the people's weapons against poverty also gets jettisoned.[61]

The complexities of the management of security pose very real challenges for governance in plural societies like India. The elite form the 'national security' constituency, while it is the deprived that are most concerned about human security.[62] These twin foci of security—human and national—are competing for attention more forcefully than before. While there is growing recognition that social conflict and economic weakness are enduring obstacles to human security, these are not configured into the formal strategic discourse, but are treated as 'non-traditional' security concerns. The political leadership is yet to create a consensus on national security. Concerns have also been expressed about the lack of interaction and coordination between the various bodies that comprise the new national security apparatus, namely the National Security Council, the Strategic Policy Group and the National Security Advisory Board.[63]

A security establishment, comprising experts from politics, administration, diplomacy, military, intelligence, sciences and economics, and possessing a multidisciplinary understanding is absent in India. There is a lack of congruence between genuine expertise and influence. However, the weakened position of the nation state in a globalized world order encourages the association of national pride with weaponization in the discourse of the political elite.[64]

The increasing levels of internal violence—religious, ethnic and caste-based—can be linked to failures of governance to meet the growing expectations of newly enfranchized groups in civil society. The growth of private armies and militias like the upper-caste Ranvir Sena in Bihar also reflects the inability of the State to provide protection or maintain order. A centralized command and control system for the management of internal security, relying on military and paramilitary forces, is not working. There are limitations on the capacity of the Indian State to cope with these problems. The compulsions of balancing a fragile 23-party coalition have made consistency in decision-making by the central government a casualty. The army's increasing involvement in internal security has not curtailed militancy. Newer arenas of conflict are growing as older ones are 'contained', apparent from the renewed insurgency in the border States of Tripura and Manipur.

Between the poles of devolution in decision-making and working Panchayati Raj institutions and the centralized secrecy of its nuclear programme, the Indian State traverses the worlds of the dispossessed and privileged, human security and state security, moral imperative and expediency. Governance patterns reflect these inconsistencies in responding to the contradictory pressures of power and entitlements.

The dilemma before the Indian State of economic growth versus equity that coloured the earlier debate on development has metamorphosed today into a concern for 'security' encompassing economic stability, equity, and empowerment. The political process to meet these concerns will require a framework for governance that sees the State and civil society in democratic partnership rather than as oppositional or complicitous. There is need to move beyond a purely tactical approach and to seize—as Amartya Sen stresses—the central connection between the moral and the prudential.[65]

By any standard, citizen satisfaction vis-à-vis the quality of governance is low. The Directive Principles of State Policy enshrined in Part IV of the Indian Constitution underscore the importance of State intervention to preserve human security, but their *non-justiciability* results in slack implementation. Rampant corruption, inordinate delays in the delivery of justice, denial of information on resource allocation, lack of transparency, police brutality, violation of rights, denial of access to civic services except by patronage or bribery, distinguish the Indian administration.

Yet, those in charge of Indian governance are over-protected. Civil servants and other public servants (which includes MPs and others under the Prevention of Corruption Act 1988) are protected for offences of omission and commission. Article 311 of the Constitution also substantially protects civil servants and judges from criminal prosecution. There is, hence, a need to develop effective mechanisms to examine complaints against public officials. They have consistently evaded the creation of a *Lokpal* (ombudsman), although the initiative has been actively debated for over a decade.

There have been some laudable efforts to streamline the essentially colonial administrative system. The *Lok Adalats*, legal aid services, and citizens watchdog groups have intervened to alleviate the harassment faced by citizens. Public interest litigation and suo motu intervention by courts to review the executive actions of the government have had a positive impact. The Human Rights Commission, National and State

Commissions for Women, Monopolies and Restrictive Trade Practices Commission and Consumer Tribunals have provided some safety shields for the public. Yet, their access to disadvantaged groups remains problematic. There has been a phenomenal growth of NGO activities from the early 1990s in the area of social development. Of late, however, some have had an uneasy relationship with the government around issues of foreign funding. There is a simultaneous realization that the State cannot abdicate its responsibility of providing human security for the least advantaged to 'civil society initiatives' alone, or the 'munificence' of market forces.

The weaknesses in national security management were recently highlighted by the ineptitude displayed after the hijacking of the Indian Airlines plane IC 814 to Afghanistan in December 1999. The hostage crisis revealed the serious lack of preparedness of the executive in national crisis management. The mishandling of relief measures following the Orissa cyclone, the ineptitude in distributing relief to earthquake victims in Gujarat, the various omissions and acts of commission that have enabled the forest brigand Veerappan to hold state governments hostage, point to the sorry state of governance, stymied by official corruption and lack of political will. The reliance on judicial intervention cannot be the permanent solution to problems of governance.

On the flip side, the success of initiatives where governments have transited from patronage to partnership with citizen participation hold out some hope for the future. The Community Food and Water Security initiatives and Education Guarantee Schemes in Madhya Pradesh, the activities around the People's Plan initiatives in Kerala, the employment of erstwhile disenfranchized groups by the National Literacy Missions in many states in India, the devolution of power envisaged by the 73rd and 74th Amendments to revitalize Panchayati Raj institutions, point to the possibilities of community management of resources, and the future management of security in India. The key to effective citizen participation, of course, lies in the right to information and the administrative and political transparency and accountability in public life which, to use Aruna Roy's phrase, 'while it is more or less a moral issue for the middle class, is for the poor a matter of life and death'.

The Indian State also needs to re-vision its response and strategy to border states. A response that includes a cross-section of stakeholders of different ethnic groupings as opposed to privileging any one group in bilateral dialogues could be an invaluable starting point. A discourse that transcends the rigid separations of *internal* versus *external* security is crucial to meet the challenges posed; the crucial interface between security and governance occurs here, but a predominantly militarist discourse shrinks such space.

ENGENDERING THE DISCOURSE

From a feminist perspective, the concept of human security opens up space for concerns about war and militarism and their impact on women and men, and power relations in society can be articulated within the discourse, rather than from the margins. The marginality of women and gender has resulted from the dominance of realists and realism in the security arena, which undervalues the expanding role of non-State actors and sees the participation of women as largely irrelevant to the determination of 'high politics', specially international political security and economic analysis and decision-making.[66]

Yet, women as refugees, widows and as workers without personal or family security have become markers of the emerging international landscape that cannot be ignored. The internal and transregional wars shaping the global landscape are being fought not only on battlefields, but also in homes, communities, cities and villages. Despite the multiple roles[67] of women in conflict, their 'voice' is seldom heard in the 'hard' issue areas—security, foreign policy, finance and trade. The concept of human security helps to foreground the issues integral to feminist perspectives but not exclusive to feminist discourse: its questioning of realism and notions of security as a zero sum game; the separation of the public sphere from the private; its critique of war, gendered citizenship and nationalism; its emphasis on respecting 'difference' in democratic arrangements and its stress on the links between patriarchy, militarism, intolerance and violence. These are issues integral to humane governance.

With women constituting nearly 50 per cent of the population in India, any discourse on security and governance cannot continue to rely on analysis that is gender neutral and carried on only by men. Women and their concerns will *have* to be made more visible. Women as victims and combatants in conflict, women as workers, women as consumers, are all impacted by the manner in which States depend on particular constructions of the domestic and private sphere to govern and to provide 'security' to their citizens.[68] Yet, women have remained on the margins. . . . It is time their concerns begin to inform the discourse.

NOTES

1. 'Humane governance' is described as that good governance which fosters human development comprising three inter-linked dimensions: economic, political and civic. Of a list of 58 countries, India ranks 55 and Pakistan 54th in Human Development and 42 and 52 respectively in the Humane Governance Index. See *Human Development in South Asia*, Karachi: OUP, 1999.
2. Khadija Haq, *Human Development in South Asia*, 1999, p. 113.
3. Ibid., p. 113.
4. Ibid., p. 115.
5. Ibid., p. 115.
6. Ibid., p. 45.
7. Ibid., p. 116.
8. Ibid., p. 113.
9. P.R. Chari, ed., *Perspectives on National Security in South Asia: In Search of a New Paradigm*, New Delhi: Manohar, 1999, pp. 418–19.
10. P.R. Chari and Ayesha Siddiqa-Agha, *Defence Expenditure in South Asia: India, Pakistan and Colombo*, RCSS Policy Studies 12, 2000, p. 11.
11. Achin Vanaik, 'India's Place in the World', in Partha Chatterjee, ed., *India's Place in the World*, New Dehi: OUP, 1999, pp. 61–86.
12. Lloyd Axworthy, 'Canada and Human Security: The Need for Leadership', *International Journal* LII, 2 (Spring), pp. 183–96.
13. Kanti Bajpai, 'The Idea of a Human Security Audit', unpublished paper, New Delhi, 1999.
14. Nirija Gopal Jayal, *Democracy and the State*, Delhi: OUP, 1999, p. 257.
15. I owe this characterization to the line of argument developed in Jayal, ibid. pp. 239–48.
16. Amrita Basu and Atul Kohli, eds., *Community Conflicts and the State in India*, New Delhi: OUP, 1998, pp. 2–3.
17. The term 'Hindutva' is not identified with 'Hinduism', but is used to indicate the contemporary communal organizations and movements that use this banner primarily for political and cultural mobilization. See Tapan Basu et al., *Khaki Shorts and Saffron Flags: Tracts for the Times*, New Delhi: Orient Longman, 1993, pp. 112–13.
18. Tanika Sarkar, 'Woman, Community and Nation', in Patricia Jeffrey and Amrita Basu, eds., *Appropriating Gender: Women's Activism and Politicized Religion in South Asia*, New York: Routledge, 1998, p. 104.
19. Ibid., p. 97.
20. Quoted by Hasan Suroor, 'Dismal Scenario, Dangerous Agenda', *The Hindu*, 1 November 1998.
21. The Justice Shri Krishna Commission, in its report submitted in 1998, connected the demolition of the Babri Masjid in December 1992 to the outbreak of riots the following month. The report, through a detailed judicial process, in which hundreds of witnesses testified and were cross-examined by representatives of all involved parties, confirmed the culpability of the Shiv Sena in the riots. It held its chief Bal Thackerey responsible for intentionally inciting communal violence through his inflammatory and communal writings in the party's mouthpieces,

Saamna and *Navakal*. The BJP–Shiv Sena Government in Maharashtra, in power at the time, rejected the report, labelling it as 'anti-Hindu'.

22. It is significant that while the estimated number of cases of violence reported against Christians between 1964 and 1996 were 38, this figure increased to 136 in 1997–8.
23. KumKum Sangari, 'Which Diversity', *Seminar* 484, December 1999, pp. 24–30.
24. Ibid., p. 28.
25. Neera Chandoke, 'Rethinking Minority Rights', *IIC Quarterly*, Spring 1996, pp. 125–36.
26. The UN Human Rights Commission (established in 1946), appointed a subcommission on Prevention of Discrimination and Protection of Minorities. The formal recognition of the crime of genocide in Nuremberg in 1945 provided the underpinnings for the concern for the preservation of the rights of groups that constitute a distinctive minority culture, and is reflected in Art. 27 of the International Covenant on Civil and Political Rights.
27. See for example, 'The Rights of Minorities: A Declaration of Liberal, Democratic Principles Concerning Ethno-Cultural and National Minorities and Indigenous People's Conference on Human Rights and Minorities', Germany, *Liberal Times*, vol. III, no. 3, October 1999, New Delhi.
28. Veena Das, 'Communities as Political Actors: The Question of Cultural Rights', in Nivedita Menon, ed., *Gender and Politics in India*, New Delhi: OUP, 1999, pp. 441–69.
29. Zoya Hasan, ed., *Forging Identities: Gender, Communities and the State*, New Delhi: Kali for Women, 1994, p. xi.
30. For a well-documented background to the judgment, see Radha Kumar, *The History of Doing*, New Delhi: Kali for Women, 1993, pp. 100–71. Also see Asghar Ali Engineer, 'Maintenance for Muslim Women', *The Hindu*, New Delhi, 7 August 2000.
31. See Zoya Hasan, 'Gender Politics, Legal Reform and the Muslim Community in India', in Jeffery and Basu, eds., *Appropriating Gender*, New York: Routledge, 1998, p. 86.
32. For a well-argued exposition of the changing positions and how they compel a rethinking on the dominant discourse on 'secularism', see Nivedita Menon, 'Women and Citizenship', in Partha Chatterjee, ed., *Wages of Freedom*, New Delhi: OUP, 1998, pp. 241–66.
33. Nivedita Menon, *Gender and Politics in India*, New Delhi: OUP, 1999, p. 11.
34. This is evidenced by two landmark judgments by the Calcutta High Court in the Shakila Pervin case, and the Mumbai High Court (July 2000), where the courts have read into Sec. 3 of the Muslim Women's Act, fair and reasonable provisions for maintenance for life, and not restricted to the *iddat* period alone. These have not evoked any adverse reaction from the community so far.
35. Menon, *Gender and Politics*, pp. 30–2.
36. Menon, op. cit., n. 32 above, pp. 265–6.
37. Rajni Kothari, 'The Democratic Experience', in Chatterjee op. cit., pp. 23–36.
38. Chatterjee, *Wages of Freedom*, p. 16.
39. Jayal, op. cit, pp. 235–6. Jayal has shown that the beneficiaries of development are also, on the whole, the beneficiaries of democracy, and the victims of development do not generally enjoy much purchase in the democratic system.

40. Vinod Raina, 'Why People Oppose Dams', *Inter-Asia Cultural Studies*, vol. I, no. 1, 2000, p. 158. Raina uses this term to contextualize the psychological dimension of being displaced and uprooted that is extremely debilitating for a people whose belief system ties them to a land.
41. Conceived as a multipurpose dam on the river Narmada between the Satpura and Vindhya ranges at the Madhya Pradesh–Gujarat–Maharashtra border, the Sardar Sarovar Project is envisaged to irrigate 1.8 million hectares in Gujarat, 75,000 hectares in Rajasthan, generate 1,400 MW power and provide water to 8,000 villages and 131 municipalities and industrial towns. It is estimated that the reservoir when complete will submerge 40,000 hectares of forests and an equal amount of prime agricultural and non-agricultural land each, displace 3,50,000 indigenous people and endanger the lives and livelihood of some 1.2 million forest dwellers, farmers and fishermen. In 1988, the dam and its irrigation canals were estimated to cost Rs. 6,400 crore. Today, the official estimated cost of the project has increased to Rs. 18,000 crore, and it has not so far met the promised targets in any sector.
42. The World Bank, in 1991, following efforts of the NBA, commissioned an independent review of the project, popularly known as the 'Morse Commission'. The exhaustive report which assessed the impact of the dam on environment, resettlement and rehabilitation stated that the Sardar Sarovar Projects as they stand are flawed. Although neither the World Bank nor the Government of India officially accepted the Morse Report, in March 1993, the World Bank pulled out of the Sardar Sarovar Project. The Supreme Court had, in 1995, ordered that work on the dam be suspended until further notice. The judgment was passed on the grounds that the rehabilitation of displaced people had not been adequate.
43. See Ramaswamy R. Iyer, 'A Judgment of Grave Importance', *Economic and Political Weekly*, 4 November 2000, pp. 3913–16 and 'Troubled Waters—No Justice for Narmada Displaced', *Times of India*, 10 November 2000 and Jai Sen, 'The S.C. and the Narmada Case', *The Hindu*, 6 and 7 November 2000.
44. What emerges from the report of the World Commission on Dams released in London on 16 November 2000 is not a happy picture. The 45,000 large dams worldwide have displaced 40 million to 80 million people, affected 60 per cent of all rivers, have fallen short of their irrigation targets, have failed to recover costs, have had extensive negative impacts on rivers, watersheds and aquatic systems, many of them irreversible. Mitigation measures, where they have been taken, have usually proved ineffective. The record suggests that this is not always possible, and the costs may not be worth the putative benefits even in terms of spread of irrigation generated by hydroelectric power, flood management or increase in urban water supply.
45. Anand Patwardhan, 'Judgment and After', *The Hindu Magazine*, 26 November 2000, p. viii.
46. Verghese Koithara, *Society, State and Security: The Indian Experience*, New Delhi: Sage, 1999, p. 384.
47. Sumona Dasgupta, 'Militarization of the Indian State Since the 1980s', *International Studies*, vol. 35, no. 4, 1998, New Delhi: Sage, p. 442.
48. These were the Preventive Detention Act, The Maintenance of Internal Security Act (MISA) and the National Security Act.

49. There have been attempts to renew TADA, with the Law Commission, on the request of the Ministry of Home Affairs recommending the adoption of the Prevention of Terrorism Bill, 2000 (POT). The Human Rights Commission has opposed POT saying that it would legitimize the violation of human rights on a large scale.
50. I am grateful to Anuradha Chenoy for sharing these insights from her forthcoming book *Militarism and Women in South Asia*, New Delhi, Kali for women.
51. The figures for Kashmir are staggering. By 1993, most of the 150,000 Kashmiri Hindus were in refugee camps. Women were particularly traumatized and often at the mercy of male supervisors. Rough estimates show that the number of orphans due to militancy is anywhere between 10,000 and 20,000. There are at least 9,000 women whose husbands have died during the conflict. See Kalpana Sharma, 'The Other Side of Conflict', *The Hindu*, 10 November 1999.
52. Dasgupta, op. cit., pp. 447–53.
53. K. Subrahmanyam, 'Challenges to Indian Security', K.M. Cariappa Memorial Lecture, 28 October 2000, p. 4. Similar positions are also reflected in Raja Menon, *A Nuclear Strategy for India*, New Delhi: Sage, 2000, and Koithara, *Society, State and Security*, op. cit, pp. 388–90. Foreign Minister Jaswant Singh too writes of the alleged lack of 'territorial consciousness' as a historic Indian failing.
54. Rajesh Basrur, 'Some Observations on Indian Strategic Culture', in A. Subrahmanyam Raju, ed., *Nuclear India: Problems and Perspectives*, New Delhi: South Asia Publications, 2000, pp. 21–6.
55. Gopalji Malviya and W. Lawrence S. Prabhakar, 'India's Nuclear Culture', *The Hindu*, New Delhi, 20 May 2000.
56. Amartya Sen, 'India and the Bomb', *Frontline*, vol. 17, no. 19, 16–29 September 2000.
57. Chari and Siddiqa-Agha, 'Defence Expenditure', pp. 10–11.
58. K. Subrahmanyam et al., *From Surprise to Reckoning: The Kargil Review Committee Report*, New Delhi: Sage, 15 December 1999, p. 258.
59. Lt. Gen. V.R. Raghavan (retd). , 'A Debatable Nuclear Doctrine', *The Hindu*, 24 August 1999.
60. Here, the position of the International Court of Justice on 8 July 1996 to the question put to it by the General Assembly is pertinent. The court, while not directly establishing illegality, held that the use of nuclear weapons would be a serious danger to future generations, ionizing radiation containing the potential to damage the future environmental food and marine eco-system, and to cause genetic defects and illness in future generations.
61. Amulya Reddy, 'Technology and Violence', *Seventh Saadath Hassan Manto Lecture*, Centre for the Study of Developing Societies, New Delhi, 13 June 2000, p. 5. The World Economic Outlook of the IMF suggests that the rate of decline of poverty from the mid-1970s may have actually slowed down in recent years. In 1951, India's poor numbered 164 million; in 1993–4, the number is 312 million, indicating that the percentage of the population below the poverty line declined by less than 1 per cent per year. It is significant that the Union Budget for 2000–2001 has proposed a Rs. 10,000 crore increase in the total defence outlay over the revised post-Kargil estimate for 1999–2000. Increase in defence spending will be 20 per cent more than the budgeted growth in spending on all Plan programmes this year. According to the Economic Survey of 1999–2000, in recent years, social

sector *spending* has consistently fallen short of the budgeted amount and currently stands at 1.66 per cent of GDP, further highlighting the dramatic failure of planning and administrative structures in meeting targets in so crucial an area.

62. A rural survey undertaken by the *Peoples' Science Network* in 18 states from 1998 onwards shows that almost 60 per cent of the rural population was against the nuclear bomb—ranging from 54 per cent in Assam to 80 per cent in Tamil Nadu. The main concerns were related to housing, health, employment and educational opportunities.
63. K. Subrahmanyam, Cariappa Memorial Lecture, 2000, New Delhi and J.N. Dixit, 'Security Alert', *Hindustan Times*, New Delhi, 7 December 2000, p. 10.
64. Gautam Navlakha, 'National Security vs Peoples' Insecurity', *Economic and Political Weekly*, vol. XXXI, no. 52, 28 December 1996, pp. 33–52.
65. Amartya Sen, 'India and the Bomb', Dorothy Hodgkin Lecture, Cambridge, 8 August 2000, reprinted in *Frontline*, vol. 17, 16–29 September 2000.
66. Mahnaz Ispahani, *Background Note on Women's Leadership and the Gender Lens in International Cooperation*, New York: Ford Foundation, April 2000, p. 2.
67. Massive refugee flows, comprising mainly women and children, dominate the human landscape. Rape is now a recognized instrument of war. But women are not only victims, they are combatants. They create and manage anti-war efforts and mothers' movements for peace. They play vital roles in conflict, providing support for fighters, sending their children to war and acting both as combatants and economic providers. Yet, in post-conflict situations, women are retired to the private sphere or the social sector to address 'women's issues'.
68. Cynthia Enloe, *Bananas, Beaches and Bases*, University of Berkeley: California Press, 1990, pp. 197–8.

CHAPTER 4

Governance and Security in Plural Societies: The Case of Nepal

Lok Raj Baral

This paper opens a discourse on the generalities and specifics of pluralist democracy and the constraints of tradition, history, and the processes of change in Nepal. Its authoritarian tradition based on a rigid caste-based social structure, which impacts on Nepal's security environment cannot be studied in isolation. Nepal's standing army of about 50,000, especially its upper hierarchy, is traditional in its composition with the Rana, Shah, and other Chhetri clans dominating the structure, though representation of some hill ethnic groups—Rai, Limbu, Gurung, and Magar—is slowly rising. The Tarai people (*Madhise*) complain about the discriminatory policies of the Nepali State, since it has not encouraged Tarain recruitment in the Army, despite assurances given to their supporters like the Nepal Sadbhawana Party. The Tarai people see this recruitment pattern as being discriminatory, which weakens the Nepali State and makes it conflict-prone.

Nepal has followed the Westminster model of parliamentary democracy whilst trying to indigenize it. Unlike Britain and India, the political parties in Nepal did not evolve out of a long parliamentary tradition or struggle for independence. They were formed in the 1940s to fight the local Rana oligarchy. Many parties have undergone processes of permutation and fragmentation, but have failed to develop any intrinsic strength to sustain them in adversity. Personality differences and lack of a democratic culture have heightened their basic organizational weaknesses. Emboldened by these weaknesses the monarchy, whose power had been stripped by the Ranas for over a century, stepped forward in 1960 to dismantle the multiparty system and pave the way for a partyless regime under its 'active and supreme leadership'. This partyless regime continued until it was dismantled by the mass movement launched by the Nepali Congress (NC) with the support of a broad coalition of left parties and other professional groups in the country.

In 1990, Nepal entered a new era of multiparty democracy following a mass movement against the 30-year old royal regime. Nepal is now governed by a democratic Constitution; in practice, however, politics has increasingly been mired in bad governance due to the failure of political parties to achieve the minimum expectations of the people. This is reminiscent of the period following the end of the Rana regime in the 1950s. Within a brief span of 10 years, the country has experimented with several types of governments—single-party majority, minority, right-left coalition, right-left-centre coalition, and majority government led by the NC party. These efforts have not been without value because people's awareness, supported by the international system, has allowed the democratic system to develop.

Internal politics is an independent variable for influencing the security environment; without clean and effective governance, procedural democracy, riddled with systemic aberrations, can only lead to atrophy of the system, and raise apprehensions about its longevity. If endemic crises linger for long periods, external and internal linkages of forces could occur that are bent on destabilizing plural society and polity. Performance of the system is crucial, hence, serious questions arise about the viability of the nation state and the democratic system, since internal and external resource mobilization remains negligible whilst politicking continues unabated.

CONCEPTUAL ISSUES REGARDING GOVERNANCE AND SECURITY IN PLURAL SOCIETIES

This paper addresses three different interconnected issues—plural society, governance, and security. The sociological basis of plural society derives from the multiplicity of its social categories, specially its ethnic, tribal, and religious groups possessing a distinct cultural identity whilst coexisting with predominantly larger groups (*jatis*) with smaller ethnic groups. How ethnic pluralities or dominant group homogeneity can create positive or negative consequences for security is increasingly being recognized in the security discourse. Since 'ethnicity and nationalism are not "givens"', as Paul Brass states, 'but are social and political constructions',[1] the centralizing tendency of the 'state-nation' rather than the dynamics of a 'nation-state' provides legitimacy to power elite, both authoritarian and democratic. Democratic elites who achieve power on their own reinforce their elitist positions based on inherited social hierarchy or acquired status, making them status quo-oriented. This heightens popular cynicism about the legitimacy of the democratic system.

Elite formation reveals interactive but conflictual relations between the State and the ethnic minorities, pointing to the impossibility of change if existing social imbalances remain. Moreover, plural groups in society find that, in the absence of a rational approach to mitigating disparities—social, economic and political—ethnic assertions develop around language, culture, territory, and religion, although they may be too feeble to create an impact on governance. However, the democratic process provides space for articulating their interests, hence the possibility of mitigating these grievances is there. What a nation is and how ethnic loyalties manifest themselves becomes significant, because the concept of a nation is people-specific.

The description of ethnic or tribal groups in a 'plural society' was first conceptualized by J.S. Furnival in 1939. He defined a plural society as 'comprising two or more elements or social orders which live side by side, yet without mingling, in one political unit'. In his postulation, plural society is distinct from a homogeneous one. Later sociologists have improved upon this concept by noticing the plural existence of various social categories. According to Rabushka and Shepsle, 'a society is plural if it is culturally diverse and its cultural sections are organised into cohesive political sections'.[2]

Ethnic groups or ethnicity have significance in today's politics because this phenomenon is associated with several forms of conflict, hence, we need to understand the accepted attributes of ethnic groups or ethnicity. Various elements have to coalesce to form an ethnic community. Schermerhorn has defined an ethnic group as a 'collectivity within a larger society having real or putative common ancestry, memories of a shared historical past, and a cultural focus on one or more symbolic elements defined as the epitome of their peoplehood. Examples of such symbolic elements are: kinship pattern, physical contiguity, religious affiliation, language or dialect, tribal affiliation, nationality, phenotypic features, or any combination of these.'[3] *Ethnic* groups generally exhibit, albeit in varying degrees, six main features:

1. a common proper name to identify and express the 'essence' of the community;
2. a myth of common ancestry, a myth rather than a fact, a myth that includes the idea of a common origin in time and place and that gives an ethnie a sense of fictive kinship, what Harowitz terms a 'super-family';
3. shared historical memories, or better, shared memories of a common past or pasts, including heroes, events and their commemoration;
4. or more elements of common culture, which need not be specified but normally include religion, custom, or language;
5. *a link homeland*, not necessarily its physical occupation by ethnie, only its symbolic attachment to the ancestral land, as with diaspora people;
6. *a sense of solidarity*, on the part of at least some sections of the ethnie's population.[4]

These attributes suggest that only some shared elements evoke a sense of commonality among and between similar communities despite their ethnic and tribal biases. When conflicts between dominant and non-dominant groups arise, smaller ethnic groups with similar social, racial, and cultural traits mobilize themselves. The broad unity formed between the Mongol ethnic communities of Nepal to pressurize the dominant Brahmin and Chhetri castes to pursue a policy of greater accommodation and social justice is an example. In the later part of the twentieth century, many countries were either balkanized or were in the throes of ethno-national turbulence. The centralized State structures in the advanced industrialized and developing states left little space for 'sub-national' ethnic identities. When majority communities monopolize resources, ethnic mobilization movements designed against exploitation get encouraged.

The dalit movement in India is aimed at ending the rigid caste and class structures. The demand of the tribal hill and Tarai groups in Nepal to reduce disparity, the continuing insurgencies in north-east India and elsewhere are manifestations of this sense of deprivation. In some cases ethnic wars also become class wars. The Maoist people's war in Nepal has tried to link the sense of economic and social exploitation with an ethnic psyche. Many social scientists have urged that democratic pluralism in plural societies becomes problematical when ethnic cleavages are sharp and rampant.

Robert Dahl, the guru of pluralist democracy, has said that polyarchy, which is a more advanced form of liberal democracy, is better suited to relatively homogeneous countries than countries with subcultural pluralism, 'but he does not regard the survival of democracy as impossible in plural societies'.[5] Pluralism in politics requires institutional arrangements for ensuring an active involvement of its citizens to affect the course of policy. Does active participation alone fulfil the requirements of pluralism? What would be the fate of the system if non-participants swell, and what would happen to the polity if too many participants 'immobilize policy makers if and when a decision on any significant issue offends too many interests'? David Apter calls it the 'pluralist paradox', which has been elaborated by Samuel P. Huntington in his pioneering article 'Political Development and Political Decay'.[6]

The political dimensions of pluralism reflecting diversity and 'accountability and consent are diffused throughout society'.[7] Plural views and associations exist even in authoritarian regimes but their pluralism is limited as manifest in several Asian, European and Latin American authoritarian countries. Pluralism demands more freedom and opportunities and not the 'constructive criticism' demanded by the erstwhile monarchical authoritarian regime in Nepal. So political pluralism requires greater participation, coordination and accountability, which is a facet of good governance. Good governance is a more extensive concept and is expected to be efficient, less corruptible, the provider of social justice, people-based and task-oriented. It should also be simple, austere and accessible to the ordinary people.

Democracy in India is being treated as a laboratory for the developing world. Plurality in Indian politics in terms of parties, societies and centre-state relations lays the basis for real or 'cooperative' federalism in which the states find political space. The political landscape in India has changed now with various regional parties, both big and small, developing a feeling of togetherness in the midst of political and social diversity. Thus, instead of pulling apart, the Indian experiment illustrates the hypothesis that democratic pluralism and social diversity are not incongruous. Taking Nepal as a case study, the concept and dynamics of a plural society is not incompatible with its ongoing democratic process, because ethnic pluralities have found political space and channels for articulation of their interests. Moreover, a 'syncretic form of Hinduism, encompassing much that is Buddhist or 'animist' in derivation is the dominant religious and cultural form throughout much of Nepal . . . this does not mean, of course, that non-Hindus have always accepted the imposition of Brahmanic Hindu values willingly or that the synthesizing process has been painless'.[8] Thus, in Nepal, despite being a 'polyethnic kingdom',[9] to use Urmila Phadnis' term, the correlationship between the democratic system and ethnic conflict has not yet emerged; its crises of democratic governance can be squarely attributed to the failures of its leaders and parties.

The foregoing theoretical discourse on social and political pluralism emphasizes the need to blend the two pluralities that are inseparable for good governance in plural societies. The term 'social pluralism' refers to such societies 'whose populations are not homogeneous but divided by tribal, ethnic, racial, and religious cleavages and where . . . several factors combine to increase the propensity for conflict rather than compromise'.[10] Yet, there can be exceptions where the propensity to conflict is determined by the inability of the governing elites to address the core demands of ethnic and other social groups. Governance qua governance can turn into ritual exercises to destroy the nation and democracy, which emphasizes the need for security in the conventional and comprehensive sense. The dislocation or breakdown of the system and its subsystems would create an adverse security situation in the country, more so in the context of 'comprehensive security' that includes aspects of politics, economy, society, environment, external factors and so on.

A pluralist society has greater propinquity for violence—both structural and non-structural—and to societal and political upheavals. Nepal's 10-year exercise in pluralist politics is now under scrutiny as the public is dissatisfied with politicians and parties, though not with democracy, since its legitimacy is ensured through periodic elections and political dissent is guaranteed by the Constitution. However, people are now questioning the rationale of electoral politics as having become a mere ritual that aims at ensuring the legitimacy of power, whilst its actual legitimacy lies in the government's performance. 'Governance' is a neutral concept that can be applied to all forms of governments—authoritarian, monarchical and democratic, whilst 'good governance' is generally believed to possess universally accepted norms such as accountability, transparency, efficiency, legitimacy, and participation. Though value-loaded, all governments must be democratic. Otherwise they cannot be effective in areas like security.

SECURITY AS A DISCIPLINE

The third element of this paper is security in the context of plural societies and plural politics. It transcends military security or conventional security because several variables are involved that ensure or diminish security. Moreover, departing from the traditional focus centring on its military and diplomatic aspects, the present fashion includes comprehensive security. Individuals, societies, State structures, nation building agendas and their failures, along with interactions between various formal and informal groups within and outside nation states are involved that include several areas of citizens' interests. Globalization pressures having elements promoting integration and disintegration catalyse this interactive process. Globalization is integrationist, and nation states having absorptive and assimilative capabilities strengthen such trends. On the contrary, security will be adversely affected if nation states lack these attributes. Barry Buzan recognizes the overarching elements of security when he states:

> A large and flourishing literature exists on the empirical side dealing with contemporary security problems and issues. Most of this comes out of the sub-field of Strategic Studies, for which security is the core concept. The foreign, military and economic policies of states, the intersection of these policies in areas of change or dispute, and the general structure of relations which they create, are all analyzed in terms of national and international security. But the concept of security is seldom addressed in terms other than the policy interests of particular actors or groups, and the discussion has a heavy military emphasis.[11]

Taking security to be an 'underdeveloped concept', Buzan postulated 'individual' and 'national security', which the succeeding generation of security experts have expanded and extended in the discourse on security studies. If one takes the individual as the unit of analysis, the conceptual and operational aspects of security will cover all these areas of human security. The state-centric approach, having its major pre-occupation with building state structures and military-bureaucratic combines, undermines the concept of comprehensive security, which is concerned with the security of the territorial State, its citizens and others belonging to the region, besides the world at large. So the basic needs of citizens—–food, shelter, water, social justice, law and order, freedom—have an inextricable nexus with national security.

Good governance becomes inseparable from security for managing all these elements of national security. State monopoly has 'given way to multicentric forms of governance; economic governance is now a function that can be performed by a wide variety of public and private, State and non-State, sub-national, national, regional and international institutions and practices'.[12] It does not mean that the state's role has been overtaken by a laissez faire approach to the global economy. In truth, nation states are in the throes of transforming the democratic process. In South Asia, however, non-State actors or civil society have not yet eroded the dominance of the State.

Security in a plural society is primarily based on the security perceptions of the citizens. For Nepal, it is a people-centric concept with implications for comprehensive security. People-centric security covers military, social, economic, political, bilateral, regional and international spheres. Citizens as a national community and citizens as individuals should have a sense of security within the neighbourhood, district, zone and nation. Today, the erosion of authority and power, and the callous indifference of State structures to mitigate complaints and threats ranging from the absence of civic amenities to larger issues of human and State security predispose citizens to feel insecure. He/she finds a total vacuum of authority in his/her surroundings, as the authority of the State and civil society has either broken down or is unavailable when crises arise.

If the State police fails to come to his or her rescue, the faith of the people in governance gets eroded. Thus, the loss of faith in State authority and civil society is the major source of insecurity 'Freedom from fear', which is one of the four freedoms enunciated in the 1940s, has evaded both state-oriented security and other forms of security. The idea of security has become amorphous but includes elements of good governance, social equilibrium, justice by guaranteeing basic needs, alleviation of poverty, a fair electoral system, demographic management, enlightened foreign policy incorporating the trend towards globalization and integration and so on. The Nepalis are not greatly concerned with external threats. No country in the world has the will or capacity to invade other countries and extend its national boundaries, notwithstanding the temptation to promote cross-border terrorism or irredentism. Still, ethnic groups with similar identities in countries having common borders may try to mobilize external support—the obvious example being the nexus between the state of Tamil Nadu in India and the Tamils in the northern and eastern parts of Sri Lanka fighting for a separate Tamil Eelam (homeland).

The vulnerability of small States like Nepal arises from its internal problems—failure of the State, abysmally slow development, rampant corruption, lack of sound policy decisions and their implementation, erosion of institutions, crisis of leadership, aberrations within the system and the failure of politicians to correct them, and influence gained by external powers and financial institutions over the decisions of the government. Lack of people's faith in institutions like the Parliament, judiciary, bureaucracy, military and the police are other areas of critical concern. A cartoon published in the leading dailies of Kathmandu showed the Speaker of the House of Representatives addressing an empty House; the presence of a mouse aptly reflected the disinterest of the people's representatives in the institution. The major components of security/insecurity exist in the context of resources and overall national and international objectives. The security priorities for Nepal cannot obviously be compared to those of India, although both face similar problems like poverty, unemployment, population, water, health and corruption.

For Nepal, even a small problem becomes large and complex if not addressed. When pulls and pressures from different parties and lobbies working at cross-purposes hamstring the government, the failure of its command structures and decision-making centres become apparent. The Maoist people's war has been sustained by various agencies that have neutralized the operational strategies of the government. Prime Minister G.P. Koirala, for example, emphasized the role of the National Defence Council, a constitutional arrangement for tackling wide-ranging security issues and problems, including the Maoist insurgency. But he retracted his own statements subsequently without elaborating the reasons for his volte-face. This led to doubts about the government's commitment to the letter and spirit of the Constitution.

The elected Prime Minister and other senior leaders are haunted by the 'active monarchy' of the past regime, and see the King as 'one of the three centres of power', the other two being the Nepali Congress and the Communists; this is apparent in the last 10 years of democratic governance. The haste with which the Constitution was finalized, bypassing the Constituent Assembly, and the statements made by hard-core leaders show that they had little confidence in themselves and expected a backlash from the supporters of the former regime. Moreover, many of them lost credibility after they displayed their disregard for implementing the Constitution in its true spirit. Insecurity has its origins in the malfunctioning of governments, and the failure of the development of political parties and their leaders erodes the system.[13]

The foregoing clearly reveals the nature, conduct and ramifications of security policies. Is the security environment neglected in a pluralist system of governance? Or has it better scope for rationality and pragmatism? Can conventional approaches to security ignore the larger issues of human security and manage the crises emanating from different sources? Such questions can only be answered by merging the conventional and non-conventional approaches to security that are seminally related. The remaining part of this paper would examine the issues of governance and security in Nepal.

NEPAL'S SECURITY ENVIRONMENT: HISTORICAL AND RECENT

The modern Nepali rulers have accepted the view of King Prithvi Narayan Shah, the founder of modern Nepal, who compared Nepal with a yam between two stones—India and China. Though the geopolitical and geostrategic situation has undergone a change following the modernization of the country, and the presence of the People's Republic of China in Tibet since 1950, Nepal's relations with both its neighbours remains the same. After establishing diplomatic relations with Communist China in 1955 and opening the northern Himalayan route to Tibet, the manoeuvrability of Nepal's foreign policy increased. This flexibility was apparent when King Mahendra took advantage of the strained relations between China and India in the late 1950s and early 1960s, particularly after the flight of the Dalai Lama in 1959. Emboldened by the growing animosity between India and China, on the one hand, and his adroit mobilization of political forces against the elected Nepali Congress Government, on the other, the King abolished the multiparty system and the elected government on 15 December 1960 and arrested the Prime Minister, ministers and others who were not supporting him.

It is interesting that the King, like other coup leaders in developing countries, took this step on the basis of unspecified charges—anti-national activities, corruption, favouritism, politicization of the bureaucracy, and ineffective economic policies. Though King Mahendra, an ambitious and shrewd ruler, had hinted at this move, making his plan an open secret, but his impatience led to dissolution of the system itself, and charted another political road map to suit an active monarchical leadership.[14] Defence of the Koirala Government was not lacking despite the serious charges levelled against it. Rose has remarked: 'B.P. Koirala's credentials as a bona fide nationalist, primarily concerned with protecting Nepal's national interests, had been firmly established during his eighteen months in office. There was no more substance to the allegations that he was an Indian agent or even 'biased' toward India than there was later to the charge that King Mahendra was pro-Chinese'.[15] An end to the era of party politics in 1960 and the partyless panchayat system introduced by the King thereafter revived the traditional authoritarian political culture. Armed with absolute power, the monarch went about consolidating his rule by a two-pronged strategy, consolidating the new regime internally, and cultivating relations with various foreign powers externally.

Relations with Pakistan and China helped counterbalance Indian pressure via the Nepali Congress leaders to minimize Nepal's contacts with China. The King was thus enabled to give short shrift to Indian opposition against the construction of the 104-kilometre Kathmandu–Kodari (Tibet) Road in 1961. Many felt this development was the 'beginning of the cold war' in the Himalayan region. The opening of the Tibet road dramatically enhanced India's security problems in the north. It provided Nepal an alternate trade route to Tibet, and a large quantity of consumer goods floods the Nepali market today. India surrounds Nepal on three sides that makes Nepal dependent on the Indian seaports; the Kathmandu–Kodari road was a symbol of Nepal's diversified foreign, security and economic policies.

The first crisis from Nepal's diversified policies followed the unilateral Indian decision in 1989 to discontinue its Trade and Transit Treaty obligations after its expiry. The reasons behind this action, which many Nepalis called a 'blockade', was Nepal's decision to import arms from China without consulting India in terms of the Treaty of Peace and Friendship of 1950. Besides, in 1965, Nepal had also entered into a secret understanding with India according to which only India, Great Britain and the United States could supply arms. Taking this to be a serious breach of the Treaty, Prime Minister Rajiv Gandhi provoked by many other incidents and misunderstandings, stopped the flow of goods into Nepal. Although Nepal managed to weather this crisis, the cost and difficulties faced by the Nepalis was enormous. Normalcy could only be restored after the collapse of the partyless system in 1990. The interim government formed after the successful democracy movement restored the bilateral relationship on the basis of the traditional ties as determined by the 1950 treaty.

The foregoing narration focuses on the limitations of Nepal. Whatever advantages and countervailing role Nepal might have acquired by its diversified economic and security policies, it suffers from the same earlier constraints in the domain of external security. Examples abound regarding the compromises made by Nepal on various issues and projects whenever its two neighbours, more so India, wants a reversal of the decisions arrived at by Nepal.[16]

INDIA, THE ISI AND THE MAOISTS

From the Indian standpoint, Nepal is increasingly becoming a base for anti-Indian activities, specially by the Inter-Services Intelligence (ISI) of Pakistan, which increased its role after the restoration of the multiparty system in Nepal. For its part, Nepal has met such Indian concerns either by cooperating with India to apprehend the culprits or by taking appropriate decisions not to allow Nepal from becoming an ISI base. Reports have been published in the Indian press giving detailed accounts of arms and explosives flows across the Indo-Nepal borders. Shops were identified in Kathmandu to establish the veracity of these reports. Nepal has taken great pains to explain that it would cooperate with India because these nefarious activities are as much a threat to Nepal as to India.

In June 2000, during the visit of a high-power delegation led by the Indian Prime Minister's Special Secretary and National Security Adviser, an Indian intelligence report was published by an Indian weekly and on the Internet detailing the widespread tentacles of the ISI in Nepal. It covered politicians, journalists, individuals, businessmen and teachers, in addition to a number of other persons working as conduits between the underground gangs. How the schools—madrassas—are working as networks for ISI activities was also highlighted. *India Today*, whilst divulging the report, tried to link the consolidation efforts by the ISI after an Indian Airlines plane was hijacked in December 1999 by terrorists operating across the India–Pakistan Line of Control in Kashmir. As *India Today* writes, 'Prepared after the hijacking of the plane, it probes the extent to which Pakistan has spread tentacles in Nepal. It also looks at the demographic changes that have come about due to the mushrooming of NGOs and Madrasas which are spreading terror'.

The report, as quoted by the magazine, says: 'Smuggling, which was the exclusive preserve of elite groups during the three-decade-long Panchayat Raj in Nepal, flourished on a grand scale after the restoration of multi-party democracy.'[17]

Prime Minister Koirala dismissed the report as baseless, lacking proof of the involvement of many people identified in it. However, the manner in which the report tried to establish connections between the politicians, the press and other individuals would definitely cast a shadow on bilateral relations. Indians seem to have been fed such stories in the 1990s, and now the report, presumably leaked by official sources, has only reinforced mistrust between the two countries. What new strategies they would adopt in the context of these new security threats needs some more time to evolve.

Meanwhile, presumably stung by the US State Department Report on 'Patterns of Global Terrorism 1999', and also by the dent made by the fundamentalist forces in Pakistan, the military government has outlined an ambitious campaign to curb the militant networks that have taken roots in Pakistan and Afghanistan. Spelling them out, the Interior Minister of Pakistan said that these networks threaten Pakistan by 'fanning sectarian violence and poisoning people's minds'. And the thousands of religious schools (madrassas) are the recruitment centres for mounting jihad or holy wars. Hinting at a government decision to curb such activities, the minister said, 'I feel this is good for Pakistan. . . . I am not following anyone else's agenda. Pakistan ought to become a progressive, modern and tolerant, secular state.'[18]

Bowing to American pressure, however, specially after President Clinton's visit to Islamabad and the report on Global Terrorism prepared by the State Department branding Pakistan as a major source of terrorism, leading to its further isolation in the international community, the military government seems to be toying with the idea of curbing religious militancy. The State Department report identified South Asia as the source of terrorist threats to the United States, and Pakistan and Afghanistan as the main sources of terrorism, saying:

> Pakistan continues to send mixed messages on terrorism. Despite significant and material cooperation in some areas—particularly arrests and extradition—the Pakistani Government also has tolerated terrorists living and moving freely within its territory. Pakistan's government has supported groups that engage in violence in Kashmir, and it has provided indirect support to terrorists in Afghanistan.[19]

The Pakistani connection is emphasized here in view of the growing Indian concern over ISI activities allegedly conducted from Nepal.[20] What would be the Nepali response to tackling this situation in the context of Indo-Nepal relations? Taking advantage of the open border between the two countries, many persons have started using it for various purposes—smuggling, terrorism, crime, and migration, to mention some. Although the border is delineated, it is open for the free movement of people, whose national identity gets blurred whilst using the Indo-Nepal border. Indians, Pakistanis and Bangladeshis, whose physical and linguistic identities are not dissimilar, become either Indians or Nepalis after they cross the border.

Closely connected with the open-border regime is the linkage between internal and external terrorist groups, although little evidence is available of this nexus to explain the spurt in Maoist violence over the last 5 years in more than 30 districts of Nepal. Its ideological components are Nepal-focused Maoist abstractions. They believe that the current multiparty system is irrelevant to solve the problems of poverty and exploitation, hence they need to be replaced by people's democracy. Whether this model advocated by the Maoists is an appropriate remedy for the pervading socio-economic and political malaise is arguable, but they have been successful in indoctrinating the poor and illiterate sections of the population living in the interior of the country. The insurgents have shown their prowess by killing people and the police in some districts adjoining the capital.

In the beginning (1991–4), the Maoist group took part in parliamentary elections under the title Samyukta Jana Morcha ('United People's Front') and had nine legislators in the House of Representatives. Formed to contest the elections on a common, extra-CPN(UML) platform in 1991, the UPF split before the 1994 elections: one powerful faction led by the present Maoist leader, Babu Ram Bhattarai, boycotted the polls leading to the rout of the other faction. A radical group-known as Masal (then undivided), of which many top-ranking leaders of the present Maoist group were members, contributed significantly to making the Constitution democratic by holding elections to the Constituent Assembly. This demand was not fulfilled by the major parties involved—the NC and the United Left Front—on the grounds that the reactionary forces were not reconciled to the collapse of the royal regime and would strike if the drafting of the Constitution was delayed.[21]

Frequent changes of governments due to lack of majority in the House of Representatives (Lower House) and due to the intra-party schisms in the ruling and opposition parties have given rise to disenchantment with multiparty democracy, which the Maoists have fully exploited for mobilization against the established order. During the visit of the Indian External Affairs Minister to Nepal in 1999, it was reported that Nepal had raised the issue of Nepali Maoists allegedly using some Indian states for training guerrillas, urging India to dismantle their camps. Quoting Maoist sources, a vernacular Nepali magazine reported that the Dandakaranya and northern Telengana areas of Andhra Pradesh, Chandrapur and Gadchiroli in Maharastra, southern Bastar and Bilaspur areas of Madhya Pradesh, are treated as base areas by the People's War Group of India, and are the major sites for Maoist training.[22]

With the unabated Maoist violence claiming about 2,000 lives and displacement of more than 60,000 people from the Maoist-affected areas, the security situation became serious in the summer of 2000. Both the government and the Opposition parties demonstrated their contradictions by opening negotiations with the Maoists, whilst using force against them. The police force, which lacks training and sophisticated weapons, came into the public debate centred on the issue whether the Royal Nepal Army should be deployed to curb the Maoist menace. This issue took a new turn following repeated statements by the new Prime Minister, G.P. Koirala, that he would revive Art. 118 of the Constitution dealing with the Rashtriya Surakshya Parishad. The Council consists of the Prime Minister, Defence Minister and the Commander-in-Chief, whilst the King performs 'the operation and deployment of the Royal Nepal Army on the recommendation' of the Committee, including appointment of the Chief of the Army. The Constitution does not spell out the other functions of the Army. How the Prime Minister (himself the Defence Minister) would deal with the Maoist insurgency has not been spelt out either. It seems the Prime Minister was only hinting at the possible deployment of the Army for anti-Maoist operations, because he later retracted his statement by saying that dialogue alone could resolve the crisis.

Unauthorized stories dominate the local press regarding the government's dilemma since the army is allegedly showing reluctance to involve itself in such operations in the absence of an all-party consensus. Since the Nepal Army is perceived to be the exclusive domain of the King, contrary to the spirit of the Constitution, government leaders have developed their own complex vis-à-vis the King, despite his being a constitutional monarch under the present Constitution.[23] So, use of the army remains problematic demonstrating that an elected Prime Minister is hamstrung by the weakness of the power elite themselves. They fear annoying the King if they insist upon their constitutional rights. Compromises made with the Palace have cast a shadow on the working of the Constitution.[24] While the issue of army involvement continues to be contentious, the government has decided to create a new armed police force for insurgency operations. Sophisticated arms would be supplied to the standing army, whilst the arms being used by the Nepal Army would be given to the new armed police force; an increase in the combined budget of the army and police of around 22 per cent is visualized. The police budget alone has increased by 800 times within a period of 10 years. In the 2000–1 budget allocation, 12.11 per cent of the total general budget has been earmarked for the police, including the purchase of arms and ammunition, due to the spurt of Maoist violence during the last four years. Replying to the debate in the Parliament, Prime Minister G.P. Koirala admitted that the Maoist menace had forced his government to divert resources to the police. The army claims 9 per cent of the total budget.[25]

The Maoists are pursuing a two-pronged strategy: open dialogue with the government through designated interlocutors and continued killing of the police and targetted people, specially Congress supporters. The Nepal Communist Party (NCP-Maoist) general secretary has described the government's call for talks as 'only a drama' adding that 'it has not . . . made public the whereabouts of a number of Maoist leaders. It has to publicly initiate actions if it [Government] really wants to hold talks.'[26] How the talks would proceed and what will be their outcome is yet to be seen. But the Maoist insurgency has weakened considerably due to the personality clash between Prachanda and Babu Ram, its two important leaders, that weakens the movement.

How has Nepal been increasingly dragged into the vortex of violent politics? What are the latent reasons spawning the Maoists in Nepal? Many observers see a hiatus developing between the feudal and consumerist culture of the Nepali political elite and the poor and helpless people suffering from poverty and destitution. The Nepali leaders have taken the cream for themselves, to the total neglect of the poverty-stricken people. Thus, *Maobad* (Maoism) is designated as a war against *Khaobad* (kleptomaniacs).[27] Democratic governance has suffered a setback due to the unending schisms within the ruling party, the NC, whose leaders were/are more preoccupied with wrecking their own governments rather than concentrating on socio-economic programmes and stability. Conflicting voices have been raised coupled with anarchical party discipline, which afflicts the political process itself. Since the Prime Minister is vulnerable to the shifting loyalty of his party members in the Parliament, his government's credibility is questioned.[28]

OTHER ISSUES CONCERNING GOVERNANCE AND SECURITY

Issues of critical concern are identified on the basis of severity and immediacy. Such issues are examined institutionally to yield results. Some critical areas having direct and indirect impact on security and governance can be listed, though intervening factors like a spurt in violence in the national and international sphere are relevant. Some of these issues are: (1) educational crisis, (2) poverty, population pressure and unemployment, (3) lack of space for ethnic groups and dalits, (4) nexus between politicians and criminals of all hues and nationalities, and (5) institutional decay. These issues relate to the non-conventional areas of security that could spark off short-term and long-term crises. All these issues are related to governance and the underpinnings of governance in plural society and plural polity.

The security and governance discourse should be extended to humane governance. Focusing on these areas, *Human Development in South Asia 1999: The Crisis of Governance* has clearly identified and discussed these issues in great detail under the rubric 'good political governance, good economic governance, good civic governance, measuring humane governance and the crisis of governance'. Commenting on the failure of democracy in South Asia, the report says' democracy is fast turning into an empty ritual'.[29] This general picture of systemic failures in South Asia reveals an uncertain future. How Nepal fits into this scenario needs analysis.

The current picture appears dismal because of the callous indifference of leaders and parties who are too myopic to take enlightened policy decisions. Even if Nepal achieves 100 per cent literacy—the present official figure is 52.6 per cent, a big increase from 39.6 per cent in 1992—the situation will not change because of the existing three-tier system. According to the budget speech of the Finance Minister delivered on 30 May 2000, the number of primary, lower secondary and secondary schools reached 37,397 with a commensurate increase of 52,86,000 students and 30,049 teachers in 2000. The total number of private schools was 10,833 with 6,49,978 students and 30,049 teachers.[30] Education is an important area that could spark off tensions and disorder in the country and become a threat to national security: this makes us believe that in today's context, internal sources of insecurity are more significant than external sources of insecurity.[31] The increasing social disparity arising from a highly stratified educational system, coupled with what a former Prime Minister called the production of 'troops of unemployed' young Nepalese, has the potential to cause political turbulence.[32]

There are uncorroborated accounts of the government wishing to control Maoist pressure through the army, but the latter is reluctant to join such endeavours in the absence of an all-party consensus. Contrary to the spirit of the Constitution, which visualizes a constitutional monarchy, the Nepal Army is seen as the exclusive domain for exercise of the King's powers. Government leaders have developed a complex vis-à-vis the King, not due to his intervention in the affairs of the State, but due to their own weakness and fear of annoying the King. So control over the army remains problematic, despite the elected Prime Minister being the Chairman of the National Security Council. The wrangling between the army and the government came into the open following a pre-dawn attack on the western hill district headquarters of Dopla in September 2000 by the Maoist insurgents. To the surprise of the government, the army failed to cooperate with the administration to foil the attack, which resulted in 12 policemen being killed and 40 others sustaining injuries. Criticizing the army's role, the Home Minister questioned the need for maintaining a standing army if it did not cooperate with the government in a crisis situation.

In this situation, several Maoist-type movements are possible in view of these growing troops of a half-educated but highly politicized generation. It has been estimated in the Economic Survey of 1999–2000 that about 300,000 persons enter the labour force every year. More than 5 per cent remain completely unemployed; only a fraction of the unskilled labour force enters the foreign job markets in the Gulf, East Asia and South-East Asia, while India remains the major employer. Lack of a balanced educational system widens the elite-masses gap, with members of elite families continuing to dominate the power structure and the economy. The mushrooming of private schools with better-quality education and the draining of State resources into public schools that are no competition for the private schools has further stratified Nepali society. The third category comprising 60–70 per cent of the population (the official figure is 42–50 per cent) is below the poverty line and cannot send their children to schools and colleges. Those belonging to the latter categories are prone to crime, posing a serious threat to society.

In the early 1970s, King Birendra, then Crown Prince, introduced a New Education System plan envisaging that all institutions would follow a semester system and new curricula. This scheme fizzled out after some time due to social conditions, an environment where work culture does not exist due to the failure of institutions and managers, and the authoritarian value system based on fear and compulsion, not motivation. What is more frightening is the politicization of educational institutions at all levels along party lines. The absence of a well-developed civic society that could arrest such divisive trends has led to a further deterioration in the situation. The creation of universities and colleges in the private and public sectors without addressing these issues has not changed the status quo.

The unchanged poverty level alongside slow economic development with $210 per capita income and low Growth Domestic Product is exacerbated by the population growth rate of 2.36 per cent (official figure). Although some bright spots in the economy remain unnoticed, the alleviation of poverty and general improvement in governance remain elusive areas. The fast-changing demographic structure of the country and its disproportionate spatial distribution is another source of insecurity. Nepal's total population has already crossed 22 million due to a high fertility rate, failure of population control measures, and the country's social environment, next to the densely populated states of India—Bihar, Uttar Pradesh and West Bengal.[33]

International migration and refugee flows into the country with 18 per cent land use (the rest is mountainous region) adds to these problems. Hence, the migration of refugees from Bhutan, numbering one hundred thousand, is viewed with alarm. Though India and Nepal have treaty arrangements allowing free movement across the border, voices are being raised seeking its regulation by introducing some new measures—identity cards, entry records and, finally, passport system. The two governments are in a dilemma about how they should proceed since their relations are based, not only on formal-legal arrangements, but social, economic, familial and civilizational factors. A sizeable number of Nepalis live in India for various reasons, the most important being economic, making India a 'safety-valve' for Nepal.

How should Nepal absorb its own people if relations are impaired by unexpected developments? Similarly, how should Nepal continue with the old arrangements when it has to accept migrants from other South Asian countries entering through a porous and open border? Framing this dilemma, a Nepali left leader, Man Mohan Adhikari (then Prime Minister of the CPN-UML minority government), had said: 'If 100,000 to 2,00,000 workers from Nepal go to India, this will be like a drop in the ocean. However, even if only 10,000 or 12,000 Indians come to Nepal [as workers], this will make Nepali workers unemployed.'[34] This dichotomous situation due to the open border regime can endanger the national security of both countries, but has remained outside the agenda of India and Nepal. Of late, following the alleged intensified ISI activities in Nepal, India is getting serious about establishing some joint measures for border regulation. Nepal is not clear how it should harmonize its position on the border issue despite several public statements and posturing. The demand for greater integration is the trend in today's world due to globalization and regionalism; how then could the two neighbours with civilizational and historical continuities reverse course by closing their borders?

The population dynamics, exacerbated by internal growth and transboundary migration, has reached an explosive stage, posing a serious challenge to the governance and security of Nepal. Demographic pressures 'will also tell on land, air, water, energy, environment and various natural resources such as forest cover',[35] that could affect the region. The mismanagement of city municipalities due to large population growth also presents law-and-order problems. Kathmandu, the most attractive tourist destination in the country, has already become the most polluted city due to faulty policies and the incapacity of governments; garbage disposal has become *the* permanent problem for both the Kathmandu Municipality and the national government. Social crimes are on the increase because of the rapidly spreading networks of criminal gangs and mafias. Working as a conduit for women and drug trafficking, Kathmandu is increasingly being presented to the world as a notorious place. Yet, tourists love Nepal for its beauty and serenity and continue to visit it despite this negative image. Thus, a minor management problem becomes large if authority lacks will power based on an all-party consensus.

The nexus between crime and politics has become an important issue in the national discourse in Nepal. During the former royalist regime, stories of amassing wealth by foul means and the nexus between politicians, royal relatives, and unscrupulous traders set off controversies. Now it is focused on parties, leaders, ministers, bureaucrats, police and army personnel as if the entire political and administrative machinery is working in tandem with commission agents and underground gangs. Elections have become too expensive for those who do not have money and other resources, which prompts the aspirants to seek funding agents. While describing this cruel dilemma, the Speaker of the House of Representatives confessed that some members in the Lower House had spent up to 10 million rupees (one US dollar fetched NR 68 in 1999). Moreover, political parties are not transparent about their sources of income and election funds.[36] Political party leaders have not paid attention to reform the system. Although both politicians and members of civil society have realized that democratic governance would be jeopardized if this trend continues, legal instruments alone will not salvage the system. Strong commitment by parties and leaders armed with laws may change these electoral aberrations.

Another major issue relating to security and governance is ethnicity.

Ethnicity permits mobilization of minority social groups which want to enhance their bargaining position vis-à-vis the 'dominant' groups in a given sociocultural and political context. Although the Brahmin, Chhetri and Newari castes are in a minority, with a total percentage of 30 in the population, their disproportionate share in political representation, administration and educational institutions highlights a potential source of conflict.[37]

A comparative study of the pattern of representation in various legislatures since 1959 shows the continued domination of the same caste groups with a middle-class background. During the partyless regime, the Chhetris dominated the National Panchayat (a unicameral legislature), followed by Brahmins. In the 1991, 1994 and 1999 House of Representatives, the Brahmins displaced the Chhetris with 42.7 per cent, 48.2 per cent, and 47.3 per cent of the seats, while the Chhetris had only 20 per cent, 18 per cent and 17.3 per cent of these seats. The representation of hill ethnic groups was 8.2 per cent (1991), 8.4 per cent (1994) and 10 per cent (1999), while the Tarai groups had 22.7 per cent (1991), 21.7 per cent (1994) and 18.2 per cent (1999). The Newari community, which is 4 per cent of the total population, but is well represented in the administration and business, had a 5.5 per cent (1991), 2.4 per cent (1994) and 5.5 per cent (1999) share in the composition of the Lower House. The dalits, who constitute about 20 per cent of the population and the Muslim community with 4 per cent population, have less than 1 per cent representation.

Tables 4.1, 4.2 and 4.3 show the pattern of representation in the three Houses of Representatives in 1991, 1994 and 1999.

This issue has attracted the attention of the political parties for reducing the disparity between the Brahmin, Chhetri, Newari and other less privileged communities, but it would take a long time to bring them on par due to factors like educational qualifications and political domination by the former categories. The ethnic dimension to political violence is, therefore, increasing, with the Maoist groups trying to mobilize the various hill ethnic groups for their cause. Still, an ethnic war in Nepal is unlikely at this stage. The dalits constituting 20 per cent of the total population continue to be suppressed and remain destitute. Their representation in politics and administration is much less than the hill and Tarai groups. The absence of dalits is conspicuous in almost all the cabinets formed after the 1990 pro-democracy movement since they are discouraged from becoming Members of Parliament. The composition of the parties' central committees reveals that the national parties are

TABLE 4.1: ETHNIC COMPOSITION OF MEMBERS OF HOUSE OF REPRESENTATIVES (1991)

	NC		UML		RPP		Other		Total	
Variables	No.	%	No.	%	No.	%	No.	%	No.	%
Hill caste group										
Brahmin	47	42.7	29	42.0	2	50.0	2	9.1	80	39.0
Chhetri	22	20.0	9	13.0	2	50.0	2	9.1	35	17.1
Newari	6	5.5	6	8.7	—	—	2	9.1	14	6.8
Others	1	0.9	—	—	—	—	—	—	1	0.5
Hill ethnic group	9	8.2	18	26.1	—	—	7	31.8	34	16.6
Terai group	25	22.7	7	10.2	—	—	9	40.9	41	20.0
Total	110	100	69	100	4	100	22	100	205	100

TABLE 4.2: ETHNIC COMPOSITION OF MEMBERS OF HOUSE OF REPRESENTATIVES (1994)

	NC		UML		RPP		Other		Total	
Variables	No.	%	No.	%	No.	%	No.	%	No.	%
Hill caste group										
Brahmin	40	48.2	46	52.3	4	20.0	1	7.1	91	44.5
Chhetri	15	18.1	11	12.5	7	35.0	5	35.7	38	18.5
Newari	2	2.4	9	10.2	—	—	2	14.3	13	6.3
Others	1	1.2	—	—	—	—	—	—	1	0.5
Hill ethnic group	7	8.4	12	13.6	3	15.0	2	14.3	24	11.7
Terai group	18	21.7	10	11.4	6	30.6	4	28.6	38	18.5
Total	83	100	88	100	20	100	14	100	205	100

not concerned with the uplift of dalits. Since democratic pluralism visualizes greater dalit and ethnic mobilization to change the status quo, dalit leaders cannot secure their rights without vociferously asserting their cause. Unless the situation changes, these groups may adopt undemocratic means of assertion.

Who are the new democratic elite and which socio-economic backgrounds do they represent? Are they the old *panchas*, many of whom belong to the nouveau riche? Or has a new generation of elite emerged in post-1990 politics? From the caste and class perspective no significant development seems to have occurred in creating an egalitarian society

TABLE 4.3: ETHNIC COMPOSITION OF MEMBERS OF HOUSE OF REPRESENTATIVES (1999)

	NC		UML		RPP		Other		Total	
Variables	No.	%	No.	%	No.	%	No.	%	No.	%
Hill caste group										
Brahmin	52	47.3	39	54.2	—	—	4	33.4	91	46.3
Chhetri	19	17.3	8	11.1	5	45.5	3	25.0	38	17.1
Newari	6	5.5	4	5.6	2	18.2	1	8.3	13	6.3
Others	2	1.8	—	—	—	—	—	—	1	1.0
Hill ethnic group	11	10.0	13	18.0	1	9.1	—	—	24	12.2
Terai group	20	18.2	8	11.1	3	27.3	4	33.3	38	17.1
Total	110	100	72	100	11	100	12	100	205	100

because the politicians have failed to initiate any substantive reforms. On the contrary, all political parties and their functionaries have reinforced the stratified socio-economic structure by imitating the former 'kleptomaniac' elite. Inherited social and economic status—*khandan* and *kulgharan*—and personal links and favouritism determine the careers of politicians. Since the control of money and other resources continues to define elite status, common citizens aspiring for political roles can hardly succeed in electoral politics. So the members of political parties adopt dubious means to achieve upward mobility and elite status.

Notwithstanding this uninhibited behaviour of politicians to grab power and position, the electoral exercises carried out over the years have provided political education, resulting in a change of representatives and leaders in elections by over 60 per cent. The heyday of coalition politics (1994–9) saw many aberrations creeping into public life, which placed the political elite in the dock and led to their being penalized in the elections. This process of rectification is possible in a democracy for the people can be patient, which is another aspect of democratic politics.

Pluralistic politics have to be broad-based in both symbol and substance. A change in the existing rigid structure is unavoidable by implementing radical programmes and policies. An expansion of social movements within the democratic framework or beyond can also 'enlarge the meaning of freedom'. The issue of women is no less urgent as the women-men population ratio is 50/50, but less than 5 per cent women are visible in the government and non-government sectors. Nepal has only 11 women parliamentarians (Lower House) in a house of 205. This does not meet even the constitutional provision of 5 per cent representation in the central, district and local political institutions. Stressing the need for enlarging social movements, it has been pointed out in the Indian context, which is no less relevant to Nepal that, 'It is the failure of the dominant classes and the governments to lead the process of change towards integration on an egalitarian basis. . . .'[38] This situation exists in Nepal.

CONCLUSION

Nepal's pluralist political system suffers from three dangers. First, the defenders of democracy reveal schizophrenic cultural and personality traits; they are unable to break from the past and are compromising on the essentials of democratic governance. They have revealed their feudal inclinations in the running of their parties and governments, forgetting their commitments to create an egalitarian society and polity. Second, the alternative forces, i.e. the various communist groups including the CPN (UML) have adopted fluid ideological and tactical positions vis-à-vis the obtaining political system. Their utterances and signals create dissonance, leading to misgivings about the future role of the communist parties as an alternative to the NC. All political parties have denounced the political backlash against the system, but their conflicting statements do not assure those who want to stabilize the process. In the absence of a major alternative, the future of democracy remains uncertain in Nepal today despite the widespread political awareness. Finally, the erosion of institutions has afflicted state and human security. The incapacity of the elite to arrest such trends adds to the dangers of insecurity. The only institution that remains organized is the Army which, in the general perception, works in tandem with the King despite the establishment of governments elected by the 'sovereign people'. However, the King or the Army are not independent variables for stability, plurality and security in Nepali politics. Disruptive forces are at work and their political management is becoming complex and intractable.

Paradoxically, the enabling international environment, coupled with the limited manoeuvrability of the King, provides an opportunity for the parties and leaders to correct themselves. If the political institutions continue to rot and if the political leaders fail to identify with the common people, the legitimacy issue would surface again placing the country and the polity in serious jeopardy. On balance, however, irresponsible elite behaviour flouting the norms of democratic politics provides an opportunity to the people to evaluate their leaders. Politicians indulging in unbecoming activities are looked down upon by people, despite their influence acquired by distributing largesse.

It is clear that security must be ensured within the context of a plural polity because alternative authoritarian or totalitarian models advocated by some detractors of the system on the extreme right and extreme left (the Maoists), are untenable. But if good governance remains elusive, upheavals leading to anarchical trends are likely to wreck the country and the system. What Nepal needs for safeguarding plurality, security, and governance is effective performance of the system and a good image of its elite.

NOTES

1. Paul R. Brass, *Ethnicity and Nationalism: Theory and Comparisons*, New Delhi: Sage 1991, p. 8.
2. Alvin Rabushka and Kenneth Shepsle, *Politics in Plural Societies: A Theory of Instability*, Columbus, Ohio: Charles E.Merrill, 1972, p. 61.
3. R. Schermerhorn, 'Ethnicity in the Perspective of the Sociology of Knowledge', in John Hutchinson and Anthony D. Smith, eds., *Ethnicity*, Oxford: OUP, 1996, p. 6.
4. Ibid., pp. 6–7. Categories 2 and 6 are supplied by the editors respectively from D.L. Harowitz, *Ethnic Groups in Conflict*, Berkeley: University of California Press, 1985, p. 57, and Anthony Smith, *The Ethnic Origins of Nations*, Oxford: Blackwell, 1986, Ch. 2.
5. For a more detailed theoretical discourse on pluralism and democracy, see Tatu Vanhanen, *Politics of Ethnic Nepotism: India as an Example*, New Delhi: Sterling, 1991, Ch. 3.
6. David Apter has used Robert Dahl's analysis from the latter's work *After the Revolution?* New Haven, Conn.: Yale University Press, 1970 in David E. Apter, *Introduction to Political Analysis*, New Delhi: Prentice-Hall, 1978, p. 293. For more details about the Participation-Institutionalization problem, see Samuel P. Huntington, 'Political Development and Political Decay', *World Politics*, vol. 17 no. 3, 1965 and his book *Political Order In Changing Societies*, New Haven: Yale University Press, 1968.
7. Apter, ibid, p. 299.
8. Leo E. Rose, *Nepal: Strategy for Survival*, Bombay: Oxford University Press, 1971, p. 8.
9. Urmila Phadnis, *Ethnicity and Nation-Building in South Asia*, Delhi: Sage, 1990, p. 40.
10. Apter, op. cit., p. 301.

11. Barry Buzan, *People, States, And Fear: The National Security Problem in International Relations*, New Delhi: Transasia Publishers, Indian edn. 1987, p. 3.
12. A.P. Rana, 'The South Asian State in an Age of Globalization: transcendence, transmutation or adaptation?' in B. Ramesh Babu, ed., *Globalization and the South Asian State*, New Delhi: South Asian Publisher, 1998, p. 234.
13. Drawing a more pessimistic picture, Panday has pointed out: 'The nation has been plagued by near stagnation—some might say, it is retrograding (*sic*) . . . Under the circumstances, we have to wonder if the dismal condition of the country is not the result of 'action without reflection' and 'reflection without action'. See Devendra Raj Panday, *Nepal's Failed Development*, Kathmandu: South Asia Centre, 1998, p. xv.
14. For more details, see Lok Raj Baral, *Oppositional Politics in Nepal*, New Delhi: Abhinav, 1977, Chs. 1 and 2; Anirudha Gupta, *Politics In Nepal*, Bombay: Allied Publishers, 1964; Bhuwan L. Joshi and Leo E. Rose, *Democratic Innovations in Nepal: A Study in Political Acculturation*, Berkeley: University of California Press, 1966; and R.S. Chauhan, *Political Development In Nepal: Conflict Between Tradition and Modernity*, 1950–70, Delhi: Associated Publishing House, 1971. For original sources, see *Proclamations, Speeches and Messages*, Kathmandu: Department of Information, Ministry of Communication, 1967, part 1.
15. Rose, *Nepal: Strategy For Survival*, op. cit., p. 232.
16. Shriman Narayan, *India and Nepal: An Exercise in Open Diplomacy*, Bombay: 1970. Later, many projects relating to road building won by Chinese bidders were withdrawn when India put pressure on Nepal on the basis of security, as those projects were too close to the Indian heartland. Similarly, the Chinese put pressure on Nepal not to allow the Dalai Lama to visit Nepal in 1990.
17. See Harinder Baweja, 'The Kathmandu Nexus', *India Today*, 12 June 2000, pp. 26–7. For further information, see *Deshantar Weekly* (Nepali), 11 June 2000. Not totally discounting the ISI activities in Nepal, a Kathmandu dispatch of Dhruba Hari Adhikari stated that 'sources in Nepal's security agencies . . . concede Pakistani infiltration in the form of help to Madrasas—Muslim religious schools—has increased'. See *South China Morning Post* (Hong Kong), 12 June 2000.
18. The Press Trust of India, Delhi quoting the *New York Times*, 11 June 2000.
19. See in detail, *Patterns of Global Terrorism 1999*, April 2000. For this quote, see p. v.
20. Kathmandu as the centre of dubious groups of peoples and identities has drawn regular attention. The presence of Kashmiri Muslims and their alleged nexus with the local Nepalis and other people for conducting anti-Indian activities have been partially accepted, despite the official denial of such activities. A Nepali travel writer, Prakash A. Raj in his booklet has also presented how Kathmandu had been depicted as the centre of anti-Indian activities. See Prakash A. Raj, *Road to Kathmandu*, Kathmandu: Nabeen Publication, 1994. Narrating the story, Raj writes: 'Arif Ali is an intelligence expert who flies from Dubai to Nepal. His mission is to smuggle arms and Mujahideen to India from Nepal in order to fight a 'holy war' against the infidels in Kashmir. In Kathmandu, he meets stunningly beautiful Sadhana who is a prostitute. Will he succeed in his mission?'
21. For more details, see Lok Raj Baral, *Nepal: The Problems of Governance*, Delhi: Konark, 1993; and Lok Raj Baral, *The Regional Paradox: Essays in Nepali and South Asian Affairs*, Delhi: Adroit Publishers, 2000, Ch. 5.

22. See *Himal* (Kathmandu), 3–17 October 1999, p. 31.
23. In the wake of intensified Maoist attacks on a district headquarters of the western hill district of Dolpa killing 22 policemen in September, 2000 and the disclosure of the Home Minister about the uncooperative attitude of the Army to help the police and local administration, the Army-government relations came into sharp focus. According to the Home Minister, if the Army would have cooperated on the basis of a previous understanding, the disaster could have been averted. Reacting to the role of the Army, the leader of the Opposition and former Chief Justice, who was also the Chairman of the Constitution Drafting Commission in 1990, said that according to the Constitution of the Kingdom of Nepal, 1990, the Army is under the government. Later, it was believed that the agitated Prime Minister had taken up this matter with the King to clarify the position of the Army. For details, see *Kantipur, Himalaya Times* and *Kathmandu Post*, 30 September and 2 October 2000.
24. The erosion of the role of the elected Prime Minister can be illustrated by a number of instances during the 10 years multiparty exercise. The nomination of the members of the National Assembly (Upper House), the controversial appointment of the Chairman of the Human Rights Commission, the Prime Minister's failure to get the House of Representatives dissolved on his advice, etc., demonstrate how the Prime Minister is becoming increasingly helpless. Their own fears of the King getting annoyed could partially be the reason for their decline. The former Chief Justice and Chairman of the Constitution Drafting Commission, Bishwa Nath Upadhyaya, has not dwelt on this reality while showing his displeasure with the compromises made by the Prime Ministers. See his interview with *Bimarsha Weekly* (Kathmandu), 2 June 2000, and *Khabar Kagaj*, 1 June 2000.
25. See in detail, *Budget Speech of the Fiscal Year 2000–2001*, Kathmandu: HMG, Ministry of Finance. See also *Deshantar Weekly*, 2 July 2000.
26. *Nepal Press Digest*, vol. 44. no. 24, 12 June 2000.
27. The former Speaker of the House of Representatives, Daman Nath Dhungana, used this word to expose rampant corruption and the strong temptation to amass wealth by politicians. According to him, continuation of feudalism and overall backwardness became a cause for the Maoist people's war.
28. Reports of quarrels within the Nepali Congress often dominate the headlines of dailies and weeklies. The members of Parliament belonging to the dissident camp hold meetings to censure some disliked ministers, so the government headed by any leader feels insecure. For a detailed report of intra-party conflict and their power games and also the declining morale of the police force, see *People's Review* and *Katmandu Post*, 15 June 2000.
29. See *Human Development in South Asia 1999: The Crisis of Governance*, Karachi: OUP, 1999, p. 4.
30. See the *Budget Speech for the Fiscal Year 2000–2001* and the *Economic Survey: Fiscal Year 1999–2000*, Kathmandu: Ministry of Finance, 2000.
31. P.R. Chari, 'Newer Sources of Insecurity: The Crisis of Governance in India', monograph, Colombo: Regional Centre For Strategic Studies, 1998.
32. Sher Bahadur Deuba has presented a frightening picture of unemployment on several occasions.
33. For a detailed account of the population picture in Nepal, see Harka Gurung, *Nepal: Social Dimensions of Expressions*, Kathmandu: New ERA, 1998, Ch. 1.

34. *Kantipur Daily*, 9 January 1995. For more details on Indo-Nepal migration, see Lok Raj Baral, 'India-Nepal Migration: Solution Beyond Formalities', in Jayanta Kumar Ray, ed., *India-Nepal Cooperation Broadening Measures*, Calcutta: K.P. Bagchi, 1997, pp.106–20.
35. V.A. Pai Panandiker, 'Demographic Challenges to Governance', in V.A. Pai Panadiker, ed., *Problems of Governance in South Asia*, Delhi: Konark, 2000, p. 29.
36. For more details about the election system and its problems, see Dev Raj Dahal, 'Reforms in the Election Process of Nepal', *Comparative Electoral Processes in South Asia*, Kathmandu: Nepal South Asia Centre, 1999, pp. 55–75. In a BBC interview on 12 June 2000, the General Secretary of the Nepali Congress, Sushil Koirala, was grilled by the questioner to disclose his party's funds and its management system. But Koirala simply evaded the question saying that the NC depended on the donation of party members. This situation prevails in other parties too.
37. For more details, see Lok Raj Baral, 'Ethnicity and Constitutional Reforms in Nepal', in Iftekharuzzaman, ed., *Ethnicity and Constitutional Reforms in South Asia*, Delhi: Manohar, 1998, pp. 84–105; Gurung, *Nepal: Social Demography and Expessions*, Kathmandu: New Era, 1998, pp. 41–3. and Dilli Ram Dahal, 'Ethnic Cauldron, Demography and Minority Politics: The Case of Nepal', in Dhruba Kumar, ed., *State, Leadership And Politics In Nepal*, Kathmandu: CNAS, TU, 1995, pp.148-69; and Krishna B. Bhattachan, 'Ethnopolitics and Ethnodevelopment: An Emerging Paradigm in Nepal' , ibid., pp. 124–44.
38. Manoranjan Mohanty, 'Introduction: Towards a Creative Theory of Social Transformation', in Manoranjan Mohanty, Partha Nath Mukherji and Olle Tornquist, eds., *People's Rights: Social Movements and the State in the Third World*, New Delhi: Sage, 1998, p. 15.

CHAPTER 5

Ensuring Devolution of Power Enhances Human Security: Some Key Issues and an Indicative Model

Shahrukh Rafi Khan

INTRODUCTION

Pakistan was taken over by a military government on 12 October 2000. This is not the first time this has happened, and history may repeat itself yet again. In the increasingly democratic world political culture, when the military does intervene, it faces immense national and international pressure for the restoration of civilian rule. However, the problem the military confronts is devising an 'exit strategy' acceptable to it and also acceptable nationally and internationally. The current military government has viewed the devolution of powers to the grass-roots level as its key political initiative to move the country from a 'sham' to a 'real' democracy. This is fortuitous because, while political parties view such

* Paper prepared for an author's conference on Governance and Security sponsored by the Regional Centre of Strategic Studies, Sri Lanka, New Delhi, 19 August 2000: a version is forthcoming in the *European Journal of Development Research*. Many thanks for comments to P.R. Chari, project leader of the Governance and Security component of the RCSS project on Human Security and those of the discussant. Thanks are due to Omar Asghar Khan, Minister of Local Government and Rural Development, Pakistan and Rashida Dohad of The Asia Foundation for initiating this work and to Rashida Dohad for ongoing discussions and valuable comments. Thanks are due to colleagues in SDPI for comments, particularly Saba Gul Khattak, Foqia Sadiq Khan and Sajid Kazmi, and also to Samina Ahmad, Haider Nizamani, and particularly Tariq Banuri for extensive and valuable comments. Many thanks are due to Lt. Gen. Syed Tanvir Hussain Naqvi (retd), Chairman, National Reconstruction Bureau (NRB), for sequentially and crisply posing the problems to address and asking challenging questions and to all members of the NRB who engaged with us in lively discussions. Financial support of The Asia Foundation and RCSS is gratefully acknowledged.

devolution with suspicion, it is probably the only viable exit strategy that the military government has.[1] Without condoning military interventions and the suspension of the political process, one can assert that, if this does occur, there are lessons to be learnt from the power devolution exercise currently under way in Pakistan. These lessons can also be of value for other developing countries contemplating more democratic governance.

This is not the first time Pakistan has wrestled with the notion of local government.[2] A newspaper symposium on the issue organized by the News International is quite illustrative of various views on devolution. Rahman (1999) has a valuable account of the experience to date with local government under both military and elected governments, none of which, according to him, came close to an 'ideal' of local self-government. Yusafzai (1999) points out how the current provincial politicians, many of whom were thrown up in the partyless local government elections ordered by the last military dictator Gen. Zia-ul-Haque, have now got a vested interest in preventing the devolution of power to lower tiers, such as the district level. Finally, civil-society representatives are suspicious of local government elections under a military government, since, based on past experience, they are viewed as a cynical attempt at bypassing provincial and national representatives and building a constituency at lower tiers. Even so, this is an issue of far-reaching long-term significance for effective and participatory decentralized community management of its own affairs.

Among scholarly sources, Bengali (1999) is particularly instructive in his review of local government in Pakistan.[3] An important insight concerns the institutional anarchy that results from the parallel systems for local government and hence the non-rational jurisdictions that are currently in place.[4] Unlike India, Pakistan currently has no explicit constitutional cover for local government. Provinces are empowered to establish local bodies (possibly elected) such as municipal corporations, town committees, district and union councils (reporting independently to the provinces) and frame rules and regulations for them. By the same token, they are empowered to suspend or abolish them. Thus, the provinces exercise complete legislative, financial and administrative control. The local bodies fall under the jurisdiction of the Provincial Ministries of Local Government. In addition, there are provincial line departments of ministries such as health and education that are expected to deliver services at the grass-roots level. Finally, there is the provincially controlled civil service administration, in charge mainly of the law and order, magistrate and the police functions going down to the division, district and tehsil level, but in effective authority on other issues as well.[5]

The issue is also of much broader regional significance, particularly in South Asia. A conference in Sri Lanka brought together participants from South Asia and the papers from Bangladesh (Rahman 1999) and India (Sharan 1999) indicate that similar concerns with local government issues are being dealt with in other South Asian countries.[6] For an extensive discussion of the advantages of devolution in a wider and rural development-related context, refer to Manor (1999: 87–115) and Blair (1998: 11–12).[7]

The concern in this paper is with the effective devolution of the power and functions to the grass-roots level as a first in a sequence of devolutions to attain democratic governance. Using the case of Pakistan, it will focus on some of the key issues required for effective power devolution, which include, in particular, the benefits of devolution, the prerequisites of successful devolution, and finally the level to which devolution should take place. A recurring theme in this paper is that no major policy reform, such as devolution, can occur in isolation, but must be seen as part of a larger package of reforms. A corollary to this view is that, while devolution is pursued to enhance human security, if it is not well designed and implemented, it will aggravate human insecurity. To make the discussion more concrete, the National Reconstruction Bureau (NRB) devolution model and an alternative indicative model of devolution to the grass-roots level are presented.

WHY DEVOLVE POWER?

The theoretical debate sparked by the comparison of the centralized socialist economies with the decentralized free market economies is relevant here. Proponents of the market system, particularly those of the Austrian school such as Hayek (1944), argued that the decentralized free market system is inherently more efficient because it can quickly take advantage of the special local information related to time and place. By the time such information is passed back to the centre, digested and instructions sent back, the decisions are already irrelevant. Moreover, there are all kinds of distortions, disruptions and hindrances in the flow of information. Finally, even if such distortions did not exist, there are limits to the amount of information the centre can efficiently process and act upon. The larger the country and the larger the population, the more relevant is this limitation. Thus, it is inherently more efficient for decisions to be taken at the local level to benefit from this special information in a timely manner. While this logic was used in the socialist-market economy debate, it applies with equal, if not greater relevance, to local government where the concern is with people making decisions for their own welfare.

A similar and related reason for relying on local effort is the scale on which centralized services have to be delivered in countries with a large population like Pakistan. Devolving the delivery of services to the provincial level has not been enough, and social-sector delivery is in a state of collapse despite the Social Action Plan's attempt to boost them.[8] Once again, harnessing local effort for local services would *a priori* be expected to produce better results.

Community empowerment and involvement should also lead to less transactional costs, since individuals would not have to appeal to higher tiers for particular services. It would also reduce the culture of dependency, as individuals would be involved in various ways in the delivery of their own services. In this regard, one could argue that involving communities in the delivery of their own services is just. This should also produce better accountability, since local knowledge regarding misappropriations should build pressure for redress at the local level.

If the accountability structures could be vested for the most part at the level at which services are delivered, the existing cumbersome accountability structures could be reduced. For example, in education, due to its placement in the concurrent list of the Constitution, there are both central and provincial educational departments. Certainly, there is no need for an educational department at the federal level. Also, at the provincial level, the district education officer, assistant education officer, learning coordinator and supervisors add little value to the educational process. Thus, the devolution of services and accountability to the grass-roots level has significant economies built into the process.[9]

To sum up, devolving to the grass-roots level is a means to an end, and not an end in itself. The end is just, efficient, accountable, transparent, cost-effective and economical (in an aggregate sense) service that promotes democratic governance and enhances human security. If the end cannot be reached due to constraints or unmet prerequisites, it would be advisable to postpone or even avoid it. Thus, the constraints to effective devolution or prerequisites for successful devolution need to be explored.

PREREQUISITES OF SUCCESSFUL DEVOLUTION: THE POWER ISSUE

Several sources have addressed the prerequisites of successful devolution. For example, Banuri, Ahmad and Afzal (1995) and the World Bank (1998) rightly point out that effective devolution would require constitutional cover, and the transfer of financial powers to, and administrative capacity strengthening of, the local for the devolution to be meaningful. However, not much attention has been given to the 'power issue', which may be the most important prerequisite for effective devolution to the grass-roots level.[10] This section concentrates mostly on the power issue.

It is assumed that the benefits of devolution would result in communities working in their own best interests for the delivery of services. 'Community' at both the rural and urban levels needs to be decomposed. At the urban level, there may be a fair degree of homogeneity in a particular town committee or ward. However, in rural areas, what is referred to as a 'village community' is normally a mosaic of class and caste. If the concern is for the poorest, which is suggested in the rhetoric of devolution, than their empowerment via devolution needs to be ensured.

Suppose, in a rural setting, the devolution is to the district level, such that district-level elections will elect candidates for district councils that will have jurisdiction over the whole district. One needs to be concerned about whom, in the current socio-economic milieu, the power will devolve to for understanding the sources of power. It is argued that the real source of power is district administration, including the police and the courts. In Pakistan, the police and courts are widely perceived as being corrupt, and, instead of serving the ordinary people, are seen as oppressing them.[11]

While poor salaries are part of the problem, the other problem is that large landlords have been able to exploit these needs of the police and courts to serve their purpose. Had land been equally distributed, the abuse of police and magistrates' powers would still have been present without far-reaching police and judicial reforms. However, given the very unequal landholdings obtaining, it is likely that feudal power would subvert such reforms.[12] Thus, land concentration is a source of power that would allow the capture and subversion of district government via elections; this is a real problem in many districts.

Ultimately, whether or not landed power can be parleyed into electoral power is an empirical question. Wilder (1999), in a very insightful and valuable study, has argued, using interviews, secondary data, constituency returns and polling station returns, that voting patterns have changed in the Punjab province. Instead of feudal power and other social determinants like caste being important, the party candidates most capable of delivering 'development' or 'patronage' are likely to be elected. This is how he explained the electoral defeat of many major PPP (Pakistan People's Party) landholders by PML (Pakistan Muslim League) candidates in the 1997 elections. While the empirical exercise in fairly convincing, Wilder's analysis suggests the overlay of another dimension upon the existing social determinants of voting behaviour in Pakistan's political culture.

In other words, those reaching the assemblies may have a party identification, but may still be local notables backed by landed or other sources of power. Most Pakistanis are under the impression that the National and Provincial Assemblies are still the playing fields of major feudalists. A very easy way to test this hypothesis is to compare the mean landholding of the average members of the National and Provincial Assemblies with the average for the country and province. Adil et al. (2000: 12–14), using interviews and press reports, determined that large landlords are the largest group in the National Assembly and have managed to hold about half the seats since the 1970 elections. Beyond that, electoral politics have become a preserve for the rich.

Another way of looking at this issue is via the perception of people at the grass-roots level regarding the barriers to empowerment: 42 people's assemblies were conducted by public interest organizations in 2000 at the local level. The results of the 31 reports released show that feudalism is viewed as one such barrier almost universally.

Some have argued that feudalism in Pakistan is dead due to a natural process of land fragmentation resulting from Islamic inheritance laws, and sometimes inheritance dissipation. Perhaps this is so in some districts and tehsils. However, aggregate statistics suggest an increase in concentration of operational landholdings. Table 5.1 presents the size distribution of farm holdings which highlights this point.[13]

The 1990 agriculture census results are the latest reported to date. Three points are particularly noteworthy. First, perhaps due to corporatization of agriculture, large farms accounted for a negligible number of total farms in both 1980 and 1990, but the area they cultivated has more than doubled from 3 per cent to 7 per cent.[14] Second, it is evident from Table 5.1 that the middle farm-size categories are thinning

TABLE 5.1: CHANGE IN PERCENTAGE OF PRIVATE FARMS AND CULTIVATED AREA BY FARM SIZE ACROSS THE CENSUS PERIOD

	1980		1990	
Farm size (acres)	% of farms	% of cult. area	% of farms	% of cult. area
< 5	74	38	81	43
5–10	17	26	12	23
10–20	6	17	5	15
20–60	3	16	2	12
> 60	-	3	-	7

SOURCES: *Economic Survey 1992–3*, Statistical Supplement, p. 77 for the 1980 numbers and *Economic Survey 1995–6*, Statistical Appendix, p. 53 for the 1990 numbers.

NOTES: 1 acre = 0.4047 hectares.
— = non-significant percentage statistically.

out and there is greater cultivation in the smallest and largest farm-size categories.[15] Finally, since the numbers involved are not large, particularly if the accounting is done in terms of households, land reform would not be a large exercise.[16]

Other than land, wealth or income legally or illegally acquired by smuggling, drugs and gun running, is a source of electoral success as noted by Wilder (1999: 205–8). He also indicates how this commercialization of politics has corrupted the bureaucracy. Finally, he cites the view expressed to him in interviews that while politics was originally perceived to be a way of preserving wealth, it is now being used for generating wealth. In the sections that follow, the NRB and an indicative model for devolution of financial, administrative and accountability authority to the grass-roots level have been presented.

THE NRB MODEL OF POWER DEVOLUTION

The Local Government Plan (2000) is designed to devolve power to district (*zila*), tehsil and union council levels. It identifies the following three structural changes that the NRB views as central to its plan:[17]

- Unifying rural-urban governance via *zila* government.[18] This is to be achieved mainly at the tehsil level, since tehsil government is to be responsible for both rural and urban municipal functions;

- Integration of the local bureaucracy with the local government; and
- Develop a coherent and reformed police and *zila* administration answerable to the elected local representatives.

The change in power balance is expected to provide local empowerment, protection against non-professional transfers and undue political interference from the higher levels. Apart from reporting to elected representatives, accountability in service delivery is also to be ensured via village/town councils, citizen monitoring boards, regular evaluation and the free flow of information via the establishment of Management Information Systems (MIS) offices at the *zila* level.

Various other checks and balances are also built into the system at all tiers. Thus, the 'Nazim' (governor) at any tier level could be recalled, after at least six months in office, by a motion carried in any of the respective assemblies. If the motion is not carried, the mover and the seconder lose their seats. If the motion is carried, the removal of the Nazim would require a two-thirds majority. The provincial chief minister can also move a motion with a simple majority of the provincial assembly. The provincial governor could endorse the decision or send it back once for reconsideration.

The checks and balances via the various institutional mechanisms mentioned above are expected to provide better service delivery. Villages are to be recognized for the first time as municipal entities. The union council is to cater to the village municipal needs via local effort and via coordination with the tehsil officer, municipal standards and coordination.

The elected nazim and naib nazim of the union council are automatically the members of the tehsil and zila assemblies respectively. Also, the nazims and naib nazims of the higher tiers are to be indirectly elected by the counsellors of their respective assemblies.[19] This process is expected to produce a highly integrated and well-coordinated local government structure. The various tiers are also expected to have a high level of fiscal autonomy via fiscal transfers and local tax authority.

In order to address the power issue, separate seats are reserved for women (33 per cent), workers and peasants. This is expected to bring new faces into the political arena. However, the real issue of empowering the grass-roots level has still not been addressed, since those delivering a service are not answerable to those being delivered a service to at the grass-roots level.

The architects of the plan are aware of the need for empowering the grass-roots level, and the vehicles selected for this are the village councils (VC) and the citizens community boards (CCB). The VC is to assess finances, promote civic education, community learning, recreational and youth activity and gender sensitivity. The CCBs will be registered in the *zilas* and will mobilize communities, raise funds for local problems, receive cost-sharing support and work closely with the monitoring committee of the union councils. Needless to say, none of this will happen without real empowerment, and, at least this part of the plan, represents a wish list like so many government plans in South Asia. Thus, an alternative is proposed below that we feel has a better chance of achieving the government's stated objective of empowering the grass-roots level.

AN ALTERNATIVE INDICATIVE MODEL FOR POWER DEVOLUTION TO THE GRASS-ROOTS LEVEL

BACKGROUND

Power is to be distributed across five tiers, i.e. centre, provinces, districts, tehsils and union councils. We argue that villages/towns or wards would be the most appropriate lower tier for the devolution of power.[20] The premise is that more effective devolution and participatory democracy will result by starting to build upwards from the grass-roots level. Other than the main objective of using devolution as a mechanism to build democratic governance, the other expressed policy objectives include building an institutional structure that empowers the poor and, hence, gives them a vested interest to protect; ensuring cost-effective service delivery via collective action; and ensuring the delivery of speedy justice at the doorstep of the poor. All these are worthy objectives that would enhance human security and are likely to be achieved, as elaborated below, if the lowest tier is the village.[21]

Power is a zero-sum game. Achieving the empowerment of the poor at the grass-roots level may mean disempowering other groups. At the district and grass-roots level, this would include the elite who derive their power from land or other sources of legal or illegal wealth; local, provincial and national politicians who have a stake at all levels including the grass-roots level; district administration; and local government. An ideal solution would be to take a long-term view of achieving the kind of far-reaching reforms needed to effectively devolve power to the grass-roots level. Thus, it would require diffusion of power via land reform and electoral reforms to prevent the capture of power at the grass-roots level, far-reaching public-sector reforms to eliminate redundancy, and judicial and police reform at the district level to ensure effective dispensation of justice. In practice, political compulsions require quick action, but also constrain the nature of reforms that can be effected. In this regard, a model for achieving the desired objectives, with the least possible demands for fundamental structural reform, is presented.[22] However, there are some minimum conditions for power devolution and these will be specified. In addition, the issues of capacity building at the grass-roots level will be addressed. Given that such reforms result in social and political disruption at the local level, it may be wise to implement these reforms via a process of conducting pilot projects. The two subsections that follow contain a model for power devolution to the grass-roots level and explore a mechanism for the interaction of local government with district government.

MODEL[23]

The case for devolving power to the village is based on the principle of subsidiarity, viz., that power should be devolved to the lowest possible level at which it can be effectively discharged.[24] This has been argued to be both more efficient and more just in the preceding section. Such devolution would also address all the above-stated objectives, particularly that of ensuring cost-effective service delivery via collective action. The services being referred to include, inter alia, education, health, drinking water supply, sanitation, feeder roads, environmental conservation, local irrigation works and justice. The scope of what a village could handle would change with technology and the growing expertise/capacity over time.

The main difference in this model and that proposed by the NRB is that local knowledge will be used for local action rather than passed up the ladder via village councils and citizen's monitoring boards to district authorities. In this regard, while the NRB model has institutional innovations, it stops short of embodying them with executive authority, and without that, there is not much to chose between the status quo and the NRB model.

Elections to Village Assemblies[25]

The formation of an elected village assembly that corresponds to district, provincial and national assemblies is proposed here. About 10 or so members (depending on population) could be elected based on safeguards to ensure the diffusion of power.[26] For village assemblies, land reform would be one such critical safeguard. In its absence, various electoral safeguards could be used as a poor second. These could include bifurcating the candidates into agricultural vs non-agricultural occupations. In the agricultural category, there would be a need to ensure that there is an adequate representation by size of farm and for those who are landless.[27] Special affirmative action seats should be reserved for women and minorities. However, separate electorates have not worked in Pakistan and are not supported by the minority groups they were supposed to protect because it marginalized them.[28] Thus, all individuals should have a right to vote for all candidates in the various categories, and all individuals should have a right to fight elections from all the seats subject to the qualifications mentioned above.

The time period for which candidates are elected needs to be long enough to give them an opportunity to settle in and serve the community, but not so long that the threat of having to face the electorate is too distant. While accountability will need to exist at the village level to deal with errant behaviour, the threat of being ousted is an important democratic check if the process is allowed to continue.

Elections should be on the party basis for the following reasons:[29]

- Exclusion of the political parties, particularly those which have already announced their desire to participate in local government elections, will create social discord and rifts that will jeopardize the process. Past experience shows that political parties find a way to directly or indirectly contest the elections anyway;
- If accompanied by elections within parties, this will deepen democracy, since it will create a cadre of leaders who emerge from the local tiers and move on to higher tiers based on serving the community. This is an important feature of all good democracies. As Manor (1999: 75) notices, it will integrate elected bodies across the various tiers, which is an important building block for a healthy democracy;
- If parties are excluded, it will create political insecurity and tensions, and create the impression that the military government merely

intends to perpetuate itself, as happened with military governments in the past;

- Implementing sequential party-based elections from the lower to the higher tiers is the best 'exit strategy' for the military government. This will give it enough time to implement the fundamental reforms it would like to undertake; its announcement of such a strategy will create national and international goodwill; and
- Mathew (1996: 136) makes the interesting point that while there is often a dominant local household that captures power, local-level party elections are a means of countering this monopoly on power.[30]

Service Delivery

Committees should be constituted for all services that are delivered at the level of the village as indicated above. The chairperson of the committee would be a member of the village assembly, and other members could be elected/selected from the community as appropriate. The time spent serving on committees should be paid for at local market rates as determined by the assembly. For example, for schooling, others members of the committee could include representatives of parents, teachers and the broader community since all have a stake in children's education.[31]

The functions of the committee would need to be effective service delivery depending on the level of skills that exist at the local level. Thus, for the school committee, the appropriate functions would be to ensure that school-age children are enrolled in accordance with the law and provided appropriate incentives for this (school lunches, uniforms/ books, crèches for the poor), to monitor teacher and student absenteeism; to ensure, in agricultural areas, that the school schedule is consistent with the agricultural cycle; and to ensure that the funds allocated to the school by the village assembly are properly used. Naturally, the higher tiers may determine the curricula, but as local expertise grows, more autonomy for such functions must also reside at the village level.

All committees would report to the village assembly (i.e. the people's representatives) that would ensure that the functions of the committees are being carried out according to their mandate.[32] Thus, for example, the school committee could recommend firing a teacher to the village assembly that should have the power to accept such a recommendation. In this regard, government officers like public school teachers will become the employees of the village government and not the provincial government.[33]

Accountability

Good service would be predicated on three factors. First, repeated elections, if allowed to occur, should ensure that the community chooses those who best serve it. Second, as pointed out by Banuri and Mahmood (1997: 153–67), healthy competition might get promoted across communities in delivering good service. Third, there could be a routine audit of various service functions at the lower tiers by the line ministries and civil service, such as a schooling committee or justice committee audit, with the results provided to the village assembly for action. Finally, laws and rules would need to be framed to enable the community to take the village assembly to the district courts.[34] The basic principle that needs to be conformed with here is that accountability and authority must reside at the village level. In addition, the principle of judicial review should prevail, so that a judge could call the assembly to account for malfeasance, negligence and criminality.

Justice

Policy makers have stated that one of the objectives, as stated above, is speedy justice delivered at the doorstep of the poor. One possibility is to have a justice (or *insaf*) committee. Once again, the committee should have an elected assembly member as the chair, and there should be due representation provided to women, minorities and lower castes. The key would be the force provided by the police and district administration to the decisions of the *insaf* committee, as endorsed by the elected assembly, on matters that are deemed to be within their jurisdiction.[35] This issue will be further discussed whilst considering the interface between the district and local government.

Finance

It is now well understood that devolution of powers from the centre to lower tiers is meaningless without devolving financial authority also to the local tiers. Thus, devolving power to the village level would require that the financial base is tapped at the local level. For villages, this would primarily be a tax on land (rather than an agricultural income tax, which falls within the provincial jurisdiction). The mechanism for collecting such a tax already exists at the village level, so it would be a question of the village assembly retaining these funds rather than passing them on to higher levels. In addition, there could be a nominal fee for services such as education, health and water supply to be collected from those who can afford it as determined by the village assembly. Finally, the higher tiers could provide funding based on sales taxes collected at higher tiers of government. The transfers from the higher tiers would need to be based on the population and backwardness of the recipient community.[36]

RELATIONSHIP OF LOCAL GOVERNMENT WITH DISTRICT GOVERNMENT, CIVIL SERVICE AND LINE DEPARTMENTS

As earlier stated, even this minimalist model of power devolution presented here has far-reaching implications for restructuring of functions at various levels of the government. Thus, the challenge is to restructure the role of the civil service and line department personnel in such a way that their roles are both productive and consistent with the power devolution being advocated. The concern of the civil service or the district management group should now be explicitly concerned with the maintenance of law and order, as mandated, as they would no longer have a role in development, as that would be handled by the elected local assemblies. They could backstop the justice committees and village assemblies, engage in capacity building at the local and district level, and deal with law-and-order issues under their jurisdiction with the aid of a reformed district courts and police service.[37] Freed from their other responsibilities, they could focus on a more rapid and efficient dispensation of justice. As Manor (1999: 97) pointed out, prejudices can find more intense expression at the local level; thus, a heightened responsibility at the village level will be good for the protection of the minority rights if these are threatened at the local level.

The main functions of the line departments would include, inter alia, capacity building, technical assistance, training, passing on development grants approved by the district assemblies and maintaining the records, setting standards, data collection and periodic audits, although the latter will have to be left to a specialized agency.

Effective authority would reside with village committees and assemblies. Gross misconduct or misappropriation would be reported to village assemblies which would refer it to the judiciary. In order that they perform this task efficiently, line department officials would also need to be trained. The training of higher tiers could be managed by agencies like the NRSP (National Rural Support Program).[38]

Some rationalization of the functions of the line department would naturally be called for. For example, currently the Ministry of Local Government and Rural Development (LGRD) and Public Health Engineering Department (PHED) have both been entrusted for providing rural water supply schemes. Since rural development should be managed at the local level, relying on the line departments or the specialized agencies (rather than LGRD) for training, technical assistance and capacity building should be adequate. Village assemblies should be able to approach the elected district officials for inadequate or slow response from line departments.

CONCLUSION

The arguments in favour of devolving power to the grass-roots level to attain human security are very persuasive. These include more efficient and accountable service delivery, if participation can be engendered and local communities are involved in self-management. In addition, it would also be more just because it would reduce the transaction costs for the poor who would not have to go to higher and yet higher tiers of administrative authority for having their problems resolved. Finally, it would be more economical in the long term since, in the context of broad civil service reform, layers upon layers of the administrative bureaucracy could be eliminated since they are not adding any value anyway.

Devolution of power is not, however, a straightforward exercise. Various prerequisites need to be satisfied and, in accordance with the principle of subsidiarity, it requires the effective transfer of accountability, and administrative and financial authority to the levels at which the service is to be delivered. Since, in many cases, the service is to be delivered at the village or ward level, the focus on the tehsil and union council tiers misses the point.

The effective diffusion of economic power is probably the most important prerequisite of effective devolution, and one that has gained the least attention. Land operations in Pakistan became more concentrated between 1980 and 1990. Economic power, particularly that derived from landholdings, gets parleyed into political power, and such power, in collusion with the district administration, magistracy and police, oppresses the poor and leads to human insecurity. There is evidence drawn from electoral studies to support this view. The most recent of these studies suggests that politics in Pakistan has become completely commercialized. Thus, the road to political power appears to be derived from income generated from land, industry and illegal channels such as smuggling and gunrunning which are part of the huge undocumented black economy. While politics at one time was viewed as a means of preserving wealth, it has now become a mechanism for enhancing wealth.

The abuses mentioned above are likely to be more pronounced at the higher tiers. This is another reason why it would make more sense to start with elected multi-purpose ward/town committees and village assemblies. It may also be possible at this level to build in election safeguards to prevent the capture of power at the local levels for rent-seeking and other forms of corruption and to ensure adequate representation of women and minorities.

Power devolution is a zero-sum game, and empowerment at the grass-roots level requires disempowerment of other groups and interests at other levels. A pragmatic approach to this issue has been adopted, and the model proposed suggests how the four stated objectives of power devolution for 'building real democracy', an 'empowering institutional structure', a 'cost-effective service delivery' and 'justice at the doorstep' may be achieved with a minimum of social and political disruption. Naturally, real and sustainable grass-roots empowerment is contingent on more fundamental land, electoral, judicial and public-sector reforms. In the shorter time frame for reform that the military government in Pakistan has adopted, minimum conditions have been specified for some meaningful change to achieve these stated objectives.

It is essential that accountability reside at the grass-roots level for the functions that are within their jurisdiction. Repeated elections, the right to take village assemblies to district courts, and judicial reviews are part of the accountability process. In addition, district management and line department officials can perform periodic audits of the various service committees such as education and *insaf* (justice). However, it is vital that the results of these audits are provided to the grass-roots assemblies for appropriate action, so that accountability and authority reside at the grass-roots level.

NOTES

1. In fact, the Supreme Court decision legitimizing the military government, but allowing them a maximum of three years, represents an exit strategy. Nonetheless, an appropriate sequential devolution could represent a smooth transition back to the political process.

2. By local government, I mean the devolution of fiscal, administrative and accountability authority to the grass-roots level, i.e. village or town committee. The World Bank (1999: iii) makes a good distinction between decentralization, which implies preserving the line of federal or provincial command to the decentralized bodies and devolution, which means a transfer of substantive authority to local tiers. Manor (1999: 5), who refers to devolution as democratic decentralization, and Cohen and Peterson (nd.), are good sources for definitional issues and extensive references to the literature. Also refer to Gaventa and Valderrama (1999), who discuss this issue from a 'participation' perspective.
3. Banuri and Mahmood (1998) and Ahmad (1999) are other important references dealing with devolution in Pakistan.
4. Refer to the foreword in Bengali (1999) that cites several shocking examples of institutional anarchy. Also, the World Bank (2000: 67) provides a good summary of institutional overlap in functions.
5. For a good description of district administration, refer to Yasin, ed. (1999: 12–23).
6. Other South Asian sources include extensive reports from PRIA (Society for Participatory Research in Asia), particularly PRIA (2000) that details the experience with democratic decentralization (Panchayat Raj) in India, and Aziz and Arnold (1996).
7. Manor (1999: 120) also quite clearly and accurately indicates that this is a slow and difficult process, and certainly should not be viewed as a panacea.
8. For an example of the complete collapse of the provincial delivery system in rural education and rural water supply, see Khan et al. (1999) and Khan et al. (1998) respectively.
9. This is, of course, not a simple issue. In a country with a high unemployment rate, a human solution would have to be found for public-sector layoffs. The state should consider buy-out options which means a one time up-front cost that would allow employees to look for alternatives as a way of reducing its ongoing non-development liabilities. For restructuring of public expenditures and civil service reforms, see World Bank (1998, 1998a).
10. Exceptions include Kothari (1996: 36–7) and Gaventa and Valdarrama (1999: 7–8). Blair (1998: 9) reports that local elite takeover is the most common reason for the failure of decentralization schemes.
11. Yasin (1999: 22).
12. 'Feudal' has many meanings and in Pakistan is now commonly associated with an 'attitude' that is not only found among those with large landholdings. Here we refer to feudalism as a concentration of landholdings, and, more specifically, to large landlords.
13. This table is drawn from Khan (1999).
14. Since Pakistan is a country in which the capacity of towns and cities to deliver urban services is far overstretched relative to the demand for such services, corporatization should be discouraged. The need for building the stock of assets of the rural poor for ensuring sustainable livelihoods and preventing rural-urban migration are reasons for land reform and land distribution to the landless.
15. Khan (1999: 121–3) has shown using gini coefficients and the same data to show that the concentration in ownership and operational holdings has declined over time, but both remain high, at above 50 per cent. Also, this does not negate the

finding in Table 5.1 regarding the increased concentration of operational holdings in the largest farm category.

16. Ahmad and Qureshi (1999), who reopened the farm size and land productivity debate in Pakistan, have made the economic efficiency case for land reform. Khan and Siddiqui (1997) made the educational case for land reform by showing that absolute landed power is inversely associated with mean educational attainment in the village. The reasonable counter-argument to land reform is that if land is to be appropriated by the state, then why not industry and even other forms of private property like homes. In this regard, the anti-trust imperative of diffusing economic, and hence political, power provides justification for land reform. It is also argued that while Islamic economic philosophy, strongly advocates social justice, it also endorses private ownership. However, in Islamic economic philosophy land and other property is viewed as a 'trust' and those in [legitimate] authority have a right to bestow this trust. For these and other arguments see Khan (1985). Note, not all agree that land reform is necessary for effective devolution and, for a contrary view, refer to Manor (1999: 58).
17. Details of the highly complex plan including functions and committees at the four tiers (including village) are shown in Appendix 5.1 in the form of a flow chart.
18. Large cities will, however, be city districts.
19. This indirect election via an electoral college has caused much concern about possible electoral manipulation at the *zila* level of the nazim elections.
20. The rest of the paper refers only to villages, although, with some changes, such devolution also applies to urban local government. For useful accounts of urban local government in Pakistan, refer to the first three chapters of Zaidi (1999).
21. While it is difficult to imagine a military government achieving these objectives, the purpose here is to indicate the minimum steps and safeguards required for their achievement.
22. While the reforms suggested are quite fundamental, they fall short of the land, electoral, judicial and public sector reforms that would be ideal.
23. The Government of Pakistan (2000) has decided against devolving power to the village/ward level. Our contention is that they have not accepted the logic of the subsidiarity principle, and, as such, are not devolving to the grass-roots level.
24. Lambsdorf (1999: 41-8) has discussed 'subsidiarity' in the context of devolution. Bengali (2000) draws on Prud'homme (1994) and using externality (spillover), chargeability (user charges) and technicity (managerial capacity needed) develops an index for Pakistan to indicate appropriate tiers for devolution of different services. Many rights-based issues such as the protection of minority rights would naturally remain federal or provincial subjects.
25. There is an election sequencing issue that has not been addressed. Ideally, it would be good to start from the grass-roots level. However, since this may be logistically problematic, it would be possible to start with district elections and mandate the district assemblies to assist with village elections. Elections are being recommended here, even though some communities find them to be divisive and would prefer community selection by consensus, such as has been Pattan's (a grass-roots development NGO) experience in southern Punjab.
26. There could be a general assembly of everyone in the village/town committee,

which is more conducive to participation, but an assembly of elected representatives is likely to perform executive functions more efficiently.

27. Thus, restricting the representational rights of individuals is against fundamental democratic norms, but we recommend it nevertheless for the short term, since exclusion also results from the monopoly of economic and political power derived from land and other sources.
28. As pointed out by Moghal (nd.), minorities were only allowed to vote for their own candidates and the whole particular minority community is the constituency in national and provincial elections. The result was that Muslim candidates did not view the minorities as their constituents, hence marginalizing them, and minority candidates inevitably were elected from areas where the population of minorities was the greatest, so they were inaccessible to minorities in the rest of the country. In practice, they were also easily bought off and did not serve minority interests. See Khattak (1996) and Moghal (nd.) for details on how to practically structure the electoral process to make it just and equitable for women and minorities. Special attention also needs to be given to the lower castes called '*kamis*', who are completely powerless and disenfranchized at the local level.
29. The first three points are drawn from Manor (1999: 74–6).
30. Again, the Government of Pakistan (2000) has not proposed party elections.
31. Another inherent advantage of devolving power to the grass-roots level is being able to build on existing institutional structures. Thus, village SMCs/PTAs (school management committees/parent teacher associations) and village health committees have already been notified by the government and could be integrated into the village government structure. Similarly, the numerous grass-roots interventions at the village/ward level by development NGOs or PIOs (public interest organizations, as they are now being called) could be integrated into the new institutional structure.
32. To avoid quorum problems, it would be essential to limit the number of meetings an individual has to attend to no more than two a month. Thus, the representation of individuals in more than one sub-committee is not recommended.
33. Naturally, this will not go down well with the teachers' unions, but, as mentioned earlier, devolution does entail the distribution of power for more justice and efficiency. Public education is currently in a shambles, and research shows that the lack of effective teacher accountability has a lot to do with it. Refer to Khan, Kazmi and Latif (1999).
34. Banuri and Mahmood (1997: 153–67).
35. Naturally, affected individuals would have the right to appeal to the assembly.
36. Z.R. Khan (1996: 53) cites a range of tax possibilities at the local level including tolls, lease money, taxes on professions and events. Also refer to World Bank (2000: 78–82), Shah (1997: 533–4) and Pasha and Pasha (2000: 14) for local government tax possibilities in the Pakistani context.
37. For suggestions refer to Yasin, ed. (1999).
38. This would be an ideal use of the Social Action Plan funds.

APPENDIX 5.1: ORGANOGRAM ON THE LOCAL GOVERNMENTS PLAN

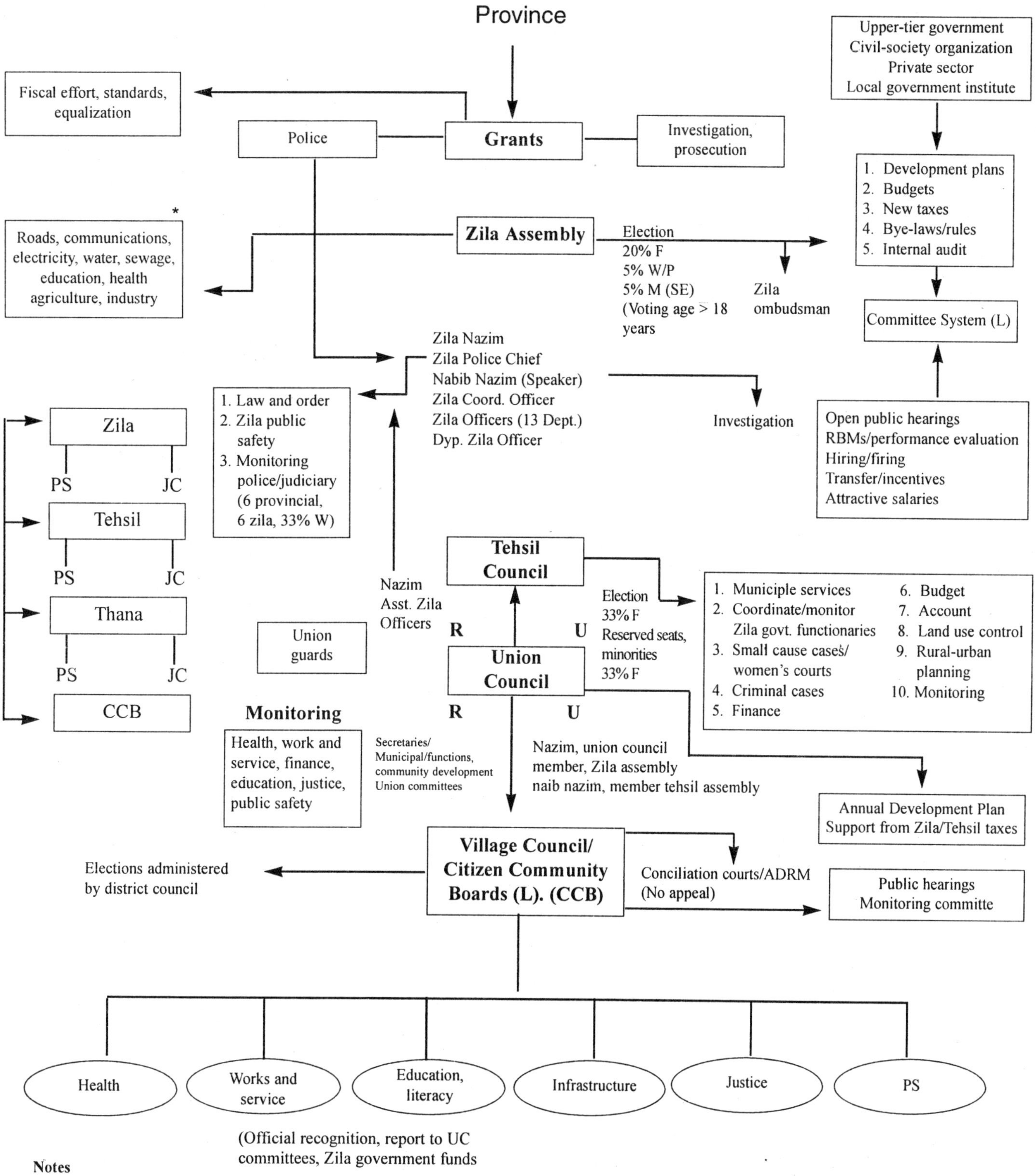

Notes

PS	Public Safety	F	Female	SE	Separate Electorate
JC	Justice Committee	M	Male	W	Worker
RBM	Result Based Matrix	ADRM	Alternative Disptute Resolution Mechanisms	M	Minority
R Rural		U	Urban	L	Linkage across all tiers
		P	Peasant		

* Initially line department, later corporatized

CHAPTER 6

Governance in Plural Societies: Sri Lanka

Paikiasothy Saravanamuttu

INTRODUCTION

At the outset, it must be stressed that any discussion of governance, and specially one of governance in plural societies, is by definition an ideological one. Certain key assumptions are invariably read into the discussion and condition the diagnosis of the problem as well as the proposed solutions. The discussion is inherently *political* in that the subject-matter is *political*. It is about the structure of power and authority in society and the relationships between groups based upon it. Therefore, a clarification of the ideological perspective of this chapter is in order.

This chapter is written from a liberal democratic perspective imbued with the values of individual liberty, democratic pluralism and faith in the belief that diversity in society must be cherished as a source of strength rather than weakness. Whilst fully acknowledging the pivotal role of the state in society, it argues that this role must be seen in terms of a facilitating framework for welfare and well-being for the pursuit and enjoyment of the good life by all. Furthermore, *the notion of governance that informs this chapter is both about the processes of mediating societal needs and tension, as well as, most importantly, the substantive content of that mediation and the values that underpin it. It is fundamentally about what should be done and why, as well as how it is to be done. Governance is not in this conception a matter of technique and technicality alone, it is first and foremost a way of looking at society stemming from a vision of the organization of society.*

Accordingly, the problem of governance in Sri Lanka stems in large measure from the failure to acknowledge the pluralism inherent in society through constitutional guarantees and through the propagation of this value in the political culture. Consequently, it gives rise to and sustains a crisis of legitimacy of the state. This is underpinned by defensive self-perceptions of the State and societal perceptions of it that range from the authoritarian and discriminatory to the corrupt and inefficient. These perceptions are mutually reinforcing and societal insecurity is thereby compounded.

What follows is an attempt to identify the sources of this problem.

For a country in the throes of a prolonged and seemingly intractable nation and State building process in which armed conflict and constitutional reform for conflict resolution have been identified as key elements, the question of an overarching political culture facilitating political pluralism assumes particular significance in respect of governance. It is allied to the question of whether 'nation state' or 'state-nation' is the better characterization of the highest unit of collective political organization in Sri Lanka. Accordingly, this *problématique* needs a general statement as central to the challenge of governance in a plural Sri Lanka.

THE NATION STATE/STATE NATION PROBLEM[1]

In Sri Lanka and South Asia in general, governmental structures still bear the hallmarks of the colonial legacy, and social relations that of pre-colonial influences. Consequently, although the dominant Eurocentric paradigm for collective political organization and economic development is the nation state and modern capitalism, in Sri Lanka the political formation is better characterized as the State-centric nation in which economic development has been uneven. Unlike the European experience of the symbiotic development of State, nation and market, here the state, essentially the colonial State, preceded nation, and has become the principal institutional agency in the creation of the nation through strategies of assimilation, integration and coercion. Development of the market has lagged behind both.

These centralizing tendencies of the State have bedevilled the objectives of developing socio-political harmony and an overarching national consciousness. Rather, the inability and/or unwillingness of the State to accommodate social diversity and provide democratic 'space' to a variety of groups, has in turn nurtured and intensified centrifugal tendencies. Moreover, the compulsions of the State to forge a nation in its thrall invariably involves the pre-eminence of coercive strategies and the gradual erosion of democratic rights and freedoms. The institutionalization of hegemony through the insistence on linguistic conformity, with its repercussions on educational and employment opportunities, and, to a lesser extent, the elevation of the majority religion to 'foremost' position, have struck at the fundamental tenets of minority identity in a representative secular democracy and have gone far in entrenching perceptions of discrimination.

There is another related factor contributing to this as well. It pertains to the political-civil society relationship, on the one hand, and to economic development on the other. It also accounts for the rise of populism and the consequent erosion of the early parliamentary democratic ethos that accompanied the initial transfer of power in 1948.

Populism rises in proportion to the widening disjunction between the pretensions and performance of the State as seen in its ability to deliver the goods to its people. And, as the State expands its role and reveals its incompetence, it becomes more authoritarian and feeds the crisis of its legitimacy. The failure of the State to deliver on its promises with regard to the good life of its citizens and its tendency to camouflage its limited capabilities with coercion and authoritarianism invariably give rise to anti-establishment/anti-systemic forces, not all of which seek to define identity in ethnic terms. They view the system of governance as corrupt, exclusive and bankrupt: thus economic development is denied democratic legitimacy.

In a context in which all power and authority is jealously guarded at the centre and concentrated in a class, a community, a party and then in a single individual, as Sri Lankan constitutional development bears out, the *raison d'être* of those who believe that the system is not working for them is to capture the system itself through armed insurrection. This is a course of action which serves only to replicate the problem as it is, by its very nature, a thoroughly statist response.

The development of a strong liberal rights consciousness, which can temper the costs and consequences of populism, has been mitigated by the overwhelming politicization of society imposed by the nation and State building imperative. When power, authority and opportunity stem from ethnic identity and partisan affiliation, the development of flourishing institutions of civil society that would serve as independent guardians of democratic rights is stymied. Secular, democratic civil society is not seen as the measure of the democratic health of society, but as a potential threat to the 'state-nation' bent on becoming the 'nation state'.

As independence is seen to be the regaining of sovereignty by the 'imagined community' of the nation, therefore, rights are initially conceived and later canvassed with an external orientation vis-à vis the international system. The multiplicity of threats that constituted the Cold War compounded this. Within the political unit, corresponding duties of citizens are stressed along with the assertion of the rights of the majority. At the international level, notions of justice have priority; at the domestic level they are superseded by arguments positing order as the higher goal. In both instances, rights and duties are collective and selective. They are not an end in themselves, but a means toward the end of forging a viable and secure collective entity—the nation state—in the image of the majority community.

The suppressing of civil society and the emphasis on allegiance from citizens to an overarching authority, uphold a particular version of collective good, which is further buttressed by the model of economic development.

The traditional notion of the state as the primary—if not exclusive—provider of the welfare and well-being of the collectivity, has been enthusiastically pursued. Again, the dominant ideology was collective and selective. The State enters the economy to control it. Consequently, the modernizing effects of economic development, specially as far as social mobility is concerned, is limited by the preponderant role of the State in controlling and distributing economic largesse under its political patronage and according to discriminatory criteria. Like civil society, private enterprise is not encouraged and is, therefore, unable to play its role in opening up alternative routes to social mobility, and, most importantly, the related function of facilitating the articulation of individual rights. The stultifying role of the State with regard to social mobility also has had the effect of allowing, by default, the persistence of feudal, caste and class considerations.

In this situation, minorities are doubly disadvantaged, as citizens, and as persons. They have responded in various ways and with mixed results, depending on their particular circumstances. Some who have acquired material prosperity and social advancement have done so on the tenuous basis of political patronage or a particular power configuration, rather than on or through solid institutional foundations. Individuals have succeeded by virtue of social class. As a group, though, minorities are disproportionately vulnerable to the vicissitudes of politics.

It is important to stress in this context, though, that the ultimate political expression of minority demands—national liberation/self-determination—is in effect a reaffirmation of the majoritarian principle and illustrative of the political culture. Other anti-systemic political forces whose leitmotif can be best described as the 'hijacking' of the State also share this anti-liberal-democratic feature. In this sense, post-Independence politics has entrenched the monolithic nation state bias of collective political organization without fostering the mediating attractions of *meaningful* constitutional and political experimentation to accommodate social diversity. The emphasis on '*meaningful*' is apposite, in that such experimentation, as there has been, has maintained the State-centric bias, and, at most, has been perceived by the minorities and the anti-systemic forces as tactical manoeuvre—the marginal tinkering with form as a smoke screen for the denial of substantive change.

The consistent denial of meaningful redress through political accommodation by the State only reinforces the belief that the system only works for some and is not intended to work for others. Therefore, it has to be abandoned, captured, destroyed or replaced. At the margins, the belief that underpins political action is that the State so designed cannot reform itself. It will always oscillate between provider and predator, and never partner. Is there a way out in Sri Lanka to create and sustain a political culture of partnership in the basic social contract between the government and the governed?

Whilst there have been changes in Sri Lanka from the description provided in the general statement made above, it should be stressed that these changes have yet to produce a durable political culture and institutions for democratic governance and conflict resolution in the future. My contention is that we are into a state of 'becoming', as opposed to a state of 'being', with regard to the question of nation and state and the answer to it in terms of democratic governance.

The horrors of the Janata Vimukthi Peramuna (JVP), or 'People's Liberation Front' insurrections (1971 and 1987–9) and ethnic conflict (in its armed manifestation since 1983), the theft and temerity of the 17 years of the United National Party (UNP) rule (1977–94), the upheaval and cultural challenge of the open economy and structural adjustment conditionality have highlighted the need for a redefinition of the status quo. There are many interests and sections of society though, which stubbornly—and, at times, even viciously—cling to the immediate past and beyond. As their insurance policy against alienation and anomie in a situation of change, they have fallen back on certainties culled from the situation that is being transformed. Fear of the future leads them to a position of going back to it.

These differences in response to change, of acceptance and accommodation or outright denial and rejection, define the political dilemma of contemporary Sri Lanka. Governance becomes a balancing act, a series of ad hoc, quid pro quos for quick fixes. The current process of constitutional reform for conflict resolution is illustrative of this, and highlights the element of good political governance identified in the 1999 Report on Human Development in South Asia as a constitution not easily amendable by any of the branches of government. It should be read together with an analysis of the ethnic conflict.[2]

ETHNIC CONFLICT: DEMOCRATIC GOVERNANCE AND CONFLICT RESOLUTION

The ethnic conflict in Sri Lanka stems from Tamil minority perceptions of discrimination dating back to the colonial era, and augmented since Independence. In the latter period in particular, discrimination was institutionalized through the Official Language policy (1956) which struck at the heart of minority aspirations regarding education and employment, and State colonization of predominantly Tamil-populated areas, seen by them as areas of their historic habitation, and, according to some formulations, as 'homelands'.

The accumulated sense of grievance and discrimination was exacerbated by the inability and/or unwillingness of successive governments to address this, and specially by their determined pursuit of majoritarianism. As attempts to seek political compromise through the established channels of elite democratic politics proved futile, extra-parliamentary militancy was nurtured and grew to the point of armed insurgency against the State. Political demands traversed the spectrum from federalism to secession, as championed by the Liberation Tigers of Tamil Eelam (LTTE).

Since 1983, a number of militant groups took up arms against the Sri Lankan State. Indian intervention in the form of a peace-keeping force and the Indo- Sri Lanka Accord of 1987 paved the way for the 13th Amendment to the Sri Lankan Constitution that provided for a measure of autonomy through provincial councils. All the militant groups entered mainstream establishment politics except the LTTE, which held out for secession, at best, and far-reaching autonomy for the north and east of Sri Lanka, at the least. Since 1990, barring intervals in which talks between them and the Sri Lankan State have taken place, the LTTE and the Sri Lankan State have been at war with each other. The LTTE fought the Indian Peace Keeping Force as well (1987–90).[3]

The ethnic conflict is reported to have cost some 60,000 lives so far, with over a million people both internally displaced and made refugees abroad. It is a conflict which has been marked by widespread terrorism and atrocity, including high level political assassinations, suicide bombings, the continued recruitment of child soldiers, traumatization and brutalization of the population and other human rights abuses. Included in this is the increase in violent crime and the deterioration in law and order attributable to army deserters. According to the figures provided by the Human Development Centre in its 1999 report on the Crisis of Governance in South Asia, the rates of murder and armed robbery are higher in Sri Lanka than in its immediate neighbours. In economic terms, the defence budget stands at 6 per cent of GDP, soaring considerably with the rearmament necessitated by LTTE successes in April/May 2000. Consequent to this, the country was put on a 'war footing' and there continue to be frequent increases in the prices of essential items—also partly attributable to increases in world oil prices.[4] A study by the Institute of Policy Studies values the cost of the conflict in the period 1984–96 alone at nearly 170 per cent of Sri Lanka's total GDP for 1996. The Central Bank in its 1999 Annual Report estimates that the conflict has reduced growth by 2–3 per cent points annually.[5]

Whilst the conduct of the Sri Lankan security forces is commonly believed to have improved considerably with regard to human rights abuses, allegations still persist and thereby feed perceptions of discrimination and the ethnic conflict. These extend from the recent massacre of Tamil inmates in the Bindunuwewa rehabilitation camp to the use and abuse of emergency regulations which have been in force for most of the last three decades, and, in particular, the recourse to the draconian Prevention of Terrorism Act (PTA), which has been in existence since 1979.[6] Large parts of the north and east of Sri Lanka, for the duration of the conflict, have been effectively governed by either the security forces or the LTTE, raising grave concerns for the observance of democratic rights and norms and the rule of law. The LTTE, on the other hand, has been internationally proscribed as a terrorist organization, and, whilst it has earned a reputation for military and political prowess, this has been overshadowed in popular perception by its fascist organization, ruthlessness and brutality in practice.[7]

The repeated failure since 1983 of either side to win an outright military victory quickly or cheaply has focused attention on a political solution, its substantive provisions and modalities. Constitutional reform has been identified as a key component for this, and is accordingly framed by the need to restructure the State and define the nation to meet the twin demands of democratic conflict resolution and governance.

Resolution of the ethnic conflict is about an attractive enough alternative for the Tamil people to the LTTE goal of a separate state of Tamil Eelam. Attempts at crafting proposals for the devolution of power will have to recognize this basic political point; they will have to contain viable, effective guarantees against discrimination, and convince the Tamil polity that they can seek the good life within a united Sri Lanka. Devolution and power sharing are now on the agenda because the Tamil minority took up arms against the Sri Lankan Government, after various attempts at political accommodation had failed. The LTTE, which seeks to establish totalitarian control and hegemony over the Tamils in the north and east of the country, is an outgrowth of the Tamil problem, and the political success of this essentially fascist organization has been its ability to acquire the rhetoric of Tamil nationalism in the absence of government attempts to effectively address Tamil grievances.

President Kumaratunga appeared to acknowledge most (if not all) of the foregoing at the outset of her first term in office (1994). However, naivete and arrogance characterized her attempt at direct negotiations with the LTTE, who, in any event, found a context of hostilities more conducive to the advancement of their totalitarian political project. With the LTTE leader Mr Prabhakaran's unilateral decision to resume hostilities on 19 April 1995, the government too allowed itself to fall back upon its primary reliance on military force for conflict resolution.

The use of force, however, is not politically neutral, and, as all the classic texts on its use point out, it releases its own dynamics. War was waged for peace, and terrorism had to be destroyed so that the Tamil problem could be addressed. However, since the Tigers have come to be synonymous with the Tamil problem in the majority Sinhala psyche in a way that they have never been in the Tamil one, the use of military force and the apparent success it met with in Jaffna in 1995 restricted the space for devolution and meaningful power sharing to resolve the Tamil problem.

The Peoples Alliance (PA) Government released an unprecedented devolution package as the nucleus of a political solution of the ethnic conflict in August 1995. It was the first time any Sri Lankan Government had ever come up with a set of proposals that entailed movement away from the unitary State. However, by the time it was presented to the Parliamentary Select Committee on Constitutional Reform as the government's proposals on devolution in January 1996, the balance of power was clearly restored in favour of the central government to allay the doubts and apprehensions voiced. The point to be noted is that the restoration of the military balance in favour of the government as a result of the intervening Riviresa military offensive was not interpreted as strengthening the government's hand in the pursuit of more meaningful devolution.

The extent of the reform of the political structures for peace and reconciliation, and, accordingly, the shift in the political culture was best exemplified by the Minister of Justice and Constitutional Affairs' explanation of the amendment to Art. 2 of the present Constitution enshrining the unitary State. The proposed amendment described the State structure of Sri Lanka as an 'indissoluble Union of Regions', and, according to the minister, in his published commentary on the proposed constitutional reforms, this is a necessary 'redefinition' of the unitary State as opposed to a wholesale jettisoning of the concept.[8] There was, in this document (and in subsequent versions including the Constitution Bill eventually presented to Parliament), a marked reluctance to make an explicit statement on the federal characteristics of the State that were being introduced.

My concern here is to understand how much is popularly understood by 'ethnic conflict', and to locate that understanding in the context of democratic governance in a plural society. The constitutional settlement is surely intended to take the ethnic conflict into account and provide future insurance against it, rather than deny its significance. Perhaps the lesson about the political culture to be discerned from the devolution debate is that, however inadequate, there are proposals along these lines, and, however distorted, there is a debate and not a riot.

The proposed new Constitution incorporating the devolution proposals was presented to Parliament on 3 August 2000 by the President, and then withdrawn when the necessary two-thirds majority of the legislators was not forthcoming for its passage. Whilst the latter was the direct reason for its withdrawal, protests and demonstrations from right-wing groups and significant sections of the Sangha (or Buddhist clergy), including a fast unto death by a monk, must be cited as reasons that would have influenced legislators, though they were by no means the only ones. It has been reported that various attempts to induce legislators to defect to the government, euphemistically labelled the 'handsome rewards scheme', were checkmated by the UNP Opposition. Sections of moderate Tamil opinion too, including the oldest Tamil political party, the Tamil United Liberation Front (TULF), and the only one in Parliament not to have resorted to arms were going to vote against the Constitution on grounds of the inadequacy of its devolution provisions.[9]

The devolution package has been through many incarnations since it was first presented as the government's basic thinking on the resolution of the ethnic conflict in August 1995. Presented as the government's proposals on devolution in January 1996, and then as the Legal draft of the Constitution in October 1997, it was not brought to Parliament till 3 August 2000, three weeks before the term of Parliament expired.

The reason cited for this delay was the unwillingness of the Opposition United National Party (UNP) to engage constructively in the process of constitutional reform and lend support to the government's efforts. The UNP at the outset positioned itself as champions of the unitary State. The absence of a bipartisan consensus between the two main political parties has been a key factor in the past that had obstructed a solution of the ethnic conflict. The UNP, for its part, has argued that the government is not really interested in a consensus and is more concerned with the consolidation of power, in the pursuit of which the government constantly alludes to the corruption, fear and terror that characterized the 17 years of UNP rule (1977–94).

Whilst the search for consensus has been stuck in partisan invective and parochialism, events on the ground have served as the catalyst for changing perspectives on the substance and modalities of a political solution to the ethnic conflict.

The government's key military offensive Jayasikuru ('Victory Assured'), in what it termed a 'War for Peace', was aimed at opening the main supply route from Colombo to Jaffna in the north. The rationale for this campaign was that it would facilitate the return of normalcy to the Jaffna peninsula and pave the way for the passage and implementation of the devolution package, which the LTTE had rejected outright. The government hoped that this could be accomplished by April 1998. They calculated on a referendum on devolution on the heels of the successful completion of the offensive, local government elections in the peninsula in January 1998, and the 50th anniversary celebrations of independence in February 1998.

Local government elections were held and hailed as a success, in that they demonstrated the desire of the population for returning to normalcy.

However, the unwillingness of the government to release the necessary funds for local government, and the series of political assassinations carried out by the LTTE destroyed the potential for the democratization portended by the elections. The LTTE also launched a bomb attack on 25 January 1998 against the Dalada Maligawa or 'Temple of the Tooth', the premier Buddhist symbol of religious and temporal power in Sri Lanka, and thereby decisively altered calculations regarding a referendum on devolution. The independence celebrations were to be held at the site of the temple in Kandy.

Launched in May 1997, the Jayasikuru military offensive was aborted in October 1998 after the LTTE overran the military camp at Killinochchi killing over a thousand Sri Lankan troops. The focus of attention then shifted to a series of provincial elections, culminating at the end of 1999 with a presidential election called over a year ahead of schedule. A mandate for the political resolution of the ethnic conflict was the stated purpose for this decision.

RECENT POLITICAL AND MILITARY DEVELOPMENTS

In November 1999, after the presidential election was announced, the LTTE scored another military victory by capturing chunks of territory in the Wanni region of the northern province, which the security forces were reported to have taken two years to capture. Consequently, the presidential election was fought under conditions of censorship of military news. Whilst intense partisan politicking dominated the contest, including allegations of a UNP—LTTE conspiracy to be at the heart of the military defeat in the Wanni, one issue came to the fore with regard to a resolution of the ethnic conflict and was the subject of considerable controversy.

Ranil Wickremesinghe, the UNP candidate and leader of the Opposition, proposed that an interim council for the north-east be set up with LTTE participation for a period of two years to prepare the ground for a lasting political settlement. He had earlier proposed that there be de-escalation of the conflict and asymmetrical devolution for the north-east. Part of the UNP strategy vis-à-vis the government's devolution proposals was to label them as irrelevant, in the face of LTTE rejection, and to argue that talks with the LTTE had to be initiated. The government, on the other hand, whilst not averse to resuming talks with the LTTE, always hoped to be able to do so from a position of military advantage. Mr Wickremesinghe's interim council proposal was roundly castigated for being tantamount to handing the north-east to the LTTE, indefinitely.[10] It brought out the entrenched fear and loathing of the LTTE, and raised questions about popular willingness to entertain a political settlement with them.

Indeed, the dilemma of conflict resolution in Sri Lanka continues to be the choice between the peace that can be sought with the LTTE and the peace that can be had without them. The former will entail incorporation of the Thimpu Principles (a statement of the principles of self-determination agreed to by all Tamil political representation in talks with the Sri Lankan Government at Thimpu in 1985) and asymmetrical devolution based on them in a constitutional settlement.[11] The latter will involve either the military and political marginalization and/or defeat of the LTTE, and the emergence and effectiveness of credible, alternative Tamil political representation to implement the devolution proposals. None of this has been forthcoming as yet.

Whilst Mr. Wickremesinghe won the bulk of the Tamil vote in the presidential election, the incumbent president Chandrika Bandaranaike Kumaratunga won the election and a second term with 51.12 per cent of the popular vote. The LTTE intervention to influence the outcome of the election extended to a suicide bomb assassination attempt on the life of the President as she was leaving her last election rally on 18 December. The unsuccessful attempt blinded her in one eye.

The configuration of circumstances following the election raised hopes that there could be a national government and that negotiations with the LTTE would be commenced in earnest. Conciliatory statements by the President, including an invitation to the leader of the Opposition to join her in the search for a settlement, were largely responsible. She revealed that she had attempted to open talks with the LTTE through the good offices of the Commonwealth Secretary General and the government of Norway, and that she had been rebuffed in both instances.[12] This had been earlier confirmed by LTTE leader Prabhakaran in his annual Heroes Day speech (26 November 1999) in which he referred to the Kumaratunga Government as a 'curse on the Tamil people'.[13]

In January 2000 it was officially announced that Norway had been identified as the third party to assist in talks between the government and the LTTE, and by February, the UNP leader of the Opposition, breaking the past pattern of bipartisan relations, announced his party's willingness to support the government's 1997 draft Constitution were it to be brought to Parliament. What followed the UNP leader's announcement was a reopening of discussions on the 1997 draft, first within the ruling PA coalition, then with the UNP and the Tamil parties. It was assumed that the consensus that emerged from these talks would be presented to the LTTE.

The PA–UNP talks stretched over a period of five months and resulted in the whittling down of the devolution proposals. Whilst the unitary State clause of the 1978 Constitution was dropped, so was the concept of a 'Union of Regions'. Tamil parties tried to restore the 1997 devolution provisions as a minimum position for incorporation in the proposed new Constitution. They succeeded to some extent, and hoped to present further amendments to the document once it was presented to Parliament in August.

The LTTE, in the meantime, scored a spectacular military success in late April 2000. They overran the Elephant Pass military complex at the entrance to the Jaffna peninsula and positioned themselves to take Jaffna town and the air and naval bases at Palaly and Kankesanthurai, respectively. They were also in a position to capture or destroy the core of the Sri Lankan Army, some 30,000 troops, who were isolated as a consequence of the Elephant Pass debacle.

In May, expectations were rife that the LTTE would take control of the peninsula—a *sine qua non*, it was believed, for their engaging in any talks. The Sri Lankan Government sought military assistance from India, and the very forces that had opposed Indian intervention in 1987 appealed to India for help. The Indian response was to offer 'humanitarian assistance' if requested. Weaponry was hurriedly acquired from Pakistan, Iran and the Czech Republic and diplomatic relations were reestablished with Israel to obtain Kfir fighter aircraft and military material. Consequently, there was a lull in the fighting, and whilst the LTTE has not advanced, it has not been ousted either.

The presentation of the new Constitution to Parliament in its dying days, plus an amendment to the current Constitution, which sought to amend the electoral system was to be debated, amended and passed: all within a space of three weeks at the most. The Constitution Bill was presented to the Supreme Court for determination as a 'bill urgent in the national interest'. Likewise, the 17th Amendment to the current Constitution, which sought to change the electoral system. In both cases, the court determined, in a space of 24 hours, as it was constitutionally mandated to, that the government could go ahead. The government had informed the court that it intended to pass the new Constitution by a two-thirds majority in Parliament, and thereafter subject it to an island-wide referendum, as required by the current Constitution. The court did not address the question whether the referendum could be held in the lifetime of a Parliament other than the one which passed the Constitution.

In the case of the 17th Amendment, the court determined that the government could go ahead with a two-thirds majority and without the requirement of a referendum. In both cases, there were a host of petitions to the court submitted by political parties, religious and civil-society organizations, citing lapses and lacunae in the process of constitution making. In the case of the proposed change to the electoral system, petitioners argued that it fundamentally affected the franchise, and, therefore, required a referendum. None of the petitions on either score were successful.[14]

The questions of process on which most of the petitions challenging the method of passage of both the new Constitution and the proposed change of the electoral system were based go to the core of the problem of democratic governance and the acknowledgement of pluralism in its institutions and processes.

The government has argued that, since 1995, there has been sufficient consultation and advocacy of the devolution proposals, and, therefore, the arguments about a 'secret' process and the lack of public participation in the constitution making on the lines of South Africa or Thailand, for example, do not hold. It charges the UNP with reneging on the understanding reached during the talks with them to support the Constitution. It also points out that a number of UNP proposals have been incorporated in the new Constitution, including the interim council concept.

Whilst it is correct that the government and civil-society groups did engage in public information campaigns and advocacy on behalf of the devolution proposals over the last five years, it is also the case that there was no time provided to the public to acquaint itself with the final composite document presented to Parliament. The question also arises as to whether the limited time provided was sufficient for parliamentary debate on two crucial issues, such as the Constitution, and the electoral system. Furthermore, there has been no record presented to the public of the various deliberations, ranging from the parliamentary select committee to the PA–UNP talks. Moreover, the Constitution is about more than devolution, it is also about the supremacy of the Constitution, fundamental rights, the independence of the judiciary and judicial review of legislation—all vital safeguards in a pluralist democracy.

The proposed new Constitution is also about the abolition of the Executive Presidency and the return to full-fledged parliamentary democracy. It contains transitional provisions in this regard. These have been the source of considerable controversy in that they provide for the current President to retain her office and enjoy the executive powers of the Prime Minister under the proposed new Constitution for a period of six years. The transitional provisions were cited by some as the basis for their opposition to the new Constitution. The President has promised to abolish the Executive Presidency—an office seen by the PA as the source of authoritarianism—by July 1995.

The new Constitution and the proposed change in the electoral system were complementary exercises, and whilst there has been public discussion on devolution, there was none on the change to the electoral system. In fact, right upto the dissolution of Parliament, the government assured the people that the impending general election would be fought on the existing electoral system.

The government's strategy seems predicated on profound distrust of the UNP and the conviction that it would vote against the Constitution at the last moment. The UNP defence has been that provisions not agreed upon were included therein, and that there was an understanding that the document would be presented to the LTTE and the Buddhist clergy (or 'Sangha') before it was introduced in Parliament.

With regard to the 17th Amendment, it is clear that the government wanted to adopt a system that would give it a two-thirds majority in Parliament. This, in turn, could have been used for, amongst other things, amendment of the new Constitution in the future, including, perhaps, agreement with the LTTE on a political solution, were that possible. The proposed 17th Amendment provided for a Parliament of 298 members, 168 to be elected on the 'first-past-the-post' basis, another 100 on district-based proportional representation, and 30 from a national list nominated by political parties and based on their share of the popular vote.[15]

The danger inherent with this process of Constitution making is that it has allowed the opponents of devolution to present themselves as the champions of the democratic process and transparency by derailing constitutional reform for the moment. Moreover, the problems of process and their impact on both democratic governance and conflict resolution could arise if the government sought to promulgate the new Constitution after the general elections on the basis of a mandate secured in that election. Given the current proportional representation system of election, it is virtually preordained that no party can obtain a two-thirds majority in the legislature.

Were a new Constitution to be promulgated on the basis of a mandate underpinned by a simple plurality of the legislature, this would clearly be unconstitutional under the terms of the present Constitution as well as the Supreme Court determination regarding two-thirds majority and countrywide referendum. Importantly, it should be pointed out that any Constitution so promulgated could be abrogated by the same pro-cedure. Accordingly, the guarantees to minorities and the devolution provisions will always be vulnerable to the vicissitudes, whims and fancies of partisan politics. Every party that has come into power since 1970 has changed the Constitution to suit its needs. There is a distinct possibility that this bad practice would be perpetuated.

The 'mandate theory' procedure for promulgating a new Constitution was compounded by the results of the general election, which made the government heavily dependent on the support of the smaller and minority community parties, and also the manner in which the elections were conducted. Serious allegations of electoral violence and malpractice implicating the ruling party were made during the elections, and grave doubts persist about the freeness and fairness of any electoral contest. The very forces that agitated against the Constitution, particularly because it was quasi-federal and departed from the unitary state, will be able to present themselves as the champions of the democratic process if the results of the referendum on the Constitution are seen to be manufactured by electoral violence and malpractice.

From the perspective of pluralist governance, process is important, because it is through process that the legitimacy crucial to the durability and effectiveness of the Constitution can be obtained. Any 'ends justifies the means' logic with regard to constitution making will imperil governance in the long term. The dilemma, nevertheless, remains as to how a Constitution that lays the foundations for a pluralist democracy can be promulgated in the face of entrenched institutional and cultural bias against it. The same forces that were galvanized against the Constitution because it espoused the devolution of power launched a successful challenge to the government's attempts to introduce Equal Opportunity legislation in September 1999. The legislation had to be withdrawn.[16]

Partisan politics defined by a zero-sum political culture militating against a political solution to the ethnic conflict has been alluded to above. It has frustrated attempts to accommodate minority grievances throughout the post-Independence period and thereby given rise to armed ethnic conflict. Despite the optimism afforded by the PA/UNP talks in early 2000, it has resurfaced in the aftermath of the general election. There are other factors worthy of comment, which relate directly to the insecurities entangled in the ethnic conflict and governance.

THE SANGHA AND THE MEDIA

The role of the Sangha is of especial significance and is linked to the perceptions of insecurity on the part of the majority Sinhala community.[17] The conflict in Sri Lanka has been described as 'one between two minorities', or one in which the majority has a minority complex and vice versa.

The extent to which the majority community too has a perception of grievance and insecurity is attested to by the establishment of a non-governmental Sinhala Commission in 1998 to ostensibly inquire into the grievances of the majority community, 50 years after Independence and 15 years after the armed ethnic conflict started. Its real target was the government's devolution proposals, and many associated with this group have joined with other groups such as the National Movement Against Terrorism (NMAT) to found a new political party named 'Sinhala Urumaya' (Sinhala Heritage). The depth of this majority-community feeling of grievance and discrimination must be measured against entrenched constitutional provisions since 1972 relating to the unitary State and granting 'foremost-place' status to Buddhism, the religion of the majority and, until the 1987 Indo-Sri Lanka Accord, the institutionalization of the Sinhala language as the official language of the country since 1956.

This majority-community perception, with its espousal of the trinity of the land, the race and the faith, arises from perceptions of discrimination under colonial rule and the fear of being dwarfed in a region in which there are some 60 million Tamils in the South Indian state of Tamil Nadu and more in South-East Asia. From this perspective, the Tamils have other options and other places to go to: the Sinhalese have only Sri Lanka. Therefore, the Tamils and other minorities must accommodate the Sinhalese.

Members of the Sangha have been amongst the most forceful proponents of this perspective. Their stance is augmented by defining the ethnic conflict as a problem of 'terrorism', and, therefore, one that should be resolved through military victory, not political negotiation.

Historically, the Sangha has been at the forefront of the development of the Sinhala language and culture, and, in the era of mass democratization, has been drawn into politics as a legitimizing force. Whilst their influence may not be as widespread now as it has been in the past, and although, in political terms, they cannot be said to constitute a homogeneous monolith of chauvinist opinion, they do retain a powerful hold on popular opinion as figures of authority and as community leaders.

Another factor that bears mention is the media, which, in Sri Lanka, is divided into the State-owned and privately-owned organs. The former are at the service of the government of the day and operate largely as the propaganda tools of the party in power. As far as a resolution of the ethnic conflict is concerned, the State media have been fully utilized to support the devolution package.

The attitude of the private media to the current government ranges from the uneasy to the adversarial, and this invariably affects their position on the ethnic conflict. That they may criticise the government's management of the conflict should not obscure the stereotype and bias it (and the State media), subscribe to in the coverage of the conflict and the attempts to resolve it.

Popular prejudices about terrorism and ethnic grievance as well as ethnic stereotypes abound. Coverage falls within the confines of the prevailing dominant paradigm, and little attempt is made to pursue stories not incorporated in official accounts. There is a discernible willingness to cover the conflict from Colombo, and to accept the version of events handed down by the publicity organs of the principal protagonists. Independent accounts are rare. Indeed, as a result of the availability of international networks, the average Sri Lankan has a better idea of what war has done to Bosnia and Rwanda, for example, than of what it has done to the Jaffna peninsula. The failure of the media in this respect is in turn a key factor in the absence of a critical mass of opinion that could be mobilized as an effective peace constituency.

In defence of the media, and from the perspective of governance, the relationship that has evolved between the State and the media must be mentioned. In the 17 years of UNP rule, in which many human rights abuses took place, and in which the crisis of democratic governance was brought to a head, the alternative media acted as sources of criticism of the regime. As a consequence, there was harassment of media institutions, and journalists were abducted and murdered. The fear of a return to this climate of fear and repression is sometimes cited as a sobering factor, inhibiting the media from violating censorship regulations covering war reporting, and adopting self-censorship in the absence of regulations. Whilst these fears cannot be discounted, they do not hold equally for all media organizations, and the extent to which the media are the repository of public prejudice and stereotyping as far as the ethnic conflict is concerned, should not be underestimated.

DEMOCRATIC GOVERNANCE: THE MEDIA, CIVIL SOCIETY AND THE ELECTORAL PROCESS

THE MEDIA

The role of the media as essential institutions of democratic governance bears further elaboration.

Government-media relations have undergone severe strain over the last six years, and have plummeted from the level of cordiality and optimism that obtained in 1994. As a consequence, acrimony, charge and counter-charge, confrontation and fear characterize the relationship between the government and the private media. The government maintains that the private media are partisan in favour of the UNP Opposition. This is a reason cited for its retention of the State-controlled media. It argues that the private media will always be used in the service of the Opposition to frustrate radical change and the realization of its progressive agenda, including the devolution of power as the basis for a solution to the ethnic conflict. The reasons for the deterioration in relations, however, go deeper and can be traced to the situation that obtained in the PA's ascent to office. Whilst this is especially true of the private alternative media, it also reflects a situation that obtains in respect of some civil-society organizations working for democratization and human rights.

Alternative media organizations and civil-society groups in this area were closely associated with the PA, and worked for the defeat of the UNP in 1994 on the grounds that such an outcome was essential for the survival of democracy in Sri Lanka. Once in office, the PA Government set up a series of committees to advance media freedom, including the reform of media laws. The reports of these committees were never published, but there have been attempts by the government to introduce legislation to control the media, like the proposed Independent Broadcasting Act of 1997. As a consequence of a campaign against it and the Supreme Court declaring it unconstitutional, the Act was withdrawn. In the wake of this, the government set up a parliamentary select committee to look into media reform. The committee has yet to release its findings.

The private media allege further instances of the government's bad faith, such as the frequent recourse to the law of criminal defamation against journalists. More recently, media organizations alleged that the Presidential Security Division was responsible for an attack on journalists covering an Opposition rally (July 1999), for violent attacks on journalists critical of the government, and for the murder of a newspaper editor (September 1999) as clear evidence of authoritarianism. In early January 2000, the state electronic media alleged that two editors of private newspapers were involved with the UNP and LTTE in a conspiracy to overthrow the government. The President herself, in an island-wide television broadcast (3 January 2000), publicly castigated two editors by name as agents of the Opposition.[18]

The private media's response to the government argument that they are flagrantly abusing the unprecedented climate of media freedom ushered in by the PA Government is the counter-argument that media freedom is not the gift of the PA, and that sections of the media played key contributory roles in the PA's ascent to power. They insist that it is their right and duty to expose lapses and lacunae in the government. Investigative reporting and exposes of continued corruption in government by certain media organs, whilst labelled as partisan by the ruling party, have raised public awareness about the impediments to governance in Sri Lanka.

An improvement in the government-media relationship and its elevation to that of a constructive interaction is necessary for governance. Unfortunately, there are no indications of an improvement in the relationship, rather a worsening of the situation following the general elections. There is no gainsaying the government argument about media bias and corresponding shortcomings in professional standards. On this score at least, there is some hope held out in the recognition by media organizations of the need for voluntary self-regulation and maintenance of professional standards, codes of ethics and conduct. This was initially flagged in the media organization's Colombo Declaration of Media Freedom and Social Responsibility issued in April 1998, which lays the foundation for a self-regulatory organization. This is expected to be convened in the near future.

CIVIL SOCIETY

As mentioned, whilst this applies to civil-society organizations working in the field of democratization and human rights as well, there are other dimensions to the relationship between these organizations and the government.[19]

The concern here is with the risk of partisan politicization of organizations whose *raison d'être* is the checks and balances of governmental power in the interests of democratic governance. Were such organizations to find themselves in either a situation of indefinite confrontation with the government, or alternatively one of co-option and subservience, democratic governance will be affected adversely. This is an issue that arises, in particular, with regard to the resolution of the ethnic conflict and the propagation of devolution and meaningful power sharing as indispensable to its resolution. Whilst on the one hand there are organizations openly hostile to this, on the other, there are those which, in their association with the government in this campaign, have laid themselves open to the charge that they are acting as its agents, as opposed to independent actors which are supportive of the government on this issue. For instance, conviction in the indispensability of devolution to conflict resolution is not synonymous with exclusive support of the government's devolution package. There is a danger here that on governance and human rights issues, these organizations could take on the role of 'service providers' on behalf of the government in these areas—a situation which occurred in the area of poverty alleviation in the late 1980s and early 1990s.

The argument for an issue-based democratic, secular, civil-society agenda may be difficult to realize in practice when the issues are hotly contested in political life and define party positions. Moreover, the relationship between the government and civil-society organizations is invariably an asymmetrical one in favour of the former. The current government, like its predecessors, has attempted to pass legislation to effectively control non-governmental organizations on the grounds that it is the government's responsibility to ensure financial probity in this sector. The effect of such legislation would be to obliterate the distinction between the governmental and non-governmental sectors and thereby weaken the prospects for democratic governance. Yet the carving out of a separate and distinct space for civil-society organizations in the face of such challenge is indispensable for the vital contribution they make to plural and democratic governance.

THE ELECTORAL PROCESS

Regular, free and fair elections with multiparty democracy have been identified in the Human Development Report in South Asia 1999 as one of the basics of good political governance. In Sri Lanka, the issue of free and fair elections has become a cause for grave concern in the last three decades, since threats to the integrity of the electoral process as the basic mechanism of choice and change in a functioning democracy cumulatively destroys public confidence in democracy itself. It should be noted that Sri Lankans have enjoyed universal adult franchise since 1931.

The issue of election violence and malpractice is inextricably linked to the zero-sum political culture cultivated and perpetuated by the main political parties. This includes the extensive use of patronage in all walks of life, as well as across-the-board partisan politicization of the institutions of civil society. Consequently, each election (even those at the level of cooperative societies in which manslaughter and murder are not uncommon, or even that of the Cricket Board) is seen as a matter of life and death in which physical safety, security and well-being are at stake.

The lack of intra-party discipline and democracy is at the core of this problem. They are reinforced by institutional and procedural decay which make extra-parliamentary and extra-judicial methods of problem solving and dispute settlement attractive in comparison, thus enabling those who are the least respectful of democratic norms to get elected, and ensuring their re-election as well. And once elected, they demonstrate that the requirements of winning an election are not only quite different to those of governance, but in direct violation of it as well.

Whilst party leaders make rhetorical commitments to non-violence and exercising party discipline on members identified as perpetrators of violence and malpractice, encouragement and promotion of such individuals by the very same party leaders is a common occurrence. The latest example is the reappointment of Gen. Ratwatte to the post of Deputy Minister of Defence, despite complaints against him by cabinet colleagues alleging major campaign and election-day violence and malpractice.[20] This is corroborated by the reports of both international and local monitors on the October 2000 general election.[21] Gen. Ratwatte's appointment to this ministry and to the cabinet is not the only such example. There are others, in a total of over 40, who have been appointed despite allegations of electoral violence and malpractice against them. During the election campaign, the President gave an assurance that such appointments would not be made.[22]

The cynicism and sense of powerlessness on the part of the voter is also compounded by the partisan politicization and undermining of the institutions charged with the conduct of elections—the Election Commission, the police and the public service. Whilst reform of the law will embolden them in the performance of their duties, the pervasive culture of patronage, violence and retribution could persist and undermine progress, as it does at present with regard to the observance and exercise of existing laws and regulations.

Civil-society groups monitoring elections have highlighted the pervasive use of violence in elections.[23] They have, in turn, been subject to vilification and attack as agents of the Opposition. This was the case in the provincial councils elections throughout 1999, with that in the north western province being widely acknowledged as an egregious example of violence and malpractice, as well as in the presidential election at the end of the year and the general elections in October 2000. The 17 years of UNP rule were no exception, and the ruling PA frequently makes the point that the excesses that occurred during its tenure in office do not match those that occurred under the UNP.

Whilst it is true that no party has a monopoly of electoral violence and malpractice, it is a sad reflection on the state of governance that bad practices are sought to be justified by reference to worse ones.

SOME ASPECTS OF ECONOMIC AND CIVIC GOVERNANCE

This chapter has paid primary attention to the political and constitutional aspects of governance in Sri Lanka. This is not intended to suggest that the areas of economic and civic governance identified in the Human Development Report are problem-free or without challenge. The situation obtaining in the fields of poverty alleviation and local governance are cases in point, and by no means the only ones, clearly indicating that there is a crisis of governance that can be identified, which is not directly or exclusively related to the ethnic conflict. It is, however, a product of the partisan politicization of all spheres, impeding and distorting service delivery, and the fair and efficient utilization of resources.

These were the issues—poverty alleviation and governance in general—along with relief, rehabilitation and reconciliation relating to the conflict and tertiary education, that constituted the agenda of the

18 December 2000 Paris Development Forum on Sri Lanka.[24] Earlier known as the 'Aid Consortium' meeting, the annual Paris discussion has been renamed to reflect Sri Lanka's middle-income status. The meeting in December 2000 was the first to be held after two years—elections had been the principal cause for postponement. The December 2000 meeting was not meant to result in pledges of assistance from donors, but billed as a listening and learning exercise between them and the Government of Sri Lanka. However, the political and public perception of the meeting was largely adjudged in terms of the government's ability to attract more donor assistance. The real issue here was not the pledging of further assistance, but the gross underutilization of funds already pledged and the deep, systemic problems in programme implementation and democratic governance, which donors specifically focused on at the Paris meeting.

The situation currently obtaining in the poverty alleviation field is that the 'Samurdhi' ('Prosperity')—as the government programme is called—animators are employed for party activities and benefits are distributed according to party allegiance. In the course of the 1999 presidential election, with the assistance of the Centre for Policy Alternatives, a petition was filed by some voters in the Supreme Court requesting it to ensure that Samurdhi workers were not used for electioneering.[25]

The World Bank, in its report entitled 'Sri Lanka: Recapturing Missed Opportunities' discussed at the Paris meeting, notes that 'it is widely acknowledged that successive poverty alleviation programmes in Sri Lanka have been designed and implemented more as vehicles for political leverage/patronage at the grass-roots level than as mechanisms to create opportunities for the poor . . . the political bias in the implementation of poverty programmes makes the poor highly vulnerable to changes in the political climate'.[26] It also states that programme officials charged with the identification of beneficiaries are political appointees, and cites documented research and surveys to show that party affiliation and voting patterns determine the allocation of income transfers to beneficiaries. The report also notes that the 'central government's control over the delivery of poverty programmes and social services devolved to the provinces has *inhibited the development of local institutions better able to represent the needs of the poor*' (emphasis in original).[27]

That the centralizing mindset of the bureaucracy and its political masters has severely affected the emergence of true local governance is a central theme of the 1999 research study done by Shelton Wanasinghe entitled, 'Effective Local Governance: The Foundation for a Functioning Democracy in Sri Lanka'. Wanasinghe too identifies the politicization of the bureaucracy and the consequent alienation of the people from the institutions of local governance resulting in corruption and a lack of commitment to public good and services. He notes that 'local government has not escaped the insidious intrusion of patronage networks that have come to characterize all levels of the Sri Lankan polity and to affect the functioning both of the electoral system as well as of the political and bureaucratic institutions at these different levels. These patronage networks have been major contributors to the pervasive corruption that characterizes the Sri Lankan polity and influences its bureaucracy.'[28] Local government, in short, is devoid of local governance, and is a mere extension and creature of the power relationships at the centre. Likewise, the bureaucracy.

CONCLUSION

The current political debate centres around the prospect of negotiations with the LTTE with Norwegian facilitation and against the backdrop of a month-long unilateral cease-fire by LTTE leader Prabhakaran, which has now been extended twice, each time for a further month. In contrast, the government insists that the two sides can talk and fight at the same time. The government is determined to ensure that it will not be inveigled into talks which will be broken off by the LTTE once it is ready and able to resume hostilities. Hard-line opinion, citing the improved performance of the Army as the better mechanism for conflict resolution, and the possibility of a UK ban on the Tigers are contributory factors. Another key element in the current political configuration is the rising cost of living, dire prognostications of worse to come. The debate also centres on Opposition and civil-society demands for independent commissions to deal with the public service, elections, the judiciary and the police.

The degree of international interest and pressure is such that both sides may have to commence talks or risk a debilitating war of attrition in the future. Both protagonists as well as the UNP Opposition favour talks, but the modalities are yet to be worked out. No doubt, political, economic and military exigencies will determine this. It is clear, though, that the need of the hour is to commence a process of negotiation. It is also clear that negotiations are not a panacea, but they do hold out the promise of a process culminating in peace, laying the foundations for democratic, pluralist governance. There will be pitfalls and challenges on the way, including public acceptance and support for the final constitutional settlement and the method of its enactment.[29]

On all fronts, the attitude towards governance has to undergo a paradigm shift. The establishment of independent commissions, for example, will not in itself ensure governance. The Commission on Bribery and Corruption established by the current government is a case in point of an institution established with great fanfare and paralysed from the outset. The Human Rights Commission also established by the government has yet to reach anywhere near its potential, and the office of the Ombudsman (whose powers were augmented through government legislation), was resource-starved and is now vacant. Moreover, there is the persistent problem of appointment to commissions. Were it to be done by politicians, the pernicious influence of political patronage could undermine them.

The partisan politicization of all aspects of governance needs to be combated. With its zero-sum culture, inherent fear and suspicion of pluralism and diversity, it is central to the crisis of legitimacy of both institutions and processes of government, and hence of governance in Sri Lanka. This will entail internal party democracy and the strengthening of those institutions meant to serve as checks and balances on the exercise of executive power and authority. It will also entail an espousal of meaningful devolution and power sharing as a sine qua non of peace and prosperity. An end to the conflict is a necessary condition for democratic governance in Sri Lanka. It is by no means sufficient, though. Yet, with it, the crucial paradigm shift in the political culture will have space to expand and be consolidated.

As Wanasinghe observes, 'Fifty years after Independence, a democratic way of life in Sri Lanka has yet to be institutionalized as a viable system of governance.' He goes on to contend that:

> . . . the experience of the first half of the century of independence has, thus, underscored the need for a strategy for the enforcement, by the citizens, of continued vigilance and accountability over the political institutions at the different levels as well as over their administrative apparatus. This is a prerequisite for the Sri Lankan polity to cease being a parody of democracy and to begin to evolve as a functioning democracy.[30]

Ultimately, it is a matter of the polity reconciling the governance it desires with what it believes it deserves.

NOTES

1. See also Paikiasothy Saravanamuttu, 'Sri Lanka: The Intractability of Ethnic Conflict', in John Darby and Roger Mac Ginty, eds., *The Management of Peace Processes*, London: Macmillan Press, 2000, pp. 195–227.
2. A valuable collection of essays on all aspects of constitutional reform in Sri Lanka is Chanaka Amaratunga, ed., *Ideas for Constitutional Reform*, Council for Liberal Democracy, Sri Lanka, and Friedrich Naumann Stiftung, 1989.
3. For analyses of the events leading up to the 1987 Indo-Sri Lanka Accord and the attempts at negotiations, see Ketheshwaran Loganathan, *Sri Lanka: Lost Opportunities*, Colombo: Centre for Policy Research and Analysis, University of Colombo, 1996; Kumar Rupesinghe, ed., *Negotiating Peace in Sri Lanka: Efforts, Failures & Lessons*, International Alert of London, February 1998; Robert I. Rotberg, ed., *Creating Peace in Sri Lanka: Civil War & Reconciliation*, Brookings Institution Press, 1999 and Paikiasothy Saravanamuttu, 'Instability in Sri Lanka', *Survival*, vol. XXXII, no 5, September/October 1990, London: Brassey's International Institute for Strategic Studies.
4. 'Government has no intention of Suppressing People through Emergency Regulations—President', *Daily News*, 4 May 2000, 'War footing' effective from 3 May 2000. The price of diesel went up by 25 per cent, kerosene by 48 per cent, LP gas by Rs. 30 per cylinder and bus fares by 15 per cent in February: 8 and 9 February 2000, *Island*. Following the 5 per cent devaluation of the rupee, prices of consumer items went up by 10 per cent in June: 20 June 2000, *Island*. A 20 per cent increase in the price of industrial gas followed in November and the price of diesel and kerosene was increased by a further Rs 2: 15, 16 and 19 November 2000. See the Budget Speech for details on defence expenditure: *Daily News*, 9 March 2001.
5. 'Sri Lanka Lagging Behind Asian Economies Because of War', *Daily News*, 4 May 2000.
6. '25 Killed in Mob Attack on Detention Camp', *Daily News*, 26 October 2000. 'Twenty Years of the Prevention of Terrorism Act', monograph of the seminar held on 11 December 1999 by the Centre for Policy Alternatives.
7. 'Britain Bans the LTTE', *The Island*, 1 March 2001. The list of 21 'terrorist' organizations was announced on 28 February. 'The Need for a British ban on the LTTE, *Daily News*, 1 March 2001. The United States proscribed the LTTE on 8 October 1997. India banned the LTTE in May 1992, and thereafter extended the ban every two years, as required.
8. Ministry of Justice and Constitutional Affairs, *Draft Provisions of the Constitution Containing the Proposals of the Government of Sri Lanka Relating to Devolution of Power, Including a Commentary on the Draft Constitutional Provisions*, 38978–50, 000(96/01), p 28.
9. 'TULF Under Pressure', *Daily Mirror*, 7 August 2000. The TULF adopted a resolution to oppose the bill due to its inadequacies regarding three key factors—the structure of the state, the unit of devolution, and the question of land.
10. 'Ranil Proposes Interim Council for North and East', *Daily News*, 19 November 1999. See also, *Daily News*1, 7, 8, 15 and 20 December 1999. Also Paikiasothy Saravanamuttu, 'Sri Lanka in 1999', *Asian Survey*, vol. XL, no 1, January/February 2000, pp. 219–25.

11. See Rohan Edrisinha, 'Constitutionalism, Pluralism and Ethnic Conflict' in Rotberg, ed., op. cit., pp. 169–89 and 'Federalism and the Case for Radical Constitutional Reform in Sri Lanka', in K.M. de Silva and G.H. Peiris, *Pursuit of Peace in Sri Lanka: Past Failures and Future Prospects,* International Centre for Ethnic Studies, 2000, pp. 163–83.
12. 'Prabhakaran Should Give Up his Politics of Terror and Come to the Negotiating Table—President', *Daily News*, 31 December 1999.
13. 'Prabhakaran Offers Talks at "Heroes Day" Speech', *Island*, 28 November 1999.
14. See *Daily Mirror*, 5 August 2000, and *Island*, 6 August 2000.
15. 'Ministers Rebel over reforms', *Sunday Leader*, 6 August 2000; 'Electoral Reforms Bill Withdrawn' *Island*, 9 August 2000.
16. 'Equal Opportunities Bill will Not be Tabled in Parliament, AG assures court', *Island*, 19 October 1999. See also *Daily News*, of 19 October 1999 and *Sunday Observer*, 10 and 17 October 1999.
17. H.L Seneviratne, *The Work of Kings: The New Buddhism in Sri Lanka*, Chicago: University of Chicago Press, 1999.
18. 'President Kumaratunga Bares her Heart out to the People', *Daily News*, 5 January 2000.
19. Paikiasothy Saravanamuttu, 'Sri Lanka: Civil Society, the Nation and State Building Challenge', in Alison Van Rooy, ed., *Civil Society and the Aid Industry*, London: Earthscan Publiations, 1998, pp. 104–33.
20. 'D.M. Fires Bombshell at Two Ministers', *Daily Mirror*, 6 October 2000, 'Hakeem Condemns Mass Scale Rigging, Violence', *Island*, 11 October 2000; 'Verdict Not Free and Fair', *Sunday Leader*, 15 October 2000.
21. 'Commission of Inquiry into Kandy Election Violence', *Daily News*, 30 October 2000; 'Was it Free and Fair, editorial, *Island*, 12 October 2000; 'Most Serious Election Violence Reported from Central Province', *Daily Mirror*, 13 October 2000; 'Prompt Action on Alleged Election Offences in Kandy', *Daily News*, 11 October 2000. See the EU Electoral Observation Mission to Sri Lanka, Final Report, 10 October 2000 Parliamentary Election.
22. 'Join Hands for New Political Culture Devoid of Violence and Terror', *Daily News*, 30 September 2000.
23. 'Vote Against Violence, say Religious Leaders', *Island*, 5 October 2000. 'Election Related Violence on the Increase'—Centre for Monitoring Election Violence (CMEV), *Island*, 18 September 2000, the CMEV is made up of the Centre for Policy Alternatives (CPA), the Free Media Movement (FMM) and the Coalition Against Political Violence. All its election monitoring reports can be accessed on http://www.cpalanka.org. Since it called for the annulment of the January 1999 North-Western Provincial Council election, CMEV has been accused of being partisan by the ruling PA and regularly attacked by the PA in the state-controlled media. The CMEV was threatened with criminal defamation in the aftermath of this provincial council election: 'Two Senior Ministers to Sue Centre for Monitoring Election Violence for Criminal Defamation', *Daily News*, 28 January 1999. Also see 'Party Leader Must Insist on Non-Violence—Peoples Action for Free and Fair Elections (PAFFREL)', *Island*, 27 August 2000. The PAFFREL monitors elections with the Movement for Free and Fair Elections (MFFE).
24. 'Paris Forum Focuses on Four Development Areas', *Daily News*, 15 December 2000.

25. 'Misuse of State Resources by the Government for Election Purposes', C.A. No. 1215/99 filed on 9 December, 1999; 'Samurdhi Niyamakas Cannot be Used for Elections', *Weekend Express*, 18 December 1999: court order issued on 17 December 1999.
26. World Bank, 'Sri Lanka: Recapturing Missed Opportunities', Report no 20430-CE, 16 June 16 2000, p 36.
27. Ibid., p 37.
28. Shelton Wanasinghe, 'Effective Local Governance: The Foundation for a Functioning Democracy in Sri Lanka', Research Studies: Governance Series No. 5, Institute of Policy Studies, May 1999, p. 5.
29. Centre for Policy Alternatives, *A Commentary- Seminar Series on Structure and Processes of Negotiations: Some Lessons & Reflections*, January 2001; and *PA-UNP Consensus on the Constitution*, Centre for Policy Alternatives, forthcoming. See also, Jayadeva Uyangoda, 'A Political Culture of Conflict', in Rotberg op. cit., n. 3 above, pp. 157–68 and Liz Philipson 'Breaking Recurring Themes in the Cycles of War and Peace in Sri Lanka', Research Paper 3, The Centre for the Study of Global Governance, The London School of Economics and Political Science.
30. Wanasinghe, op. cit., n. 28 above, pp. 2 and 3.

CHAPTER 7

The Crisis of Security and Governance in South Asia

P.R. Chari

AN OVERVIEW

The foregoing country studies have focused on different aspects of the interface between security and governance in South Asia; they offer country perspectives by the authors contributing to this volume, but there is no running theme discernible in them. To recapitulate,

- Amena Mohsin urges that the State institutions and processes concerned with governance in Bangladesh are responsible for its misgovernance. The politicization of ethnic and religious minorities and polarization in the majority Bengali community has undermined people's security. A greater democratization of State institutions is urged.
- Meenakshi Gopinath argues within the human security paradigm to urge that that the contemporary challenge to governance arises from the need to respect diversity. She describes a melange of issues pertaining to the management of security, the culture of militarism, and artificial demarcation of internal and external security to depict the crisis of governance in India.
- Lok Raj Baral discusses socio-political plurality in Nepal to interrogate the commitment of the ruling elite to good governance. Inattention to non-conventional sources of insecurity widens social and economic disparities inside the country and compromises the sovereignty of its citizens.
- Shahrukh Rafi Khan argues that devolution of powers to the grassroots in Pakistan requires more radical reform of its civil services, judiciary and electoral processes, and a major redistribution of assets. Devolution should be made to the lowest tier for ensuring good governance and human security.

- Paikaisothy Saravanamuttu's paper on Sri Lanka urges that the State's problems of governance arise from a failure to accept the pluralism of its society guaranteed by the Constitution, political institutions and cultural traditions. Pluralism and diversity must be institutionalized to derive strength for meeting its problems of security and governance.

These essays highlight the verity that a civilizational unity binds the subcontinent together, which also explains the vulnerability of its nations to similar national security threats. The inadequacy of governance processes constitutes a major threat to the security of these States and their people. Common causes underlie this crisis of governance, like the decay of political parties and democratic institutions; venality of the ruling elite and their indifference to the commonweal; resistance to devolution and decentralization of powers to the people; unimaginative dealing with minority populations; perversion of the electoral process; and the nexus between criminals and corrupt bureaucrats, politicians, and businessmen. The crisis of governance in South Asia obtains in all its countries: the difference is only one of scale, but the resulting atrophy of the administrative system underlies State and human insecurity in the region.

The authors were unanimous that a crisis of governance afflicts South Asia. The ruling elite was held squarely responsible for this parlous state of affairs, as they are impelled by no higher motive for seeking power than personal aggrandizement. Hence, the imperative need for greater democratization of the polity. Misgovernance and insecurity were linked. Misgovernance derived from such disparate phenomena as the disintegration of institutions, erosion of the parliamentary system, lack of internal democracy in political parties, commercialization of politics, and the pervasive corruption in the various adjuncts of the ruling elite.

The paradox is that whilst all the countries of South Asia, with the present exception of Pakistan, have democratic governments, their governance is not truly democratic. Except for India and Sri Lanka, democracy has not sent down strong roots in the region. No doubt, elections are relatively free and fair; participatory politics and support to those elected also exists. But if the South Asian countries were adjudged by their adherence to the standards of *liberal* democracy 'marked not only by free and fair elections, but also by the rule of law, a separation of powers, and the protection of basic liberties of speech, assembly, religion, and property',[1] they could only qualify as indifferently practising democracies.

The crisis of governance is manifested by pervasive nepotism and corruption; misappropriation of State funds for personal or familial or sectarian purposes to the detriment of the larger community; absence of transparency and accountability in public administration; lack of respect for the rule of law and ethical behaviour in public life; and a reluctance to delegate administrative or financial powers to grass-roots organizations. Max Weber described such situations as distinguishing a

> . . . patrimonial form of government: a form of government that originated in the royal household in which the ruler is not constrained by the rule of law, treats the state as a personal possession, and the affairs of the state is conducted according to his whims. . . . All power was concentrated in the hands of the monarch/dictator, all the officials of the state held office during the pleasure of the dictator and were responsible to him, and those loyal to him were rewarded by state patronage i.e. jobs, contracts, loans, opportunities for illegal gains, import permits and business licenses.[2]

This situation obtains in all the South Asian countries, which is likely to deteriorate when burgeoning globalization spreads its tentacles into the region; its rentier classes will ensure greater public malfeasance taking place with a consequent diminution of security in its several dimensions.

The continuing feudal character of South Asian society lies at the heart of this problem: only the trappings of modernization have occurred over the last half century, but the core values and mental attitudes of its leadership remains firmly embedded in the past. Apropos, modern society is defined as 'one in which at least the following characteristics must be present:

- Dignity of the individual;
- Adherence to universalistic norms;
- Elevation of individual achievement over privilege or disprivileges of birth;
- Accountability in public life.'[3]

Proceeding further, the manner in which the Indian middle class, expected to provide leadership to the country, acquiesced in the Emergency imposed by Indira Gandhi in the mid-1970 exposed its pusillanimity at one level, but also its inherent authoritarian impulses. Consequently, to expect the favoured classes to be altruistic and usher in true modernisation, is somewhat like whistling for the moon. To put it bluntly, the Indian middle class has no desire to alter the pre-modern attitude that exists in India when it comes to relations between people. In fact, they have a lot to lose and nothing substantial to gain should modernity come about.[4]

This is equally applicable to other South Asian nations. Feudal mores inform the region's ruling classes, which explains why the military aspects of security find greater resonance in them. It also predisposes them to view concepts like human security and humane governance with deep scepticism.

The inadequacy, however, of a military approach to national security in South Asia is becoming clearer for at least four reasons that derive from the seminal changes that have occurred in the international security regime.

- First, the locus of conflict has shifted from the external to the internal sphere, with non-military and non-traditional threats to security acquiring greater salience. They include such dissimilar threats to national security as

  > . . . cross-border movements of population; ethno-political, socio-economic, and communal-religious politics; terrorism, with its seminal linkages to money-laundering operations, and drugs/arms smuggling; environmental degradation spawning its related problems of deforestation and desertification; internal migration; chaotic urbanisation; and so on.[5]

  These non-military and non-traditional sources of insecurity could spark off widespread social conflict, but have not received much academic or official attention. A shift in emphasis from the military to the non-military paradigm of security is important, since

  > . . . the focus changes from security through armaments to security through human development; from territorial security to food, employment and environmental security. The fundamental components of human security—the security of people against threats to life, health, livelihood, personal safety and human dignity—can be put at risk by external aggression, but also by factors within a country. . .[6]

- Second, a new relevance has been acquired by transnational sources of conflict in South Asia; they transcend national boundaries and constitute major threats to national security. They include, apart from non-military and non-traditional threats, cross-border threats to security like the proliferation of light weapons, explosives and mines that are closely linked to the global trade in arms and drugs, international terrorism and money-laundering. The Cold War witnessed arms and drugs smuggling (besides support to religious terrorism) becoming instruments of State policy; this virus has spread quickly through the region. National governments have a limited capacity to deal with this range of security threats, highlighting the need for regional and international cooperation to mitigate them.

- Third, a new conceptualization of national security has occurred. Human security or the security of the individual is gaining increasing recognition, with the focus shifting from 'the protection of territorial integrity and political sovereignty from external aggression . . . to include people's security'.[7] Poverty and deprivation exacerbate the problem of human security in South Asia. The dismal statistics relating to infant mortality, illiteracy, population growth and gender discrimination are too well known to bear reiteration. They reveal the limited access of the people to food security, basic health and educational facilities. Unfortunately, the military security fixation of the regional elite pre-empts scarce resources for military, not human security. It would become increasingly difficult, however, for the regional governments to ignore the rising expectations of their people for a better quality of life. The electronic media and the revolution in information technology would ensure that their aspirations would strengthen, generate frustration, and incite violence.
- Fourth, Cold War dynamics also informed the national security decision-making elite in South Asia, with the competing East-West blocs using arms transfers to equip their client states against external and internal threats. Their ruling elite, thus, developed a vested interest in reinforcing the centrality of the State and appropriating its powers. Wisdom dictates that plural societies in a democratic framework be governed by decentralizing and circumscribing the powers of the State. The grant of a larger measure of autonomy to minority and ethnic populations would protect them from the tyranny of the majority and knit together the State more firmly than by deploying military force. The natural inclination of governments in South Asia, however, is to use force against signs of dissidence in the body politic rather than introspect on its causes and the failures of governance they portend.

Thus, difficult choices confront the State in mediating between military and non-military security and providing for human security when resources are scarce and need to be apportioned between competing demands. National security should obviously be assured from external and internal threats, but so must human security by strengthening the social and economic sectors of the economy. Instead of confronting these hard choices, the facile tendency of South Asian governments has been to deflect attention from their inadequacies by externalizing security threats and exaggerating the malevolence of their neighbours in exacerbating them. In practice, however, the relative weights to be accorded to the external and internal components of national security would vary from country to country. The external, including nuclear, aspects of military security are important for India and Pakistan, although the internal aspects have required greater attention in the last decade. For Sri Lanka, internal security is of primary significance, with its Sinhala-Tamil ethnic conflict showing no signs of abatement. Internal rather than external security threats are of greater relevance to Nepal, Bangladesh, Bhutan and the Maldives. Human security issues are of obvious relevance to all the South Asian countries.

THE NATURE OF THE CRISIS

The crisis of governance in the region largely arises from the inability of its States to govern, in contrast to rule, which enfeebles their ability to ensure human security but strengthens inhumane governance in the region. There are several facets of this phenomenon.

- First, the inability to govern has led these States to view citizen's protests against misrule as challenges to their authority that require to be suppressed. Such paranoia has reflected in large accretions to their police and paramilitary forces in terms of numbers, equipment and budgetary allocations. The intelligence agencies have also grown and are widely being used to sustain the ruling parties in power. The politicization of the administrative services, police, paramilitary forces and intelligence services over the years has greatly eroded their credibility, and they are generally perceived to be the political instruments of the party in power. This impression is reinforced by wholesale changes in the upper administrative echelons, corresponding to a spoils system, occurring whenever a regime change takes place.
- Second, there are identifiable enclaves in South Asia—Karachi,

north-east India, Bihar, eastern Uttar Pradesh, the Chittagong Hill Tracts, eastern Nepal, and the Jaffna peninsula—where the writ of the central authority is uncertain. This listing comprises insurgency areas, but also others where the administrative system has ceased to exist. A variety of militant groups, criminal mafias and local warlords have replaced the State here; their intimate links with the ruling elite aggravates this vacuum in the governance of the country.

- Third, instances do obtain when the security forces are not the solution, but the problem for ensuring human security in South Asia. It is well-known that the Punjab police in India 'might have managed to break the back of the terrorist movement in the state but, in the process, has become a terrorist outfit itself'.[8] This could also be said of Kashmir, where the surrendered militants were formed into a vigilante force permitting the 'co-optation of anti-social elements into the governance processes as the price for ceasing their resistance to the State',[9] and are much feared by the local population.

The crisis of governance in South Asia encapsulates these other dimensions of security threat to the State and its individuals. The erosion of the governance processes enfeebles the capacity of the State to administer and deliver social services. *A tour d'horizon* of the region reveals that its crisis of governance has a common aetiology. Three major symptoms of this malaise that have serious implications for national security are discussed below.

1. Crumbling of democratic institutions.
2. Alienation of minority populations.
3. Nexus between corrupt elements in the governing apparatus.

CRUMBLING OF DEMOCRATIC INSTITUTIONS

It has been perceptively noted that: 'the current restoration of representative regimes [in South Asia] has . . . to be viewed in a longer perspective in order to emphasise both the fragility of the process and to caution us against over-optimism'.[10] Coalition governments seem most likely to achieve power in India and Nepal in the foreseeable future; they have proved too weak and indecisive to provide the leadership needed for adequately ensuring human security. Being vulnerable to arbitrary demands made by their coalition partners and by their own parties makes it difficult for them to reach consensus or make the sacrifices needed to adequately provide military and human security.

Further, the Opposition parties in the region are notorious for indulging in irresponsible politics; often, they have opposed the very policies they had promoted in power only to embarrass the government of the day.

A different set of problems obtains in Pakistan and Bangladesh. Both countries were under long periods of military rule, which obtains in Pakistan since October 1999. Indeed, the transfer of power from a military to a civilian government or vice versa has never occurred in these countries by constitutional means. Hence their civilian governments are inherently fragile, with the military occupying an overweening presence in the background. Ironically, the population welcomed the military government when it re-established itself in Pakistan, which is a revealing indictment of the preceding venal civilian governments.

The role of the military is critical in the governance of Sri Lanka since its civilian governments are unable to bridge the country's ethnic divide, requiring their dependence on the armed and police forces to ensure the stability of the government. These forces often function outside civilian control, which is a reality that is accepted. A similar situation obtains in Nepal, with the armed forces owing primary allegiance to the monarch and the civilian government hesitating to exercise control over them. Witness the inability of the elected government to use the armed forces against the Maoist movement in the country.

This militarization of South Asian States weakens the democratic forces in their polity. This process could accelerate with the political parties decaying and their grass-roots organizations withering away. Power is now being acquired by politicians, not from the people, but from power brokers and sectional elite who deliver votes during the elections, and exact a price if their candidate succeeds in gaining public office. The limited purpose of this new political class is to derive legitimacy through the ballot box: once elected, their hold over power is blatantly misused to seek personal and familial advantage by garnering the resources of the State. The politics of manipulation has replaced the politics of mass appeal, enfeebling its democratic and heightening its unrepresentative character.

This flawed manner of choosing the people's representatives reflects in the farcical manner in which legislatures function in South Asia; devoid of sanctity, they are a travesty of being called the 'temples of democracy'. The exhibition of lung and muscle power within legislative chambers has made legislators the object of ridicule rather than respect. Hardly a session passes without its quota of walkouts, deadlocks, suspension of proceedings, forced adjournments and sometimes violence. Attendance by legislators is minimal, and maintaining the quorum is difficult: indeed, proceedings are often known to continue without a quorum and without any objections being raised. Legislators use their time during the sessions to do everything except legislate. The passage of laws and budgets without debate, and issue of ordinances during inter-session periods, reveals the pathetic state of legislative functioning in South Asia.

An offshoot of the politics of manipulation replacing the politics of mass appeal is the co-optation of the civil services into working this system. The district magistrate was the backbone of the colonial administration, owing allegiance to the British Indian regime and enjoying its complete trust. This extended to control over the district administrative machinery and unfettered use of discretionary powers to exercise that authority. This patriarchal administrative system did not survive the post-Independence reality that power had to be exercised through political authority and its representatives. The tragedy is that no effort was made to undertake systemic reforms in South Asia; the reports of committees for this purpose were either ignored or token action taken on them. The monumental Administrative Reforms Commission Report drawn up in India during the late 1960s is an object lesson in cynicism—it remains shelved.

The ad hoc policies pursued thereafter to refashion the administrative machinery have led to dissatisfaction all around, whilst the fall in efficiency and probity continues. Instead, the politicization of the administration continues, with the civil services becoming the tools of the political parties. Phrased differently, the colonial paradigm of a merit-based civil service was founded on the twin pillars of an impartial and politically neutral administration. This model was destined to fail when democratic elections based on adult franchise legitimized a self-serving political class interested in using the civil services for party and personal ends. The problem now arising is: 'How to include politics in the system of administration so that there is popular participation in government, and yet, exclude politics so that it does not use the administration for its narrow ends?'[11] There is no answer to this fundamental question: resultantly, a loss of organizational coherence has occurred.

District police chiefs lose effective control over their station [house] officers who look to their local legislator for protection in return for favours rendered and are disinclined to follow priorities established at the apex level of the organization. In course of time this pattern is repeated all the way up to the top levels, resulting in erasure of the professional expertise which is the *raison d'être* of the bureaucratic organization.[12]

The rapid deterioration in public and civic administration presages the State's incapacity to grapple with increasingly difficult challenges to national security. Instead, an easy propensity exists to strengthen the forces of repression—intelligence, police, paramilitary and armed forces—rather than wrestle with the hard questions involved in providing effective governance, like improving the quality and responsiveness of the administration, eradicating corruption, reducing redundancy in the bureaucracy, and disciplining unruly civil servants.

ALIENATION OF MINORITY POPULATIONS

All South Asian countries face a common problem of accommodating the aspirations of minorities in their political framework, and dealing with conflicts arising from ethnicity related issues. Defining 'ethnicity' is not easy, but a holistic approach recognizes its five components: '(a) a subjective belief in real or assumed historical antecedents; (b) a symbolic or real geographical centre; (c) shared cultural emblems, such as race, language, religion, dress and diet . . . (d) self-ascribed awareness of distinctiveness and belonging to the group; and (e) recognition by others of the group differentiation'.[13] Ethnic affinities are stronger than national identities; ethnicity, therefore, can be easily channelled into dissent and insurrection against the State or violence against other ethnic groups. For instance, the various ethnic movements in north-east India

> . . . have all to do with identity. Some have been fought for outright independence, the outstanding case being the Naga movement. A second lot has something to do with minority communities or sub-nationalities seeking separation not from India but from Assam or Bengal or autonomy within them in order to safeguard their identity (ethnic, linguistic, tribal). The third kind has been struggling to forestall or fight against a demographic transformation as a result of in-migration of foreigners or outsiders.[14]

Ethnic conflict within north-east India has its parallels elsewhere in South Asia. For instance, the secessionist option informs the LTTE-sponsored Eelam movement in Sri Lanka and some militant groups in Kashmir. A greater autonomy demand inspired the Chakma movement in Bangladesh, and the Mizo and Gorkhaland agitations in India that led to the creation of Mizoram and the Darjeeling Hill Council. Similarly, the fear of demographic submersion due to population movements has triggered sporadic violence throughout South Asia, e.g., against Nepali migration into Sikkim, Bhutan and north-east India, or Bangladeshi migration into India of people searching for a better quality of life. The recent carving out of the new states of Uttaranchal, Jharkand and Chattisgarh from Uttar Pradesh, Bihar and Madhya Pradesh connotes the Indian union government's acceptance of the logic that discrete geopolitical units sharing an identity based on civilizational and linguistic congruence need recognition.

The generic reason for ethnic and sectarian resentments is the sense of deprivation and discrimination informing minority groups against the State's political and economic capital being appropriated by the majority community or dominant ethnic group. These convictions have inspired movements in South Asia coming within the three categories listed above. Left unaddressed, these grievances fester and could generate conflicts between adversary ethnic groups, or between them and the State. These social conflicts are exacerbated by the State's inability to govern with any clarity of purpose, which has implications for national security.

Especial mention should be made of a new consciousness of injustice and discrimination informing the rural poor, who had been ruthlessly exploited in the past by feudal elements. The failure to carry out meaningful land reforms in South Asia due to the vested interests in their ruling elite has heightened this sense of deprivation, leading to socially disadvantaged groups organizing themselves to wrest a fair deal. This has led to caste-based violence in backward regions like eastern Uttar Pradesh, Bihar, and eastern Nepal, which could spread across South Asia. Private armies (*senas*) have sprung up in Bihar, to support the exploiting classes. They fall into two categories:

> First and the most common are the armies of the landlords. They employ musclemen to keep the peasants and tenants in their place, and ensure that taxes and rents are paid regularly. Second is the dominant caste Senas or private caste militias or armies, which have become a part of the agrarian struggle in Central Bihar. They are mainly constituted to suppress the militant peasant organisations.[15]

They are opposed by several left extremist organizations that have arisen in India and Nepal, which has imbued this social conflict with a Marxist orientation.

Ironically, the State which is charged with maintaining public order has become a helpless spectator, unable to prevent the open violence in the countryside, or take ameliorative measures to address the underlying agrarian unrest. The failure of security and governance is, therefore, manifest. The inability of the State to maintain law and order through its coercive organs has led to an anarchic situation developing. Many parts of the State are under the control of these combating groups; a form of warlordism also exists, with the State abdicating its authority here. This aspect of the crisis of governance dents both State and human security.

The polarization of political forces on caste and sectarian lines is growing apace in South Asia and weakening its civilizational ethos premised on tolerance and moderation. This polarization is fissiparous in its effects and militates against the inclusive culture of the region. The dangers emanating from the growth of fundamentalist forces in South Asia—Muslim, Hindu, Sikh and Buddhist—are reflective, perhaps, of a global phenomenon, viz., religious revivalism in the international system. A thoughtful view holds that:

> Two things unite their [religious groups] outlook and purpose. First, the movement is a reaction against the alienation of the leaders from the masses and the development of a two-tiered society: a privileged, westernised and self-seeking urban elite . . . and the vast majority who live below the poverty line. . . . And, second, while committed to the ideal of democratic governance and popular accountability, they [religious groups] are convinced that the terms of constitutional discourse are alien and incomprehensible to the great majority of the people and must therefore be made to reflect indigenous social and religious experience.[16]

These assertions are undeniable, and it is unlikely that these developments will abate in South Asia.

Our concern is with the sectarian violence distinguishing this phenomenon, which is often encouraged by the State. It is easy for the ruling elite to imbue an ethnic movement with a communal dimension to besmirch both as anti-nationalist: this informs majoritarian sentiments against the minorities to strengthen their support base. Examples of this phenomenon abound in South Asia: Sunnis in Pakistan stigmatizing Shias, Hindus in India branding Muslims and Sikhs as anti-national, and so on. The backlash against these developments has resulted in the mobilization of the minority communities (Sikhs, Jaffna Tamils, tribals and backward/Scheduled Castes) which aggravates social conflicts. Secularism may not be on the retreat in South Asia, but its weakening is clearly visible.

The patronage of religious terrorists by Pakistan (Harkat-ul-Ansar and Lashkar-e-Toiba) has led to a predictable reaction in India and the encouragement of the Shiv Sena and other Sangh 'Parivar' ('family') organizations like the Vishwa Hindu Parishad and the Bajrang Dal. Sikh extremist demands for a separate State (Khalistan) have abated, but the association of Sinhala extremism with the Buddhist clergy continues in Sri Lanka. These ideological predilections have become politicized due to bloc voting by different communities for candidates belonging to their religious persuasion, thereby widening cleavages and heralding greater sectarian strife in future in South Asia.

The distressing aspect of sectarian and communal strife is the partisan role of the State in dealing with it. That such a policy is short-sighted and designed for marginal political gains is apparent. In the context of India and Hindu fundamentalism, it has been noted that. 'The greater harm that can befall India from the pursuit of a narrowly defined nationalistic vision lies with the Hindu society itself. The divides within the Hindu faith, on account of castes and languages, are many. And each one of them is a potential faultline along which confrontations can be launched.'[17] Hence, religious fundamentalism carries the seeds of their own aggravation and destruction. Disconcertingly, however, divisiveness within the State cannot leave its integrity unaffected.

NEXUS BETWEEN CORRUPT ELEMENTS IN THE GOVERNING APPARATUS

The accumulated black money (unaccounted income) in South Asia now constitutes a parallel economy. The inability of the State to unravel this economy and proceed against tax-evaders exemplifies the bonding between corrupt politicians, officials and businessmen to defraud the exchequer. Their linkage in the matter of defence purchases and contracts is common knowledge in the region; the national-interest plea has conveniently been taken by governments to maintain opacity in such cases. Looking into the future, enormous sums of money would be involved in divestment of the public sector, deregulation of industry, and undertaking large-scale infrastructural and developmental schemes as the liberalization and globalization of the South Asian economies proceed further. Past experience informs that the scale of malfeasance would also be enormous. One judgement holds that 'all the agencies dealing with corruption, tax evasion, smuggling and other economic offences have been so politicised over the decades that prompt and proper action against the politicians is the exception rather than the rule'.[18]

This judgment, expressed in regard to India, is applicable to the entire region, although a few salutary exceptions have occurred with the conviction and sentencing of three past Prime Ministers, one past President,[19] and some other notables. It would be fair to concede, however, that these cases were the exception rather than the rule in South Asia. The rule, illustrated in innumerable other cases, has been for these worthies to avoid investigation into their misdeeds, delay their progress by the investigating authorities, then delay cases if they reach the courts by various judicial devices, and, finally, occasion more delays by appealing to higher judicial authorities should the judgment be adverse. The proverbial tardiness of the judicial process greatly assists these machinations.

The resulting politicization of crime exacerbates both the crisis of governance in South Asia and its security *problématique* in at least two ways:

- First, by accentuating the virtual immobility of the State in dealing with the growing challenges to national security, especially internal and human security. Indeed, the State organs have often become part of the problem. For instance, the police services are widely perceived as part of the State's machinery to oppress the poor, not protect them from exploitation.

  > In such circumstances the police are feared as much as the criminals... [T]o the extent that the police may connive with and protect criminals and be used by the ruling political party and by men of property to promote their interests, the forces of law and order are seen to be part of the problem of the criminalisation of society rather than its solution.[20]

  But the police and paramilitary forces continue to appropriate increasing budgetary outlays despite their patent inadequacies leading to the breakdown of law and order in large parts of the region. Disconcertingly, the paltry additions to social sector outlays and its poor management illustrate the low priority accorded to human security by the regional governments.
- Second, the criminalization of politics and its linked phenomenon, the politicization of crime, have pervaded South Asia: this greatly reduces the State's capacity to ensure national security. The entry of criminal elements into the legislative chambers and cabinets at the

federal and provincial levels should raise deep concern. This largely explains the incapacity of the State to maintain law and order and assure the physical security of its citizens, which is the most basic function of the State. The inability of the State to arrest and prosecute criminals with political connections or politicians with criminal antecedents with any celerity delineates this problem. The celebrated Vohra Committee Report[21] informed that

> . . . there has been a rapid spread and growth of criminal gangs, armed 'senas' (armies), drug Mafias, smuggling gangs, drug peddlers and economic lobbies in the country which have, over the years, developed an extensive network of contacts with the bureaucrats/Government functionaries at the local levels, politicians, media persons and strategically located individuals in the non-State sector. . . . DIB (Director Intelligence Bureau) has stated that the network of the Mafia is virtually running a parallel government, pushing the State apparatus into irrelevance.

The report concludes that 'The various crime Syndicates/Mafia organisations have developed significant muscle and money power and established linkages with governmental functionaries, political leaders and others to be able to operate with impunity.' This indictment of the Indian political system has not bestirred any systemic reform by the Indian Government; recurrent exposures of links between criminals, bureaucrats, businessmen and politicians only confirm the growing expansion of this criminalization process.

A study of narco-politics in Pakistan is also instructive;[22] it points out that no consensus was possible in the government on taking steps against drug trafficking. Frequent transfers of honest officials in the Pakistan Narcotics Control Board (PNCB) and the Anti-Narcotics Force eroded the legitimacy of political parties and people's faith in the democratic process. Another investigative report[23] informed that the drugs-army nexus was fuelled by an identity of mutual interests; the army's need for narco-money to pursue its strategic interests in Afghanistan found congruence with the mafia's interests in ensuring the safe transport of its drugs. Apparently, 'Vehicles of the army-controlled National Logistics Cell and those used to supply arms to Mujahideen have also been used as drug carriers. The PCNB and other agencies do not have the authority to check these vehicles and so they were the safest means for drug transportation.'[24]

The situation pertaining to criminalization of politics in Nepal,

Bangladesh and Sri Lanka may differ in scale, but is little different in character, establishing that the inner processes of governance in South Asia have been infiltrated. This should be a matter of concern as it could affect their national security by providing opportunities for foreign elements to influence their decision-making processes. In other words, the entry of criminals, national and international, into governing structures can provide transnational forces entry into the governing structures in South Asia, which could prejudice their national security in a direct fashion.

The question now becomes germane why people elect criminals to the legislatures, which enables them to enter Cabinets and the inner processes of governance. It would be naive to believe that the voters are unaware of their dubious character and antecedents; this would assume that the voters are collectively gullible and ignorant about the general reputation of the candidates. A counsel of despair would suggest that the lack of suitable alternative candidates is responsible for this state of affairs. Or is it possible that voters are intimidated? Or that their judgment is swayed by caste, class and communal loyalties? It is arguable, however, that South Asian citizens are not averse to electing criminals, if they can 'deliver the goods' and exercise patronage to benefit the elector. It has been realistically, if cynically, urged that

> we, in India, do not elect representatives but patrons. Both the rich and the avaricious, as well as the poor and the stricken, vote on this principle. . . .[E]fficiency, diligence and adherence to norms and procedures are of little significance in the Indian context. They are all right if you are an underachiever with negligible ambitions, but not otherwise. It is fine if one wishes to lead one's life incognito, but to make a mark it is essential to seek out a patron.[25]

This leads to the conclusion that reversing the increasing criminalization of politics in the coming years is difficult, if not futile.

The implications of this assessment are profound for governance and security in South Asia. The criminalization of politics affects the processes of governance by immobilizing the State. The entry of criminals into the legislatures and cabinets hollows out the State from within, strengthening the nexus between the pillars of government and anti-social elements. Left unattended this is a prescription for 'failing' or 'failed' States emerging. The nexus between the military, jihadist groups and organized crime in Pakistan foretells a serious crisis brewing in that country. An international dimension obtains in this matter. Interpol has informed the US Congress that:

Structural links between political terrorism and traditional criminal activity, such as drugs trafficking, armed robbery or extortion have come increasingly to the attention of law enforcement authorities, security agencies and political decision makers. There is a fairly accepted view in the international community that in recent years, direct state sponsorship has declined, therefore terrorists increasingly have to resort to other means of financing, including criminal activities, in order to raise funds.[26]

The lesson here for the South Asian countries is that encouragement of terrorism in their neighbours is sowing dragon seeds that would ultimately promote their own instability. The cancerous growth engendered within the system would become difficult to reverse, but the consequent erosion of the governance processes would only aggravate State and human security.

A FINAL WORD

The dangers to governance and security from the criminalization of politics and the politicization of crime in South Asia need greater recognition. The transnational aspect of this threat underlines the need for greater regional and international cooperation to combat its menace. This is necessary because national, regional and international criminal groups and terrorists are increasingly forging links for mutual profit. Law enforcement, consequently, has to function in an undefined national/international zone, which is difficult and costly. Money-laundering, for instance, underpins the illegal activities associated with drugs and arms smuggling; trafficking in human beings and similar nefarious activities have profound implications for governance and security. But they cannot be effectively proceeded against unless countries cooperate with each other to collectively devise an integrated strategy that addresses their economic, social and legal dimensions. Recognition by SAARC of the fuller contours of this crisis of governance in the region and its serious implications for national security is important. This could, hopefully, inform the regional countries to collectively devise national and regional measures to mitigate the problem.

A greater recognition is also required that the crisis of governance in South Asia also derives from inadequate understanding of the region's essential genius to tolerate a multicultural society; adequate space was always available in the region for plural societies and diverse communities to live together in amity and peace. The post-Independence political compulsions seem to have dictated, however, the evolution of divisive societies that are fragile and degenerate into social conflict and violence derived premised on caste, class, and communal particularities. If multiculturalism in the plural societies of South Asia is to be preserved, its governance processes must consciously create space for its practice. A new context is provided, therefore, for greater devolution and decentralization of administrative, political and economic powers to minority groups on the peripheries of the State. In short, enlarging local autonomy and accommodating the sectional interests in the State must be recognized as the *sine qua non* for good governance and security in South Asia.

All this may seem hopelessly idealistic, but the alternative of creating new political entities like states, union territories, autonomous regions, autonomous districts and so on to defuse movements for greater sovereignty, as is being attempted in India, offers no viable solution to the issue. In truth, the underlying problem of enlarging local autonomy and accommodating sectional interests would only be transferred to another level, ignoring the basic issue of strengthening multiculturalism. Indeed, the new political entities created would be less equipped to handle the problems of devolution and decentralization due to their more acute lack of resources.

The essential question remains whether the governments in South Asia have the political will to reverse the downward trend in their polities. The symptoms, as elaborated above, include the crumbling of democratic institutions, alienation of minorities and the nexus between corrupt elements in their governing elite. The answer is a resounding 'No', but it also needs appreciation that this answer will remain in the negative unless a radical restructuring of their polities occurs. How this will happen is a question whose answer remains in the void.

It is generally believed, however, as urged in the foregoing essays, that the root cause of the crisis of governance and security in South Asia lies embedded in the electoral process. This has been subverted by illicitly acquired money power, which can also buy muscle power. Hence, this dispensation serves the interests of the rich and feudal, apart from organized communal and caste elements. As trenchantly observed, 'The root cause of corruption is the role of black money in politics. Elections have become extremely expensive and all political parties spend huge sums in every election. The need to incur colossal expenditure during elections is often put forward as a justification for making illegal collection. That is, of course, a lame excuse.'[27] Besides, in an era of coalition politics, money is also required to ensure that legislators support the government and not defect to the Opposition by yielding to temptation in times of legislative stress. The politicians' career is also likely to be short-lived, hence, their need to put by funds for an 'office-less' future. The guiding principle for the South Asian politician—with several honourable exceptions, of course—is to earn as much out of a short career in public office as feasible in the quickest possible time. The expense incurred in the elections is treated, therefore, as an investment to be recouped whenever the opportunity presents itself. The electoral laws, specially those concerned with the observance of limits on election expenditure, are, therefore, observed in the breach.

It is agreed on all hands that the requirement for large funds to fight elections has befouled the electoral process in South Asia, but efforts to curb this pernicious tradition have floundered in the past. State funding of elections is unlikely to provide an acceptable solution due to valid suspicions that such funds would be spent in addition to the expenditure incurred by political parties and candidates out of their own resources. The more practicable remedy is an upward revision of the limits to electoral expenditure and a strict observance of these limits by a system of detailed declarations and audit of expenses. Infractions of the electoral laws relating to election expenditure should be prosecuted without exception; currently, they have not proceeded very far due to judicial delays and the availability of appellate courts to indefinitely delay a final decision. Hence, the need obtains to devise a system of administrative tribunals charged with delivering a judgment within specified time frames.

Still, the basic dilemma remains: How can the State reform its governance processes if the State is a party to its misgovernance, and has a vested interest in perpetuating this dispensation? The conclusion is unavoidable that reform would only be possible if the people assert themselves and demand that the country be governed and not ruled, and that the issue of misgovernance is seriously addressed. There is an obvious need for transparency in the government, lack of which is chiefly responsible for the pervasive corruption in the governance processes. Public campaigns to secure the right to information are making a dent in several states of India, which is snowballing into a mass movement. This could spearhead a radical corrective process to reduce corruption and ensure a better standard of public service, which would enhance human security in the region.

What this example informs is that the inadequacies in the governance processes, which are prejudicial to both State and human security, require a greater assertiveness by the people to ensure its rectification. This is perfectly understandable since it is the '*demos*' (people) in democratic societies who are the ultimate repositories of power, hence, greater people's activism and a people's movement to cleanse the governance processes is imperative. Before that can occur, more voices must be raised in South Asia to highlight the dangers attendant upon the current drift into political and administrative anarchy, which inheres in the bonding between misgovernance and insecurity. A conspiracy of silence would only encourage the perpetrators of the deteriorating governance processes, which is presently exacerbating the problem of security in the region.

NOTES

1. Fareed Zakaria, 'The Rise of Illiberal Democracy', *Foreign Affairs*, November/December 1997, p. 22.
2. Gowher Rizvi, 'Democracy, Governance and Civil Society in South Asia', *The Pakistan Development Review*, vol. 33, no. 4, Winter 1994, pp. 599–600.
3. Dipankar Gupta, *Mistaken Modernity: India Between Worlds*, New Delhi: Harper Collins India, 2000, p. 2.
4. Ibid., p. 10. What the author notes regarding India has relevance to the entire South Asian region in view of its common ethos and traditions.
5. P.R. Chari, *Newer Sources of Insecurity: The Crisis of Governance in India*, RCSS Policy Studies 3, Colombo: Regional Centre for Strategic Studies, January, 1998, p. 2.
6. Ramesh Thakur, *Security in the New Millennium*, keynote address, eighth Summer Workshop on Defence, Technology and Cooperative Security in South Asia, Lalitpur, Nepal, 10–20 September, 2000, p. 5.
7. *Security Sector Reform and Development Co-operation: A Conceptual Framework for Enhancing Policy Coherence*, Informal DAC Task Force on Conflict, Peace and Development Co-operation, Organisation for Economic Co-operation and Development, DCD (2000) 4/REVI, p. 3.
8. Ashis Nandy, 'Violence in our Times: In Search of Total Control', *Times of India*, 29 October, 1994.
9. Chari, op. cit., p. 15.
10. Rizvi, op. cit., p. 595.
11. S.K. Das, *Public Office, Private Interest: Bureaucracy and Corruption in India*, New Delhi: Oxford University Press, 2001, p. 223.
12. G.K. Arora, 'Bureaucracy in India: A Time of Troubles', in P.R. Chari, ed., *India: Towards Millennium*, New Delhi: Manohar, 1998, p. 79.
13. Urmila Phadnis, *Ethnicity and Nation-Building in South Asia*, New Delhi: Sage Publications, 1990, p. 14.

14. B.G. Verghese, *India's Northeast Resurgent*, New Delhi: Konark Publishers, 1996, p. 285.
15. Alok Kumar Gupta, 'Senas (Caste Armies) of Bihar', www.ipcs.org/nmt/milgroups/sena-india.html (20 October 2000).
16. Rizvi, op. cit., n. 10 above, p. 623.
17. Verghese Koithara, *Society, State & Security: The Indian Experience*, New Delhi: Sage, 1999, p. 235.
18. S. Swaminathan, 'Economic Offences and the New Class', *The Hindu*, 29 August 1996.
19. They are former Prime Ministers Zulfikar Ali Bhutto and Nawaz Sharif in Pakistan, former Prime Minister Narasimha Rao in India, and past President Ershad in Bangladesh.
20. Rehman Sobhan, 'Problems of Governance in South Asia: An Overview', in V.A. Pai Panandiker, ed., *Problems of Governance in South Asia*, New Delhi: Konark, 2000, p. 16.
21. Government of India, Ministry of Home Affairs, *Vohra Committee Report*, Mimeographed copy dated 5 October 1993.
22. Aabha Dixit, 'Narco Power: Threatening the very Roots of Pakistan', *Strategic Analysis*, vol. no. XN, May 1991.
23. Zahid Hussain, 'Narco Power: Pakistan's Parallel Government', *Newsline* (Karachi) December 1989, reproduced in *Strategic Digest*, New Delhi, June 1990.
24. Op. cit., p. 2495.
25. Gupta, op. cit., n. 3 above, pp. 144–5.
26. Written testimony presented by Ralf Mutschke to the House Subcommittee on Crime on 12 December 2000, 'The Threat Posed by the Convergence of Organised Crime, Drugs Trafficking and Terrorism'. http:/ www.house.gov/judiciary/3.htm.
27. P.S. Appu, 'Need for Thoroughgoing Reforms', *The Hindu*, 26 December, 2000.

Select Bibliography

Amena Mohsin

Barenstein, Jorge, *Overcoming Fuzzy Governance in Bangladesh: Policy Implementation in Least Developed Countries*, Dhaka: University Press, 1994.

Brautigam, Deborah, Governance, Economy and Foreign Aid, Studies in Comparative International Development (mimeo), Fall 1992.

Frischtak, Leila, *Governance Capacity and Economic Reform in Developing Countries*, World Bank Technical Paper no. 254, June 1994.

Galtung, Johan, Global Governance for and by Global Democracy (mimeo, undated).

Ghosh, Bimal, *Global Governance and Population Movement: Reshaping the International Regime for Migration Flows* (mimeo), 1993.

Hyden, Goran and Michael Bratton, eds., *Governance and Politics in Africa*, Boulders & London: Lynne Rienner, Publishers, 1994.

Kohli, Atul, *Democracy and Discontent: India's Growing Crisis of Governability*, Cambridge: Cambridge University Press, 1990.

Kothari, Rajni, *State Against Democracy: In Search of Human Governance*, New Delhi: Ajanta Publication, 1989.

Leftwich, Adrian, 'Governance, Democracy and Development in the Third World', *Third World Quarterly*, vol. 14, no. 3, 1993.

Lewis, John P., *India's Political Economy: Governance and Reform*, Oxford: Oxford University Press, 1995.

Panandiker, V.A. Pai, ed., *Problems of Governance in South Asia*, New Delhi: Konark, 2000.

Rizvi, Gowher, *Democracy, Governance and Civil Society in South Asia*, Oxford: Nuffield College (mimeo), undated.

Sobhan, Rehman, ed., *Towards a Theory of Governance and Development: Learning from East Asia*, Dhaka: Centre for Policy Dialogue and The University Press Limited, 1998.

World Bank, *Governance: The World Bank's Experience*, Washington, D.C.: World Bank, 1994.

World Bank Task Force, *Governance and Development*, Washington, D.C.: World Bank, 1992.

Meenakshi Gopinath

Basrur, Rajesh, 'Some Observations on Indian Strategic Culture', in Subrahmanyam A. Raju, ed., *Nuclear India: Problems and Perspectives*, New Delhi: South Asia Publications, 2000.

Basu, Amrita, and Atul Kohli, eds., *Community Conflicts and the State in India*, New Delhi: Oxford University Press, 1998.

Basu, Tapan, Pradip Datta, Sumit Sarkar, et al., *Khaki Shorts and Saffron Flags: Tracts for the Times*, New Delhi: Orient Longman, 1993.

Bhanot, Monica, *Order, Welfare and Legitimacy in the Regional Context of South Asia: An Ultima Thule*, RCSS Policy Studies 14, Colombo: Regional Centre for Strategic Studies, August 2000.

Bhargava, Rajiv, ed., *Secularism and its Critics*, New Delhi: Oxford University Press, 1998.

Chandoke, Neera, *Beyond Secularism: The Rights of Religious Minorities*, New Delhi: Oxford University Press, 1999.

——, *State and Civil Society: Explorations in Political Theory*, New Delhi: Sage, 1995.

Chari, P.R., ed., *Perspectives on National Security in South Asia: In Search of a New Paradigm*, New Delhi: Manohar, 1999.

—— and Ayesha Siddiqa-Agha, *Defence Expenditure in South Asia: India and Pakistan*, RCSS Policy Studies 12, Colombo: Regional Centre for Strategic Studies, June 2000.

Chatterjee, Partha, ed., *Wages of Freedom: Fifty Years of the Indian Nation-State*, New Delhi: Oxford University Press, 1998.

Chenoy, Anuradha, 'Bringing Gender into National Security and International Relations', *International Studies*, vol. 37, no. 1.

——, (forthcoming), *Militarism and Women in South Asia*, New Delhi, Kali for Women.

Chowdhury, Abrar R. and Frank de Silva, *Defence Expenditure in South Asia: Bangladesh and Sri Lanka*, RCSS Policy Studies 11, Colombo: Regional Centre for Strategic Studies, April 2000.

Cooke, Miriam and Angela Woollacott, eds., *Gendering War Talk*, Princeton, New Jersey: Princeton University Press, 1993.

Das, Veena, 'Communities as Political Actors: The Question of Cultural Rights', in Nivedita Menon, ed., *Gender and Politics in India*, New Delhi: Oxford University Press, 1999.

Dasgupta, Sumona, 'Militarization of the Indian State since the 1980s', *International Studies*, vol. 35, no. 4, New Delhi: Sage, 1998.

Drèze, Jean and Amartya, Sen, *India: Economic Development and Social Opportunity*, New Delhi: Oxford University Press, 1995.

Enloe, Cynthia, *Bananas, Beaches and Bases*, Berkeley: University of California Press, 1990.

Guha, Ramachandra and Jonathan, Parry, *Institutions and Inequalities: Essays in Honour of Andre Betéille*, New Delhi: Oxford University Press, 1999.

Hasan, Zoya, *Forging Identities: Gender, Communities and the State*, New Delhi: Kali for Women, 1994.

Iyer, Ramaswamy R., 'A Judgment of Grave Importance', *Economic and Political Weekly*, 4 November 2000.

Jayal, Nirija Gopal, *Democracy and the State: Welfare, Secularism and Development in Contemporary India,* New Delhi: Oxford University Press, 1999.

Jayawardena, Kumari, *Feminism and Nationalism in the Third World*, London: Zed Books, 1994.

Jeffery, Patricia and Amrita Basu, eds., *Appropriating Gender*, New York: Routledge, 1998.

Kumar, Radha, *The History of Doing*, New Delhi: Kali for Women, 1993.

Koithara, Verghese, *Society, State and Security: The Indian Experience*, New Delhi: Sage, 1999.

Mahajan, Gurpreet, *Identities and Rights: Aspects of Liberal Democracy in India*, New Delhi: Oxford University Press, 1998.

Menon, Nivedita, ed., *Gender and Politics in India*, New Delhi: Oxford University Press, 1999.

——— 'Women and Citizenship', in Partha Chatterjee, ed., *Wages of Freedom*, New Delhi: Oxford University Press, 1998.

Menon, Raja, *A Nuclear Strategy for India*, New Delhi: Sage, 2000.

Nandy, Ashis, 'The Politics of Secularism and Recovery of Religious Tolerance', *Alternatives*, vol. XIII, 1988.

Nauriya, Anil, 'The Hindutva Judgments: A Warning Signal', *Economic and Political Weekly*, 6 January 1996.

Navlakha, Gautam, 'National Security Vs Peoples' Insecurity', *Economic and Political Weekly*, 28 December 1996.

Raina, Vinod, 'Why People Oppose Dams', *Inter-Asia Cultural Studies*, vol. I, no. 1, 2000.

Raina, Vinod, Aditi Chowdhury and Sumit Chowdhury, *The Dispossessed: Victims of Development in Asia*, New Delhi: Arena Press, 1999.

Raju, Subramanyam A., ed., *Nuclear India: Problems and Perspectives*, New Delhi: South Asian Publishers, 2000.

Reddy, Amulya, 'Technology and Violence', *Seventh Saadath Hassan Manto Lecture*, Centre for the Study of Developing Societies, 13 June 2000.

Sarkar, Tanika, 'Woman, Community and Nation', in Patricia Jeffrey, and Amrita Basu, eds., *Appropriating Gender: Women's Activism and Politicized Religion in South Asia*, New York: Routledge, 1998.

Sen, Amartya, 'India and the Bomb', *Frontline*, vol. 17, no. 19, 16-29 September 2000.

Sheth, D.L. and Gurpreet Mahajan, *Minority Identities and the Nation State*, New Delhi: Oxford University Press, 1999.

Sinha, Mrinalini, Donna Guy, and Angela Woollacott, *Feminisms and Internationalism*, Oxford: Blackwell Publishers, 1999.

Singh, Jasjit and Pervaiz Iqbal Cheema, *Defence Expenditure in South Asia: An Overview*, RCSS Policy Studies 10, Colombo: Regional Centre for Strategic Studies, March 2000.

Subrahmanyam, K. George Verghese, Lt. Gen. (retd.) K.K. Hazari, *From Surprise to Reckoning: The Kargil Review Committee Report*, New Delhi: Sage, 15 December 1999.

Lok Raj Baral

Babu, B. Ramesh, ed., *Globalization and the South Asian State*, New Delhi: South Asian Publishers, 1998.

Baral, Lok Raj, *The Regional Paradox: Essays in Nepali and South Asian Affairs*, New Delhi: Adroit, 2000.

——— 'Non-Military Threats and Governance', in Muchkund Dubey and Nancy Jetly, eds., *South Asia And Eastern Neighbours*, New Delhi: Konark, 1999.

——— ' Ethnicity and Constitutional Reforms in Nepal', in Iftekharuzzaman, ed., *Ethnicity and Constitutional Reform in South Asia*, New Delhi: Manohar, 1998, pp. 84–105.

———, *Nepal: Problems of Governance*, New Delhi: Konark, 1993.

——— ed., *South Asia: Democracy and the Road Ahead*, Kathmandu: Political Science Association, 1992.

——— *Regional Migrations, Ethnicity and Security: The South Asian Case*, New Delhi: Sterling, 1990.

Chari , P.R., *Newer Sources of Insecurity: The Crisis of Governance in India*, Colombo: Regional Centre for Strategic Studies, 1998.

Dahal, Dev Raj, *The Challenge of Good Governance*, Kathmandu: Centre for Governance and Development Studies, 1996.

Gellner, David N., Pfaff-Czarnecka and John Whelpton, eds., *Nationalism and Ethnicity in a Hindu Kingdom: The Politics of Culture in Contemporary Nepal*, Amsterdam: Harwood Academic Publishers, 1997.

Gurung, Harka, *Nepal: Social Demography and Expressions*, Kathmandu: New Era, 1998.

Joshi, Bhuwan L. and Leo E. Rose, *Democratic Innovations in Nepal: A Study of Political Acculturation*, Berkeley: University of California Press, 1966.

Pfaff-Czarnecka , Joanna, Darini Rajasingham—Senanayake, Ashis Nandy and Edmund Terence Gomez, *Ethnic Futures: The State and Identity Politics in Asia*, New Delhi: Sage, 1999.

Panday, Devendra Raj, *Nepal's Failed Development*, Kathmandu: Nepal South Asia Centre, 1999.

Phadnis, Urmila, *Ethnicity and Nation-Building in South Asia*, New Delhi: Sage, 1990.

Klass, Morton, *Caste: The Emergence of the South Asian Social System* New Delhi: Manohar, 1993.

Kumar, Dhruba, ed., *State, Leadership and Politics in Nepal*, Kathmandu: CNAS, Tribhuvan University, 1995.

Rose, Leo E., *Nepal: Strategy for Survival*, Bombay: Oxford University Press, 1971.

Sathyamurthy, T.V., ed., *State and Nation in the Context of Social Change*, vol.1, Delhi: Oxford University Press, 1994.

Shaha, Rishikesh, *Essays in the Practice of Government in Nepal*, New Delhi: Manohar, 1982.

Vajpeyi, Dhirendra and Yogendra K. Malik, eds., *Religion and Ethnic Minority Politics in South Asia*, Delhi: Manohar, 1989.

Vanhanen, Titu, *Politics of Ethnic Nepotism: India as an Example*, Delhi: Sterling, 1991.

Shahrukh Rafi Khan

Aziz, A. and D. d. Arnold, eds., *Decentralized Governance in Asian Countries*, New Delhi: Sage, 1996.

Banuri, T., I. Ahmad and A. Afzal, 'Democratic Decentralization', in *Nature, Power, People: Citizen's Report on Sustainable Development*, Islamabad: Sustainable Development Policy Institute, 1995.

Bengali, K., 'Issues for Institutional Reform for Devolution', Karachi: Social Policy and Development Centre, 2000.

Blair, H., 'Spreading Power to the Periphery: An Assessment of Democratic Local Governance', USAID Program and Operations Assessment Report no. 21, Washington, D.C., 1999.

Cohen, J.M. and Stephen B. Peterson, 'Methodological Issues in the Analysis of Decentralization', Harvard Institute for International Development Discussion Paper no. 555, Cambridge, Massachusetts, n.d.

Gaventa, J. and C. Valderrama, 'Particpation, Citizenship and Local Government', Background note prepared for a workshop on Local Governance, Sussex: Insitute of Development Studies, 1999.

Khan, Z.R., 'Decentralized Governance and its Impact on Rural Society in Bangladesh', in A. Aziz and D. d. Arnold, eds., *Decentralized Governance in Asian Countries*, New Delhi: Sage, 1996.

Khattak, S.G., 'Women and Local Government', SDPI Working Paper Series no. 24, 1996.

Kothari, R., 'Issues in Decentralized Governance', in A. Aziz and D. d. Arnold, eds., *Decentralized Governance in Asian Countries*, New Delhi: Sage, 1996.

Lambsdoff, O.C., 'Subsidiarity Taken Seriously', *Liberal Times*, vol. VII, no. 4, 1999.

Manor, J., *The Political Economy of Democratic Decentralization*, Washington, D.C.: World Bank, 1999.

Mathew, G., 'Punchayats: The Local Self-Government System in India', in A. Aziz and D.d. Arnold, eds., *Decentralized Governance in Asian Countries*, New Delhi: Sage, 1996.

Pasha, A.G. and H. Pasha, 'Issues in Fiscal Decentralization', Karachi: Social Policy and Development Centre, 2000.

Society for Participatory Research in Asia, 'Punchayat Raj Institutions: A Balance Sheet' (mimeo), New Delhi, 2000.

Rahman, M., 'Local Governance in Bangladesh: Learning from Experience, Lessons for the Future', Workshop on Local Governance in South Asia, Colombo, Sri Lanka, 28–30 November 1999.

Sharan, S.V., 'India's Experiment with Shared Governance: Challenges Ahead', Workshop on Local Governance in South Asia, Colombo, Sri Lanka, 28–30 November 1999.

Zaidi, A.S., *The New Development Paradigm: Papers on Institutions, NGOs, Gender and Local Government*, Oxford: Oxford University Press, 1999.

Paikiasothy Sravanamuttu

Abeysekera, Charles, Rohan Edrisimha, Sumamasiri Liyanage, Paikiasothy Sravanamuttu and Jayadeva Uyangoda, *Unitarism, Devolution and Majoritarian Elitism: A Response to the Interim Report of the Sinhala Commission*, Colombo: Social Science Association, 1998.

Administrative Reforms Committee, 'Administrative Reforms in Support of Devolution', Report no. 6, Colombo: Government of Sri Lanka. 1988.

Bastian, Sunil, ed., *Devolution and Development in Sri Lanka*, Colombo: International Centre for Ethnic Studies and Konark, 1994.

Amaratunga, Chanaka, ed., *Ideas for Constitutional Reform*, Council for Liberal Democracy, Sri Lanka, and Friedrich Naumann Stiftung, 1989.

de Silva, K.M., *Sri Lanka: Problems of Governance*, International Centre for Ethnic Studies, 1993.

de Silva, K.M. and G.H. Peiris, eds., *Pursuit of Peace in Sri Lanka: Past Failures and Future Prospects*, International Centre for Ethnic Studies, Kandy and Sridevi Printers, Dehiwela, Sri Lanka, 2000.

de Silva, K.M. and Howard Wriggins, *J.R. Jayewardene of Sri Lanka: A Political Biography*, 2 vols., London: Leo Caper, 1994.

Edrisinha, Rohan, and Jayadeva, Uyangoda, eds., *Essays on Constitutional Reform*, Colombo: Centre for Policy Research and Analysis, University of Colombo, 1993.

Ghai, Yash, ed., *Autonomy and Ethnicity: Negotiating Competing Claims in Multi-Ethnic States*, Cambridge: Cambridge University Press, 2000.

Government of Sri Lanka, Report of the Presidential Commission on Youth, Sessional Paper no. 1, 1990, Colombo, March 1990.

Human Development Centre, *Human Development in South Asia 1999: The Crisis of Governance*, New York: Human Development Centre, 1999.

Loganathan, Ketheshwaran, *Sri Lanka: Lost Opportunities*, Colombo: Centre for Policy Research and Analysis, University of Colombo, 1996.

Manor, James, *The Expedient Utopian: Bandaranaike of Ceylon*, Cambridge: Cambridge University Press, 1989.

Narayan Swamy, M.R., *Tigers of Lanka: From Boys to Guerillas*, New Delhi: Konark, 1994.

Rothberg, Robert, ed., *The Political, Economic and Social Reconstruction of Sri Lanka*, Cambridge, Mass: World Peace Foundation/Harvard Institute for International Development, 1998.

Saravanamuttu, Paikiasothy, 'Sri Lanka: Civil Society and the Nation-building Challenge', in Alison Van Rooy, eds., *Civil Society and the Aid Industry*, London: Earthscan Publications, 1998.

———'Sri Lanka: The Intractability of Ethnic Conflict', in John Darby and Roger Mac Ginty, eds., *The Management of Peace Processes*, London: Macmillan Press, 2000.

———'Sri Lanka in 1999', *Asian Survey*, vol. XL, no. 1, Jan./Feb. 2000.

Seneviratne, H.L., *The Work of Kings: The New Buddhism in Sri Lanka*, Chicago: University of Chicago Press, 1999.

Tiruchelvam, Neelan, 'Bandaranaike Ideology and Social Harmony', Bandaranaike Memorial Lecture, 26 September 1992.

Wanasinghe, Shelton, *Effective Local Governance: The Foundation for a Functioning Democracy in Sri Lanka*, Colombo: Institute of Policy Studies, May 1999.

Wilson, A. Jeyaratnam, *The Break-Up of Sri Lanka: The Sinhalese-Tamil Conflict*, C. Hurst, 1988.

World Bank, *Sri Lanka: Recapturing Missed Opportunities*, Report no. 20430-CE, 16 June 2000.

Current information on constitutional reform, the peace process, media reform and elections can be obtained from the Centre for Policy Alternatives website - http://www.cpalanka.org

Contributors

AMENA MOHSIN is Professor, Department of International Relations, University of Dhaka. She graduated from the Department of International Relations of the same univesity. She received her M.A. and Ph.D. degrees from the University of Hawaii, and Cambridge Univesity, UK respectively. Her areas of specialization include minority, gender and human rights issues. She has published *Politics of Nationalism: The Case of the Chittagong Hill Tracts, Bangladesh* (Dhaka: UPL, 1997). She has also published numerous articles on minority and gender issues in different national and international journals. Her forthcoming publications include chapters in Muthiah Alagappa, ed., *Coercion and Governance: The Declining Political Role of the Military in Asia* (Stanford University Press, 2001); Michael Brown and Sumit Ganguly, eds., *Language and Ethnicity in Asia* (MIT Press, 2001).

MEENAKSHI GOPINATH is currently Principal, Lady Shri Ram College, New Delhi, where she also teachers at the Department of Politics. She is Founder and Honorary Director of WISCOMP (Women in Security, Conflict Management and Peace). Dr Gopinath is a member of multi-track peace initiatives including the Neemrana Peace Initiative, Dostaana e' Kashmir and the Pakistan-India Peoples' Forum for Peace and Democracy. She has authored the book *Pakistan in Transition* and has contributed chapters and articles to several books and journals on Gandhi, the politics of Pakistan, the arts, etc. In recognition of her contribution to women's education and empowerment, she has received several awards including the Indira Priyadarshini Gandhi Award, the Shiromani Mahila Award and the Delhi Citizen Forum Award. Dr Gopinath has been a Fulbright scholar and has received several fellowships including the Australian International Education Foundation Fellowship for 1996–7 and the University Grants Commission Indo-Israel Exchange Programe 1994–6.

LOK RAJ BARAL is Professor of Political Science, Tribhuvan University, Kathmandu, Nepal. He has authored and edited 10 books, the latest being *The Regional Paradox: Essays in Nepali and South Asian Affairs* (Delhi: Adroit, 2000) and published numerous articles in leading academic journals and edited volumes in the world, and local dailies and weeklies. He has worked in various capacities Chairman of the Department of Political Science, Visiting Professor, president of different organizations and centres, member of the delegation to the United Nations General Assembly, Chairman of the Government's Task Force, and editor. He is now the Executive Chairman of the Nepal Centre for Contemporary Studies and was a member of the International Research Committee of the Regional Centre for Strategic Studies, Colombo. He served as Nepal's Ambassador to India in 1996–7.

SHAHRUKH RAFI KHAN is Executive Director of the Sustainable Development Policy Institute. He was formerly head of the Public Policy Section at the Pakistan Institute of Development Economics. He has taught economics at the State University of New York, Oneonta and at Vassar College. He has published numerous articles in refereed journals. The books written, edited or co-edited by him are *Profit and Loss Sharing: Economic Analysis of an Islamic Financial System* (Oxford, 1987), *Higher Education and Employment Opportunities in Pakistan* (UNESCO, 1988) and *Just Development* (Oxford, 1997). He has also written or edited the forthcoming books *Government, Communities and NGOs in Social Sector Delivery: A Study of Collective Action Rural Drinking Water Supply* (Ashgate), *Fifty Years of Pakistan's Economy: Traditional Topics and Contemporary Concerns* (Oxford), and *Reforming Pakistan's Political Economy* (Vanguard). His latest edited book is on the issue of Trade and the Environment.

PAIKIASOTHY SARAVANAMUTTU is currently the Executive Director of the Centre for Policy Alternatives, an independent research and advocacy public policy institute focusing on democratic governance and conflict resolution. He received his first degree and doctorate in International Relations from the London School of Economics and Political Science, University of London in 1979 and 1986 respectively. During 1984–92, he lectured in International Relations at the Univesity of Southampton, UK. He has written and been quoted widely on the political situation in Sri Lanka in both the international and local print and electronic media.

P.R. CHARI is a former member of the Indian Administrative Service. He served in several senior positions at the central and state levels, including the Ministry of Defence. He was Director of the Institute for Defence Studies and Analyses (1975–80), International Fellow, Centre for International Affairs, Harvard University (1983–4), and Research Professor, Centre for Policy Research (1992–6). Currently, he is Director of the Institute for Peace and Conflict Studies. He has published over 100 monographs and major papers in learned journals and chapters in books in India and abroad. His publications include *Indo-Pak Nuclear Stand off: Role of the United States* (1995); co-author, *Brasstacks and Beyond: Perception and Management of Crisis* (1995); co-author and co-editor, *Nuclear Non-Proliferation in India and Pakistan: South Asian Perspectives* (1996); editor, *India: Towards Millennium* (1998); editor, *Perspectives on National Security in South Asia: In Search of a New Paradigm* (1999); and co-author and co-editor, *Kargil: The Tables Turned* (2001).

Index